C000066732

WORDS OLD AND NEW

Words Old and New

Gems from the
Christian Authorship of all Ages

SELECTED BY
HORATIUS BONAR

EDINBURGH:
THE BANNER OF TRUTH TRUST
1994

THE BANNER OF TRUTH TRUST
3 Murrayfield Road, Edinburgh EH12 6EL
P.O. Box 621, Carlisle, Pennsylvania 17013, USA

*

First published 1866
First Banner of Truth edition 1994
ISBN 0 85151 643 2

*

Printed in Finland by WSOY

CONTENTS

INTRODUCTION[1]

Of the four sons of Andrew and Marjory Bonar of Edinburgh, three were to be colleagues in the ministry of the Church of Scotland and the Free Church of Scotland. John James Bonar was born in 1803, Horatius in 1808, and Andrew in 1810. For over forty years these three men were to work together and not a year would pass without their supporting one another by preaching in each other's pulpits during communion seasons. Many references to Horace, as the family called him, will be found in *Andrew Bonar: Diary and Life*.[2] But more significant than the family relationship is the fact that, in their work, Horatius and Andrew belonged to a spiritual brotherhood which, in the words of Alexander Whyte, 'had an immense influence on the religious life of Scotland'. On the Sunday after Horatius Bonar's funeral in Edinburgh in 1889, his brother Andrew sat in the vestry of Horace's church during the morning service 'listening to the prayers and singing of the

---

[1] Almost all the following information is drawn from *Horatius Bonar, A Memorial*, London, 1889; *Memories of Dr Horatius Bonar* (Edinburgh and London, 1909) and *Hymns by Horatius Bonar*, H. N. Bonar (London, 1904).

[2] *Andrew A. Bonar: Diary & Letters,* ed. M. Bonar (London, 1893), *Reminiscences of Andrew A. Bonar,* ed. M. Bonar (London, 1895), reprinted in one volume, Banner of Truth, 1984.

congregation assembled for devotion'. He says in his *Diary*: 'Once or twice I almost realised what it may be to hear the great congregation singing together as they welcome a brother arrived in glory!', and then his memory went back to the 'beloved companions' who had gone before—'M'Cheyne, John Milne, William Burns, Dr Chalmers, James Hamilton and hundreds of such'.

The main facts of Bonar's life can soon be told. Born in a godly home, where his much loved father died when he was thirteen, he was educated at the Edinburgh High School where his brilliance as a classical scholar was evident even by his early teenage years. He entered the University of Edinburgh and then its Divinity School, where his principal instructor was Thomas Chalmers, the greatest Christian, in his opinion, that he ever knew. His first work was as an assistant in the parish of St John's, Leith (the port of Edinburgh) from whence he was settled at Kelso in 1837. Bonar's first sermon in the North Parish Church at Kelso was from Mark 9:29, 'And he said unto them, this kind can come forth by nothing but by prayer and fasting'. For the next thirty years Bonar's ministry in Kelso was lived out in the spirit of that text.

It was his happiness to have been called into the service of the gospel at a time when, in many parts of Scotland, there was a new thirst for the Word of God. The year 1837, in fact, may be taken as the year when in various places there was the beginning of a true reviving amongst the churches. Such is certainly Bonar's own opinion, for, speaking of the year 1843, he writes:

The tide of blessing which, from 1837, had been flowing without intermission, had not yet begun to ebb. Many were daily added to our living membership. The Church's true work went on happily in parts where it had already commenced; and it began in many places to which it had not yet reached. We look back on these months with thankful joy. Gladly should we live them over again, with all their tear and wear of body and mind, had we but our former strength, and the hope of like success. No one who passed through them would wish either to forget or underestimate the privilege of having been one of the 'labourers' in the reaping of that blessed harvest.

Elsewhere he gives the following description of this momentous period in Scottish church history:

During this season there were all the marks of a work of God which we see in the account given of the preaching of the gospel by the apostles. The multitude was divided, families were divided; the people of God were knit together, they were filled with zeal and joy and heavenly-mindedness; they continued steadfast, and increased in doctrine and fellowships, being daily in church and in prayer-meetings, and numbers were constantly turning to the Lord.

It would be misleading to suppose that Kelso in any sense lay at the centre of this period of awakening, yet Horatius Bonar's ministry in the Scottish Borders was long to be remembered for its fruitfulness. Later, in 1909, Robertson Nicholl, one of his successors at Kelso, was able to say of Bonar's ministry:

He set himself to evangelise the Borderland. His name was fragrant in every little village and at most of the farms. He conducted many meetings in farm kitchens and village schoolrooms, and often preached in the open air. The memory of some sermons lingered, one in particular on the Plant of Renown. The chief characteristic of his preaching was its strange solemnity. It was full of entreaty and of warning.

In 1866 Bonar became minister of a new charge, the Chalmers Memorial Church, at Grange, Edinburgh,[1] in which office he remained until his death, being dependent upon a colleague in the few final years. For a meeting to celebrate his jubilee as a minister on April 5, 1888 he started to prepare an address of an autobiographical nature but his preparation was never concluded. He laid down his pen for the last time in the middle of a sentence and could not be present at the celebration. His last sermon to his people had been preached on September 11, 1887 and its concluding words, characteristically, were 'In such an hour as ye think not the Son of Man cometh.'

---

[1] Now named St Catherine's-Argyle Church

Had a biography of Bonar ever been written it is apparent that his love of children and young people would have been a prominent feature. His first work at Leith was mainly among that age group and when he left there for Kelso in 1837, 283 girls and boys—all carefully named in one of his notebooks—were present at a meeting to bid him farewell. At Kelso it is said that 'his sermons to the young were peculiarly attractive'. On Wednesday afternoons it was his custom at Kelso to hold a Bible class and many years later one of the young people who attended recalled the 'bright, happy band of schoolgirls, sitting around listening to his earnest, loving, faithful teaching'. She went on: 'I see Dr Bonar seated at the end of a long table with a large Bible spread out before him, the Bible-hymnbook in his hand, his dear handsome face beaming, and the pleasant smile which lighted it up, as some of us gave a fuller, clearer answer than he expected to the question asked.' His son, H. N. Bonar, gives us some insight into his father's appeal to young people. He speaks of the happiness of his disposition and of the skill with which he guided his children:

He very rarely said 'don't' to me—not that he did not indicate very strongly what he would like me to do. . . All my holidays were passed with him. We boated together, we walked together, we swam together, we climbed hills together. Stern! No, he was never stern in my boyish eyes. I can remember another little personal incident—you will pardon me for mentioning it in this connection. Once an officious neighbour came to him to complain of one of my misdeeds. I fancy I had been climbing to the rooks' nests in Warrender Park, then unbuilt on. He reported this to my father, and wound up by saying, 'I hope you will give the boy a good thrashing.' My father replied, 'If I thrashed the boy for that, what would I do if he told me a lie?'.

It is interesting to note that Bonar's best remembered work, namely his *Hymns*, seems to have arisen out of his concern to help young people. His first hymns were written for the young people's class at Leith, one of these being 'I was a wandering sheep'.

It should be added that his own personal spiritual needs led to some of his finest hymns and poems. In 1843 he married Jane Catherine Lundie (1821–83). They were to lose five children in successive bereavements and something of what they felt can be seen in his poems, 'Lucy' (who died at the age of four), and 'The Blank'.

In 1845 he published a little collection of 300 hymns, *The Bible Hymn Book*, 'designed both for general use and for Sabbath schools'. This contained some sixteen of his own pieces with no name attributed to them. More than twenty years elapsed between his first hymns and their publication as a collection with his own name attached. What is now known worldwide as a communion hymn, beginning 'Here, O my Lord, I see Thee face to face', was first written at his brother John's request to be read aloud at the close of a communion service at Greenock in 1855.

While several of Horatius Bonar's hymns remain well-known today, it ought to be a matter of surprise that he is so little remembered as an author. He was clearly one of the most valued evangelical writers of the nineteenth century and he has to be bracketed with J. C. Ryle and C. H. Spurgeon in his understanding of the power of the press and in putting it to extensive use. He began with some thirty-six Kelso tracts. They were followed in 1845 by *The Night of Weeping* and the next year by *Truth and Error, or Letters to a Friend*. A regular flow of other books was to follow, including sermons, expositions of Scripture, poetry and biographies. His first biography, *A Stranger Here*, the life of an unnamed Christian woman, was published in 1853. His best biography, and surely one of the very best of the last century, was his *Life of the Rev. John Milne of Perth*, 1869. His last major work was also a biography, *The Life and Work of the Rev. G. T. Dodds*, 1884, who was his son-in-law and a missionary in France.[1]

---

[1] When Dodds died suddenly in 1882 his wife returned to her parental home, with their children. Her father wrote to a friend: 'God took five children from me some years ago, and He has given me other five to bring up for Him in my old age.' Another daughter of Horatius and Jane Bonar married the Rev. D. C. MacNicol whose book, *Robert Bruce, Minister of the Kirk of Edinburgh*, was republished by the Trust in 1961.

As though all this writing were not enough, Bonar was also editor of *The Quarterly Journal of Prophecy* from 1848 to 1873 and of the very widely read *Christian Treasury* from 1859 to 1879.

As well as being an author in his own right, Bonar repeatedly sought to bring the attention of the Christian public to the heritage of literature which exists in the English language. He did this on a large, and more specialised scale, in his reprint of John Gillies classic, *Historical Collections Relating to Remarkable Periods of the Success of the Gospel.*[1] This present book, now reprinted, is a more popular attempt to introduce readers to a considerable number of the best authors, ranging from the Fathers of the early church down to men (and one woman) of the nineteenth century. First published in 1866 by James Nisbet, the leading evangelical publishers of that period, it is no hastily compiled anthology but was clearly the fruit of his own reading and study over many years. Pithy statements which he had found of help himself he thus passed on to a wider readership.

Appendices, giving biographical information on the authors, and also listing their books re-issued by the present publishers, have been added to this edition of *Words, Old and New*.

The Publishers
Edinburgh, June, 1994

[1] Edinburgh, 1754, and Kelso, 1845.

WORDS OLD AND NEW.

CLEMENT (OF ROME).

BORN (ABOUT) 30—DIED 102.

1. Let us lay aside all vain and empty cares, and let us rise up to the glorious and venerable rule of our calling. Let us look stedfastly to the blood of Christ, and see how precious His blood is in the sight of God.

2. They gave Rahab a sign that she should hang out of her house a scarlet rope, shewing thereby that by the blood of our Lord there should be redemption to all who believe and hope in God.

3. Let us hold fast to those who follow peace, and not to such as only pretend to desire it.

4. Consider the trees. Take the vine for an example. First it sheds its leaves; then it buds; after that it spreads its leaves; then it flowers; then come the sour grapes; and after them follows the ripe fruit. Of a truth, yet a little while, and His will shall suddenly be accomplished; the Holy Scripture itself bearing witness that He shall quickly come, and not tarry; and that the Lord shall suddenly come to His temple, even the Holy One whom ye look for.

5. Let us consider, beloved, how the Lord continually shews us that there shall be a future resurrection, of which He has made our Lord Jesus Christ the first fruits. Let us contemplate the resurrection that takes place every season before our eyes. Day and night declare a resurrection to us. The night lies down, and the day arises; again the day departs, and the night comes on. Let us behold the fruits of the earth. The seed is sown. It fell into the earth dry and naked; in time it dissolves; and from the dissolution the power of the Lord raises it again; and of one single seed many arise and bring forth fruit.

6. We also, being called by the same will in Christ Jesus, are not justified by ourselves, neither by our own wisdom, nor knowledge, nor piety, nor the works which we have done; but by the faith by which God Almighty has justified men from the beginning; to whom be glory for ever and ever. Amen.

7. March on, men and brethren, with all earnestness in His holy laws.

8. Wherefore are there strifes, and anger, and divisions, and wars amongst us. Have we not all one God and one Christ? Has not one Spirit been poured out upon us? Have we not one calling in Christ?

9. In love did the Lord join Himself to us. For the love He bore toward us, our Lord Jesus Christ gave His own blood for us, by the will of God; His flesh for our flesh, His soul for our souls.

10. Let us every hour expect the kingdom of God, in love and righteousness, because we know not the day of Christ's appearing.

IGNATIUS.

BORN (ABOUT) 40—MARTYRED 107.

1. Let fire and the cross, let wild beasts, let all the malice of the devil, come upon me; only may I enjoy Jesus Christ.

2. It is better for me to die for Christ than to reign over the ends of the earth.

3. Stand firm and immovable as an anvil when it is beaten upon. It is the part of a brave combatant to be wounded, and yet to overcome. But especially we ought to endure all things for God's sake, that He may bear with us. Be every day better; consider the times; expect Him, who is above all time, eternal; invisible, though, for our sakes, made visible; impalpable and impassible, yet for us subjected to sufferings, enduring all things for our salvation.

4. Him I seek who died for us; Him I desire who rose again for us; He is my gain laid up for me. Suffer me to imitate the passion of my God.

5. I have no delight in the bread that perisheth, nor in the pleasures of this life. I long for the bread of God, the flesh of Jesus Christ, of the seed of David; and the drink that I long for is His blood.

6. If any speak not of Jesus Christ, they are monuments over the dead, on which are written only the names of men.

7. The objects dear to me are Jesus Christ, His cross, His death, His resurrection, and the faith which is in Him, through which I seek to be justified.

8. The last times are come upon us; let us therefore be very reverent, and fear the long-suffering of God, that it be not to us unto condemnation.

9. It is better for a man to be silent, and *be* a Christian, than to *say* he is, and not to be.

10. He that has the word of Jesus is able to hear His very silence.

11. Why are we not all wise, seeing we have received the knowledge of God, which is Jesus Christ?

12. It is meet that we should not only be *called* Christians, but *be* so.

13. Do not speak with Jesus Christ, and yet covet the world.

14. My love is crucified; and the fire that is within me does not desire any water.

15. A Christian has not the power of himself, but must always be at leisure for God's service.

16. It is meet that you should, by all means, glorify Jesus Christ, who hath glorified you.

17. There is one Physician, both fleshly and spiritual; made, and not made; God incarnate; true life in death; both of Mary and of God, passible and impassible; Jesus Christ our Lord.

18. Ye are the stones of the Father's temple, prepared for His building, and drawn up on high by the cross of Christ.

IRENÆUS.

BORN (ABOUT) 130—MARTYRED 202.

1. How could we obtain salvation, if it had not been God who has wrought salvation? Or, how can man come into fellowship with God, if God has not come to man? How was it possible that Christ should overcome the strong one, who held man under his dominion, and let the vanquished go free, if He were not Himself stronger than man, who had been vanquished?

2. What profit is there in that honour, which is so short-lived, as that, perchance, it was not yesterday, neither will it be to-morrow? Such men as labour for it are but like froth, which, though it be uppermost, is yet altogether useless.

3. He united man to God; for, if man had not overcome the adversary of man, the enemy could not have been overcome.

4. If man had not been united to God, he could not have been a partaker of immortality.

5. It behoved the Mediator between God and man, by His relationship to both, to bring both into agreement with each other.

6. The Word of God, almighty as well as perfect in righteousness, set Himself against the apostasy, to redeem His own property from Satan, who had borne rule over us from the beginning, and had seized what was not his own.

This redemption was not effected by violence; but the Lord redeemed us with His own blood, and gave His life for our life, His flesh for our flesh, and so effected our salvation.

7. Our Lord would not have gathered together these things to Himself, and have saved, through Himself, what was lost in Adam, if He had not actually been made flesh and blood. He, therefore, had flesh and blood, not of a kind different from what men have; but He gathered into Himself the very original creation of the Father, and sought that which was lost.

8. The Word of God, Jesus Christ, out of His boundless love, became what we are, that He might make us what He is.

9. Then from the heavens, in clouds, shall the Lord come, in the glory of his Father, to cast Antichrist, and all who follow him, into the lake of fire. Then shall He introduce the days of the kingdom to the just, that is, the rest, the hallowed seventh day, restoring to Abraham his promised heritage; in which kingdom, many shall come from the east and the west, to sit down with Abraham, Isaac, and Jacob.

10. To those who abide in His love, He gives communion with Himself. And communion with God is life and light; the fruition of all the good that is with Him. On those who stand aloof from Him, He inflicts the separation which they have chosen for themselves. But separation from God is death; and separation from light is darkness. Separation from God is the loss of all good that there is with God. Besides the loss of all good,

they incur the infliction of all punishment. And as the good that is with God is eternal, so its loss is eternal, and without end.

11. Three times did the Lord conquer Satan; three times did He repulse him (in the temptation) and drive him off, lawfully vanquished. And thus Adam's breach of the law of God was cancelled by the obedience of the Son of man, keeping the statutes of God.

12. Justly, then, was he led captive, who had unjustly led man into captivity; and man, who had been taken captive, was delivered from the power of his master, according to the mercy of God our Father, who pitied his own workmanship, and gave him salvation; restoring him through the Word, that is, Christ; that man might know by experience that, not from himself, but the gift of God, he receives incorruption.

13. As in the evening it was that God spoke to Adam, seeking after him, so is it in the last times that He has visited Adam's race, seeking after them.

14. It is by the flesh and blood of the Lord that we are saved.

CLEMENT (OF ALEXANDRIA).

BORN (ABOUT) 150—DIED 220.

1. Those who adorn only the exterior, but neglect the inner man, are like the Egyptian temples, which present every kind of decoration upon the outside, but contain within, in place of a deity, a cat, a crocodile, or some other vile animal.

2. Wealth is like a viper, which is harmless if you know how to take hold of it; but, if you do not, it will twine round your hand and bite you.

3. Remember, that unless ye become children by a new birth, the Scripture plainly testifieth that ye shall never be able to recover your true Father, nor to enter His heavenly kingdom; for that is inaccessible to the stranger and the alien; and he alone who is enrolled and made free of that city, and hath regained his heavenly Father, shall there dwell in that Father's house, receive His inheritance, and enjoy communion with His true and beloved Son. Such is the church of the first-begotten, written in the heavens, and rejoicing around the divine throne with myriads of angels. Does God freely offer so great salvation, and will you still blindly rush into destruction?

4. 'Awake,' He saith, 'thou that sleepest, and arise from the dead, and Christ shall give thee light.' 'To-day, if ye will hear his voice, harden not your hearts;' and

this to-day shall last till that word can be used no more. For the day of instruction shall endure until the consummation of time itself; until the real and unfading day of God shall be co-extended through eternity. Oh, if an entrance into that eternity could be purchased, were not the whole of Pactolus too small a price? Yet, to you it is freely offered, and requires but the treasure of a living faith, and love placed in your own possession. Yet, how many cling to this world, as the sea-weed to the rocks of the shore, and regard not this glorious immortality; but true religion can be learned effectually from God alone. He is the only perfect teacher. He alone has power to renew in man the likeness of His own image.

5. We must impart our wealth benevolently; avoiding the extremes of meanness and ostentation. We must not let our love of the beautiful run into selfishness or excess; lest it should be said of us, ' His horse, or his farm, or his servant, or his plate, is worth fifteen talents, while he himself would be dear at three farthings.

6. The Lord has made man after His own image, that he might be a fair self-breathing instrument of sweet music.

7. The Saviour is many-voiced, and in many ways strives to effect the salvation of man.

8. He who has opened the door, hitherto shut, will reveal what is within, and will shew those things which no one could know before, unless he entered by Christ, through whom alone God is perceived.

9. Call hither your Phidias, your Polyclitus, your Praxitiles, your Apelles, and all your noble artists; not one of them can make a breathing image, not one of them can

mould his clay into flesh. Who softened the marrow? who hardened the bones? who swelled the veins, and poured the blood into them? who spread the skin over all? who of you all is able to construct an eye that shall see? who can breathe a soul into his work? who will bestow righteousness? who will promise immortality? He alone, who is the Creator of the universe, the great Artist and Father, who formed man to be His living image. Your Olympian Jupiter, the image of an image, is the vain work of Attic hands; but the true image of God is the WORD, the Son of the Eternal mind, the divine reason, the light given forth by the primal light of all.

10. I urge thee to save thyself. This is Christ's will. He presents thee with life.

11. Till the ground if thou be a husbandman; but still, amid thy labours learn to know God. If thou be a seaman, follow thy calling, but call upon the heavenly Steersman.

12. The man in whom the WORD dwells is become like God; and is fair without striving to seem so. This is real beauty.

13. Man is loved of God; for on his account was the only-begotten Son sent from the bosom of the Father.

TERTULLIAN.

BORN (ABOUT) 160—DIED (ABOUT) 240.

1. Truth set out with being hated; as soon as she appeared, she was reckoned an enemy; as many as are strangers to it, so many are its foes.

2. Christians are *made*, not *born* such.

3. Scattered abroad, wanderers, banished from their own clime and land, they (the Jews) roam about the world with neither man nor God for their king; to whom it is not permitted, even in the right of strangers, to greet their native land, with so much as the sole of their foot.

4. Two advents of Christ are declared : the first, which hath been already fulfilled, in the lowliness of the human nature; the second, which remaineth yet to come, to close this world, in the majesty of the divine.

5. Men sit not down to meat, before tasting, in the first place, of prayer to God.

6. O Glory, allowed because it has a human object! Therefore it is not deemed foolhardy to despise death and shame! And, it is permitted to men to suffer for country, for empire, for friendship, but not for God!

7. We spring up the thicker the oftener we are mowed down. The blood of the martyrs is their harvest-seed.

8. It mattereth not where you are *in* the world, if ye be not *of* the world; if ye have lost any of the joys of life, ye

may count it goodly traffic to suffer somewhat, that ye may gain the more.

9. If earthly glory have such power, how much more the heavenly? Is the piece of glass so precious? How much more the true pearl?

10. In the world all things are shadowy, nothing real.

11. He that is the Head of the man, and the beauty of the woman, and the Husband of the Church, Christ Jesus, what crown did He put on for both man and woman? Of thorns and briars, as a figure of those sins which the lusts of our flesh has brought to us, but the power of the cross has taken away.

12. The theatre is especially the shrine of Venus. The theatre of Venus is also the house of Bacchus. Christian, thou must hate these things!

13. On such sweets let the world's guests be fattened; the places, and the times, and the inviter to the feast are their own. Our feasts, our marriage, is not yet. We cannot sit down with the world, nor they with us. Things go by turns; now they are glad, and we are sorrowful.

14. But what spectacle is that near at hand? It is the coming of the Lord, manifest, glorious, and triumphant. What is that joy of the angels? what the glory of the rising saints? what the kingdom of the righteous? what the city of the new Jerusalem? And there remain other spectacles; that last and eternal judgment-day, when all the ancient things of earth, and things just rising into existence, shall be consumed in one fire.

15. It is prayer alone which overcometh God.

16. Prayer is the wall of faith, our armour and weapons.

CYPRIAN.

BORN (ABOUT) 200—MARTYRED 258.

1. Christ willed to become what man is, in order that man might become what Christ is.

2. Him therefore we accompany; Him we follow; Him have we for guide of our journey; Source of light; Author of salvation, who promises heaven and the Father to them that believe. What Christ is shall we be, His imitators.

3. Gaudiness of ornament and apparel are fit for none but the immodest. They are really richest in dress who are poorest amid their modesty.

4. The foe flatters and misleads, transforms himself into an angel of light, and clothes his ministers as servants of righteousness. These are the maintainers of night for day, of death for life; giving despair while proffering hope—Antichrist under the name of Christ.

5. He cannot possess Christ's garment who splits and divides Christ's Church.

6. We need to be girded about, lest, when the day of march cometh, He find us hindered. Let us be awaiting the sudden advent of the Lord, that, when He knocketh, our faith may be on the watch, and win from the Lord the recompence of its watchfulness.

7. Does he think himself a Christian who is ashamed or afraid to be one? Can he be joined to Christ who

feels either the disgrace or the danger of belonging to Him.

8. We pray for the coming of that our kingdom, which has been promised to us by God, and was gained by the blood and suffering of Christ, that we who have continued His subjects in the life below may reign in His kingdom according to His own word, 'Come, ye blessed, inherit the kingdom.'

9. Riches are not only to be despised, but full of danger; in them is the root of seductive evils, misleading the blindness of the human heart by a subtle deception.

10. If He prayed, who was without sin, how much more ought sinners to pray! If He offered continual prayer, the whole night long, how much more ought we to add prayer to prayer, and to watch thereunto by night!

11. Let him fear to die who, not born of the Spirit, is the property of the eternal fire. Let him fear to die who is to pass from death here to the second death.

12. In persecution, earth is shut, but heaven opens; Antichrist threatens, but Christ protects; death enters, but immortality ensues; the world is taken from us, but Paradise is awarded; the life of time is quenched, but the life of eternity is accomplished.

13. Let us consider, beloved brethren, that we have renounced the world, and are passing our time here as strangers and pilgrims. We embrace the day which assigns each to his home, which restores to Paradise and a kingdom, us who have been plucked from the world and set free from worldly snares. Who would not hasten home? Paradise we count our fatherland, and the patri-

archs our fathers. Why should we not hasten homewards to salute our parents? There the mighty multitude of dear ones awaits us,—the crowd of parents, brothers, sons, longs for us, already secure of their own safety, and now solicitous about ours. How great the joy to us and to them, of beholding and embracing each other! What the blessedness of these celestial realms; without fear of death, and possessed of an eternity of life, how supreme and abiding the felicity! There the glorious choir of apostles; there the crowd of exulting prophets; there the innumerable throng of martyrs crowned because of victory in conflict and suffering; there the triumphant virgins who subdued the desires of the flesh; the compassionate rewarded, who, obeying their Lord's command, transferred their earthly patrimony to a heavenly treasure-house. To these, brethren most beloved, with eager desire let us hasten, longing to be speedily with them and with Christ. These our desires and purposes, let our God, and our Lord Christ, behold, who will give the larger reward of His glory to those who after Him have had larger desires.

ATHANASIUS.

BORN 296—DIED 373.

1. Miserable are those who measure the authority of a doctrine by the numbers receiving it. Truth always overcomes, though for a time it is found among the few. He who, for proof, betakes himself to numbers, confesses himself conquered. Let me see the beauty of truth, and immediately I am persuaded. A multitude may overawe, but cannot persuade. How many myriads could persuade me to believe that day is night, that poison is food? In determining earthly things we do not regard numbers, shall we do so in heavenly things? I reverence numbers; but only when they produce proof, not when they shun inquiry. Can you confirm a lie by numbers?

2. He strips us of the raiment of skin which we put on in Adam, that, in its place, we might be clothed with Christ. He allows his garments to be divided, that we may have the undivided Word of the Father.

3. The Saviour is delivered up, and being so, He shrinks not from death, but hastens to meet it, pursuing the flying serpent.

4. It will matter little to the faithful what their sorrows may have been in this vain world, since no trace of them will remain when they enter on that ineffable peace which is in store for them in the life to come.

5. I can do nothing without the help of God, and that

from moment to moment; for when, so long as we are on the earth, is there a single instant in which we can say we are safe from temptation or secure from sin?

6. We need grace alike to keep us from breaking the weightiest commandment of the law, and from falling into the most trifling vanity of the age.

7. The truly humble Christian does not inquire into his neighbour's faults; he takes no pleasure in judging them; he is occupied wholly with his own.

8. True religion abhors all violence; she owns no arguments but those of persuasion.

9. The will of Jesus Christ is, that those who belong to Him should walk exactly in his footsteps; that they should be, as He was, full of mercy and love; that they should render to no one evil for evil, but endure, for His sake, injuries, calumnies, and every outrage. To them all anger and resentment should be unknown.

10. I would not have you ignorant that there is a second epiphany, illustrious and divine; not in lowliness, but in His own glory; not in poverty, but in His own majesty; not to suffer, but to bestow the fruits of His cross, that is, resurrection and immortality; not to be judged, but to judge according to the things done in the body; to give the kingdom of the heavens to the righteous, but the everlasting fire and the outer darkness to the evildoers.

MACARIUS (THE EGYPTIAN).

BORN 301—DIED 391.

1. He who thinks favourably of himself, or highly of his own soul, because he has partaken of grace, has not yet begun to lay his foundation right. Consider Jesus: from what height did He, the Son of God, Himself God, descend! and to what sufferings! even to the death of the cross; for which humiliation He was exalted to sit at the right hand of the Father.

2. The lowly man never falls; for whither should he fall who is already below all men? Wherefore, pride is, indeed, great lowness; but humility, great exaltation, dignity, and honour.

3. Every soul that is without concern for itself, proves itself to be held by unbelief; through which it suffers day after day to pass by, without receiving the word. Oftentimes it buoys itself up with empty dreams, not sensible of the inward conflict, which is hidden from it by its own conceit; for conceit is the blindness of the soul, which will not suffer it to perceive its own infirmity.

4. Every one is willingly captivated by the object which he loves, because he will not give up the whole of his love to God. Thus, one man loves his estates; another, his money; another, eating, or some other bodily indulgence; another, skill in speech, for the sake of a fugitive glory; another loves command; another, honour

and applause from men; another, anger and revenge, deeming it something noble to devote himself for his friends; another, idle companies; another, merely to be singular in conversation, or to propound doctrines to attract the admiration of men. One man yields himself up to indolence and unconcern; another to the ornaments of dress; this one to sleep; that one to jests and witticisms; and another to some other great or trifling object of this world, which holds and chains him down, and will not suffer him to raise himself up.

5. Purity of heart cannot otherwise be effected than through Jesus; for He alone is the substantial and very Truth, and without that Truth it is impossible to come to the knowledge of truth, or to obtain salvation.

6. If at any time, when we have received the word of the kingdom, we find ourselves moved thereby to tears, let us not derive confidence from those tears, nor cherish any complacency in ourselves, as if we ourselves had sufficiently well employed our ears for hearing, or our eyes for reading; for there are other ears, other eyes, other tears, and another intelligence and soul, namely, those of the divine and heavenly Spirit, which must hear, and weep, and pray, and understand, and perform the will of God in us in truth.

7. Woe to the soul that can receive no convincing sense of its wounds, and that thinks itself free from evil, only through the magnitude and excess of its evil! Such an one the Good Physician neither visits nor heals; forasmuch as it cares not for its own wounds, but esteems itself to be healthful and sound. For 'they that are whole

need not a physician' (said He), 'but they that are sick.'

8. It behoves us vigilantly to look about us, and to observe on every side the machinations, deceits, and artifices of the enemy; for, as the Holy Spirit became in Paul 'all things to all men, that he might gain all,' so likewise the evil one strives 'to become all things,' that he may impel all men to their destruction. For he affects to pray with those who pray, that he may seduce them into conceit by the opportunity of prayer; he fasts with those who fast, desiring thus to deceive them into a good opinion of themselves. In the same manner, he beguiles those who possess a knowledge of the Scriptures, wishing to ensnare them by the form of knowledge; and so, also, those who have been gifted with any light of revelation. For Satan 'transforms himself into an angel of light,' that, by the appearance of a false light, he may draw them to himself; and, in a word, he transforms himself into everything, and to every one, that he may subdue them by the speciousness of appearance, and so receive them to destruction.

9. The more the evil one discharges his fiery darts against us, the more it behoves us to inflame our hearts with faith in God; being well assured that it is all His will, in order to bring to proof the affection of those who truly love Him.

10. A thousand years of this world, compared with that eternal world, are as if a man should compare a single grain of sand with all the sand upon the sea-shore.

EPHRAIM (THE SYRIAN).

BORN (ABOUT) 310—DIED 379.

1. Beloved, if you would strangle the lion, grasp him boldly, lest he crush you to pieces like an earthen vessel.

2. He, who will not serve the Lord alone, must be the slave of many masters.

3. Terrible would it be for me to perish with thirst, when supplying others with water ; which yet must be the case, if I do not discipline my own soul.

4. By love, God the Word came upon earth ; by love, Paradise has been opened to us.   Being enemies to God, by love we were reconciled.

5. From my childhood I have been a vessel unprofitable and dishonourable.   Warning others, I have fallen into their evils twofold.   Woe is me !   Whence can there be any refuge, unless the mercies of God shine quickly upon me ?   Nor is there one hope of salvation from works.   While I speak of purity, I am thinking of uncleanness ; while I am uttering rules for the conquest of the passions, my own are inwardly raging night and day.

6. Shall I despair of salvation ?   By no means.   This the adversary desires in order to destroy me.   I do not fling myself away.   I trust in the mercies of God.   I pray Thee, cast me not away ! Thou knowest the wounds of my soul ; heal me, O Lord, and I shall be healed !

7. Do we neglect to call for his help when He loves

and pities us? Hath He redeemed and enlightened us? He hath given us to see and taste His grace, that we might seek Him without ceasing. Happy he who hath tasted of His love, and seeks to be always filled with it. Filled with this love, he admits no other.

8. Who would not love such a Master, worship Him, and confess His goodness? From His immense height, and the blessed bosom of the Father, did He not descend to us? The invisible became visible! Oh wonder, full of fear and trembling;—a hand of clay, formed of the dust, smote the Creator of heaven and earth!

9. Blessed is he who shall be counted worthy to see that hour, in which all that loved the immortal Bridegroom are taken up into the clouds, to meet Him.

10. I remembered that day (of Judgment), and trembled, and wept, till I had no more power to weep.

11. My days have passed on and my iniquities have been multiplied. Woe is me, my Beloved! O gracious lover of souls, by Thy compassions I adjure Thee, place me not at the left hand with the goats. Sinner as I am, I knock at thy door without ceasing; slothful though I be, yet I walk in Thy way.

12. I beseech Thy goodness; heal my wounds and enlighten my understanding. Thou alone knowest how my soul thirsts after Thee, as a dry land. Send Thy grace, that I may eat and drink and be satisfied. Distil one drop of Thy love, that it may burn as liquid fire in my soul, and consume its thorns, even my evil lusts.

GREGORY (OF NAZIANZUM).

BORN 328—DIED 390.

1. Is my body in health? It wars against me. Is it sick? I languish with it in sympathy. It is at once a companion that I love, and an enemy that I dread. It is a prison that terrifies me, a partner with whom I dwell.

2. Such is the shortness of our life, that we pass out of one grave into another; out of the womb of our own mother into that of the earth, which is the common mother of us all.

3. Do they cast us out of the city? They cannot cast us out of that which is in the heavens. If they who hate us could do this, they would be doing something real against us. So long, however, as they cannot do this, they are but pelting us with drops of water, or striking us with the wind.

4. There is one life,—to look forward to the life above. There is one death,—sin; for it is this that destroys the soul. All things else, however prized by some, are the mere shadows of dreams, the phantoms of the mind.

5. The predestined day is near. Sorrow is not immortal. Let us not aggravate our light griefs with ungenerous thoughts. If we have been bereaved of blessings, we have enjoyed them too. To be bereft is the lot of all; to enjoy, is not the lot of many.

6. I exist;—what does that word mean? Teach me, O God.

7. The only thing we have really to be afraid of, is fearing anything more than God.

8. Wonder at the love of God! He receives our prayers as if they were things of value. He longs that we should love Him; and he receives our petitions for blessings as favours done to Himself. He has greater joy in giving than we in receiving.

9. Floods of tears flow from my eyes, but they cannot wash away my sin.

10. The paschal lamb of the Jews was a type of that of Christians. We have escaped the tyranny of Pharaoh. Crucified with Christ, we are also glorified with Him. He died; we die with Him. He rose; we rise with Him. Let us sacrifice everything to Him who has sacrificed Himself for our redemption. Let us do for Him what He has done for us.

BASIL.

BORN 329—DIED 379.

1. Life is a journey which commences when we enter the world, and ends at the grave. We are like voyagers on the ocean, wafted by winds towards the port, whilst asleep in the vessel, and who, insensible of the progress made, arrive there before they are aware.

2. Angels are distributed around us in great numbers. They form an army, an encampment, according to the Scriptures ; and a numerous army, a well-regulated camp, are not afraid of the attacks of the enemy.

3. Never let us say of anything, it happened by chance ; there is nothing that has not been fore-arranged, nothing which has not its own special end, by which it forms a link in the chain of appointed order.

4. To blaspheme the Holy Ghost is to attribute His operations to the devil.

5. Many go to hear a preacher, not as learners, but as spies, anxious to find out the weak parts of his discourse ; and who, even in the Scriptures, seek matter for criticism, not edification.

6. The slanderer harms three persons at once : him of whom he says the ill, him to whom he says it, and specially himself in saying it.

7. The rose delights me ; but I never look on it without remembering the sin that caused the earth to bring forth thorns, which before it knew not.

8. Pray without ceasing; not in mere words, but in thought and desire, so that your life shall be one long and perpetual prayer.

9. Has any one spoken evil of you? Reply by blessings. Does he treat you ill? Be patient. Does he persecute you? Think of Jesus Christ. Can you suffer as he suffered?

10. The earth does not contain one inhabitant whose life is perfectly happy. Is there a stream whose waters are always clear? It is God only who is happy, completely and unchangeably.

11. He calls Himself the Light of the world, both to indicate the unapproachable glory of His Godhead, and to shew that He illuminates with the splendour of the knowledge of Himself the purged eyes of sinners.

12. Christ was 'made of a woman.' Not *by means of,* but OF a woman, to shew the identity of the nature produced with that of hers who produced it.

13. Life runs on in a continuous current, which carries us unconsciously along with it. We sleep, and as we do so, our brief space of time flies silently over our heads. We wake to a thousand cares, and, while struggling with them, life pursues its ever rapid course.

JEROME.

BORN 331—DIED 420.

1. Whether I am eating or drinking, or whatever I am doing, that voice seems always to sound in my ears, Arise, ye dead, and come to judgment. Whenever I think of that day of judgment, I tremble all over, heart and body. Whatever of pleasure there is in this present life, it is so to be tasted as that the day of coming judgment may never be lost sight of.

2. He is rich enough who is poor with Christ.

3. You err, my brother, you err, if you think that anywhere a Christian is not to suffer persecution. Then chiefly are you assailed when you know not that you are assailed.

4. Read again and again the divine Scriptures; nay, let the holy book never be out of your hands. Learn, that you may teach.

5. Of Christ's minister, let the mouth, the mind, the hands, be ever in harmony.

6. Shun the feasts of the worldly; specially of those who are puffed up with honours. It is not seemly in a minister of the poor and crucified Christ, to have lictors and soldiers standing guard before his door.

7. It will come, it will come, that day when as victor you shall return home; when as a crowned warrior you shall march through the heavenly Jerusalem.

8. To *be* a Christian is the great thing, not to *seem* one.

9. Far rather would I have pious rusticity than learned blasphemy.

10. Lord, let me know myself, that I may better know Thee, the Saviour of the world.

11. The economy of the world, visible and invisible, before and since creation, has reference to the coming of Jesus Christ to earth. The cross of Christ is the centre to which everything tends, the summary of the history of the universe.

12. The praiseworthy thing is, not to have been at Jerusalem, but to have lived well there. The city which we desire, is not that which slew the prophets and shed the blood of Christ, but which the river of life gladdens ; which being set upon a hill cannot be hid ; which the apostle calls the mother of the saints, and in which he rejoices to have his citizenship with the just.

13. The heavenly hall is equally accessible from Britain as from Jerusalem.

14. O lust, thou infernal fire whose fuel is gluttony, whose flame is pride, whose sparkles are wanton words, whose smoke is infamy, whose ashes are uncleanness, whose end is hell !

15. You walk as one loaded with gold ; beware of the robber. This life of ours is a race ; here we strive, that hereafter we may be crowned. No one can walk securely amid serpents and scorpions.

16. It is difficult for the human soul not to love something ; and our affections must go out somewhere. Carnal love is overcome by spiritual love ; desire is quenched by

desire ; and that which is lost on the one hand is gained on the other. Therefore cry out and say upon your couch, In the night I sought Him whom my soul loveth.

17. Let the foolish virgins wander abroad, do you remain at home with the Bridegroom.

18. Let the doors of your hearts be opened to Christ, but closed against the devil.

19. Like Daniel, have your windows open to Jerusalem, whence the light shall enter, and you shall behold the city of the Lord.

CHRYSOSTOM.

BORN 347—DIED 407.

1. The Book of the Evangelists is the history of the life and teaching of Jesus Christ. The book of the Acts is the record of what has been said and done by the Holy Spirit.

2. Thus men, when a son is to shew himself at his coming to the estate and dignity, clothe even the servants with a new and bright garment, to glorify the heir,—so will God also clothe the creature with incorruption for the glorious liberty of the children.

3. Prayer is a haven to the shipwrecked man, an anchor to them that are sinking in the waves, a staff to the limbs that totter, a mine of jewels to the poor, a healer of diseases, and a guardian of health. Prayer at once secures the continuance of our blessings, and dissipates the cloud of our calamities. O blessed prayer ! thou art the unwearied conqueror of human woes, the firm foundation of human happiness, the source of ever-enduring joy, the mother of philosophy. The man who can pray truly, though languishing in extremest indigence, is richer than all beside ; whilst the wretch who never bowed the knee, though proudly seated as monarch of all nations, is of all men the most destitute.

4. There are charitable Christians, who are so drily,— barren fig-trees, with leaves only. There are also some

whose souls are narrow, who are charitable by fits, who will give once or twice and no more. Let us resemble the olive,—let us bring forth abundant fruits, the fruits of peace and mercy.

5. We are ready to reckon up our trials, but are we equally so to keep account of the sins which draw them down upon us?

6. You will perhaps be amazed when I tell you that it is not so necessary to watch against great crimes as against faults which may appear to us small and indifferent.

7. There is not anything in the Scriptures which can be considered unimportant; there is not a single sentence of which does not deserve to be meditated on; for it is not the word of man, but of the Holy Spirit, and the least syllable of it contains a hidden treasure.

8. A boat overladen sinks, so much wealth drowns men in perdition.

9. A rock, though beaten on by winds and waves, is immoveable; so faith, grounded on the rock Christ, holds out in all temptations.

10. The devil's first assault is violent; resist that, and his second will be weaker; that being resisted, he proves a coward.

11. Intemperance is a hydra with a hundred heads. She never stalks abroad unaccompanied with impurity, anger, and the most infamous profligacies.

12. The venial faults, of which you take no account, become the root of the greatest crimes.

AUGUSTINE.

BORN 354—DIED 430.

1. No one can be robbed of his delights whose joy is Christ. Eternal is his gladness who rejoices in an eternal good.

2. Be not alarmed, O Christian, because the things believed are deferred ; although the promise has not come to light, let prayer persevere in hope. Press on in works, increase in holiness ; so shall the stedfastness of thy faith be proved, and the glory of the recompence be increased.

3. God is said to remember when He does a thing, to forget when He does it not. For in God there can be no forgetfulness, seeing he changes not ; neither can there be remembrance, because he forgets nothing.

4. When thou doest good, do it cheerfully ; for whatever good thou doest sadly, it may be said to be done by thee, but thou doest it not.

5. Faith opens a way for the understanding, unbelief closes it.

6. God counts that free service, which not necessity but love dictates.

7. Night does not extinguish the stars, so this world's iniquity does not obscure the minds of believers clinging to the firmament of holy Scripture.

8. The anger of God is no furious agitation, but the judgment, which awards punishment to the sin.

9. Let not man complain when suffering adversity; for by the bitterness of the lower he is taught the love of the higher. Let not the traveller going to his native land prefer the stable to his home.

10. When shall I see that city whose streets are paved with pure gold, in which shall be sung the song of gladness, and through all the streets of which the hallelujah shall be uttered by all. O holy city! O beautiful city! from afar I salute thee, I cry for thee, I entreat for thee, I long to see thee, and to rest in thee; but kept still in the flesh, I am not permitted. O city to be longed for! thy walls one gem, thy keeper God himself, thy citizens always rejoicing, for they exult in the vision of God. In thee there is no corruptibility, nor defect, nor old age, nor anger, but perennial peace and festal glory; joy everlasting, festival unbroken. In thee there is no yesterday nor to-morrow, but an unchanging to-day. To-morrow is as yesterday, and the long ago is eternally the same. To thee belong salvation, life, and endless peace. To thee God is all. In thee there is no fear, no sadness; each desire passes at once into joy; all that is wished for is at hand, and all that is longed for abounds.

11. Sigh for the eternal Jerusalem! whither your hope has gone before, let your life follow. There we shall be with Christ.

12. If you would be armed against temptation in the world, let the longing for the eternal Jerusalem grow and be strengthened in your hearts. Our captivity shall pass away, our felicity shall come, the last enemy shall be destroyed, and beyond death we shall triumph with our King.

FULGENTIUS.

BORN 468—DIED 533.

1. There our love will not be less than our praise, nor our praise inferior to our love ; for our praise will be full, because there will be in us the perfect love of God and of our neighbour. Then we shall praise and possess ; we shall possess and love ; then we shall be satisfied with delight, and delight with satiety.

2. Then there will be in us true, perfect, lofty humility; since in the flesh and mind there shall remain no corrupt desire ; the spirit shall not be exhausted with cares, nor the body wasted with labour. There shall be no more any anxiety about the conflict, but the perfect security of peace.

3. This grace which God freely gives to the vessels of mercy, begins with illuminating the heart. It does not find man's will good, but makes it so. It chooses first, in order that it may be chosen ; nor is it received unless it first work in the heart of man. Therefore, both the reception of grace and the desire for it are the work of grace itself.

4. That men may become sons of God, they must receive the Son of God by faith ; and this power of believing they receive from the Lord.

5. Grace first chooses in order that it may be chosen. No man can desire or ask for, nay, not even so much as know it, unless it has first laid hold of him.

6. Let humility of mind grow in you. This is the true and genuine loftiness of a Christian. Know that the more humility of heart abounds in you, the more is the grace of God increasing.

7. Let those who, in days of joy, have despised the compassion of God, when brought under the rod of discipline, tremble before his sorrow.

8. It was necessary Christ should be both God and man, to work our redemption. As He was God, He was able ; as He was man, He had aptness. No man nor angel could have effected it. Not man ; for how could he, who was dead in sin, give life to others? Not the angels ; for they had not sufficiency to stand upright themselves.

9. Though thou be in the dark, yet pray, for thy Father is light. Thou canst not lie hid from His eye ; and, therefore, neither faint in thy devotion nor dissemble in hypocrisy, for thy God hears thee in secret as well as sees thee.

10. Though thou be banished, yet Christ is thy associate ; though amongst thieves or wild beasts, though at sea in tempests, or on land in troubles, though in hunger, cold, or nakedness, thy Captain stands and sees the combating. Hold out, then, for He will crown thee.

11. If he shall have judgment without mercy that hath not shewed mercy, what judgment shall he receive that hath done others injury?

12. Christ died for men and angels: for men, that they might rise from sin ; for angels, that they might not fall into sin. For them, that they might not be wounded; for man, that he might be healed of his wounds. He took

infirmity from man, and gave confirmation to them.　He
was the wisdom of the Father to enlighten, the power of
the Father to uphold.

13. Let us be careful not to revenge our own wrongs,
but remember that we ought to suffer much more than we
do for the sake of Christ.

14. The thoughts and affections do follow love's direction ; wherefore the Truth saith, 'Where your treasure
is, there will your heart be.'　Therefore, if our treasure be
in heaven, our affections will be in heaven.　To lay up
this treasure, mark thy thoughts ; so thou shalt know thy
treasure by thy love, and thy love by thy thoughts.

15. If they go to hell, not because they took away the
garment from the naked, but because they did not clothe
them ; not because they took away the bread from the
hungry, but because they did not give their bread to
them,—what shall become of them who do not give nor
clothe, but do strip off and rob the indigent ?　Remember the torment of the rich man, and relieve Lazarus, that
thou mayest escape damnation.

16. If barrenness be cast into the fire, what shall covet-
ousness deserve ? or what shall covetous rapacity receive,
when want of charity shall be tormented in hell-fire ?

GREGORY (THE GREAT).

BORN 550—DIED 604.

1. As the word of God exercises the understanding of the wise, so does it nourish the simple. It furnishes that with which the little ones may be fed; it contains that which higher minds may admire. It is a river both shallow and deep, in which the lamb may have footing and the elephant may swim.

2. As ointments, unless they are stirred, are not smelt afar off, and as aromatic scents do not give out their fragrance unless they are burned, so it is in their tribulations that the saints give forth their excellencies.

3. For the enlightening of the night of this present life, each star in its turn appears in the face of heaven, until towards the end of the night,—the Redeemer of man rises like the true Morning Star. In order that the radiance of the stars may suit itself to the darkness of our night, Abel comes to shew us guilelessness; Enoch to teach purity of practice; Noah to give lessons of endurance in hope and in work: Abraham to manifest obedience; Isaac to shew an example of chastity in wedded life; Jacob to introduce patience in labour; Joseph the repaying of evil with good; Moses for the shewing forth of meekness; Joshua to form us to confidence against difficulties; Job to shew patience amid afflictions. Behold what sparkling stars we see in the sky, that our feet may

never stumble as we walk this our night journey! As many saints as He has raised up, so many stars has He sent forth into the sky, over the darkness of erring man, till the true Morning Star should rise, who, being the herald of the eternal morning, should outshine the other stars by the radiance of His Godhead.

4. We sin with our lips two ways, either when we say unjust things, or withhold the just.

5. At the appearing of the eternal Judge, the life of the church's pilgrimage is completed. She then receives the recompence of her labours, when, having finished the time of her warfare, she returns to her native country.

6. The dawn is the new birth of the resurrection, when the church rises to contemplate the vision of eternity; for, if the resurrection were not a birth, it would never have been said of it, 'In the REGENERATION, when the Son of man shall sit upon the throne of His glory' (Matt. xix. 28).

7. Good men dread prosperity in the world more than adversity.

8. The Bridegroom hides Himself when sought, that, not being found, He may be sought for with the more ardent affection.

9. We do not render true service to God so long as we obey from fear, and not from love.

10. He that knows the grace of the Redeemer, and longs for a return to his native land, groans under the burden of his pilgrimage. He that loves to sojourn abroad, instead of his own country, knows not how to grieve even in the midst of grief.

HILDEBERT.

BORN 1057—DIED 1134.

1. He came the first time in the guise of humanity; He is to come the second time in brightness, as a light to the godly, a terror to the wicked. He came the first time in weakness, He is to come the second time in might; the first time in our littleness, the second time in His own majesty; the first time in mercy, the second in judgment; the first time to redeem, the second to recompense, and recompense all the more terribly because of the long-suffering and delay.

2. By the wisdom of the serpent we were deceived, by the wisdom of God we are delivered. The former is called wisdom, though it is our folly; the latter is called folly, though it is great and incomprehensible wisdom.

3. The devil may advise, but cannot force, to sin. If the devil alone were advising, and God keeping silence, man might excuse himself. But God, by reason, by the Scriptures, by ministers, cries, SIN NOT. God is on the right hand, Satan on the left; man is in the midst. God persuades man to good, Satan dissuades; but man yields to the devil, not to God!

4. Unhappy soul! Led captive by the devil, despised by man, forsaken by God; after so many and so great apostasies, in which, forgetting thy Saviour, thou hast cast His words behind thy back,—TURN and RETURN from thy

miserable and hurtful gladness to the spiritual and celestial joy, in the Lord Himself.

5. Brethren beloved! ye have been sleeping, now awake; ye have lain long enough in sin.   It is time to arise from sleep.   Our sleep is the darkness of sin ; and so long as we remain in sin, we dwell in darkness, and see not our wickedness.   Let us come to the light ; let us blush for our iniquity.   Oh, what luxury amongst us! what intemperance, what evil-speaking, what falsehood, what treachery to the Lord !   We are of the day, because we have believed ; because we have put on Christ.   But he who is of the day, and yet walks naked, walks dishonourably. Put on the garments of holiness, lest ye be found naked in the presence of the Lord.   Be ready, for in such an hour as ye think not the Son of Man will come.

6. One thief is saved, and cries, ' Lord, remember me;' the other, persisting in his sin, dies on the cross unsaved. How different these two !   Both intimate a coming judgment, in which, by His cross, Christ will save some, and condemn others.   How different the paths !   One ascends to heaven, the other descends to hell.   The one is an example to sinners, not to despair, seeing in the very hour of death Paradise is found.   The other is a terror to the unbelieving and impenitent, who die in their sins.   Yet equally near to both, and equally available for both, was the death of Christ.

7. The day of our redemption is at hand ; the deliverance from captivity begins.   It is now time that, as the true Jacob, we feast our Isaac—at whose nativity God made our Sarah to laugh—on the best and choicest of our

dainties, lest we be condemned for our thanklessness.   To
the great Father of the family, whose guests we are, let
us present the offerings of faith, righteousness, and meekness, for with the proud He will not eat.   They who so
eat and drink are His friends just now, and, in the time
to come, His best beloved, when, from being Jacob, they
shall become Israel; from being wrestlers with God, they
shall be beholders of God ; from faith they shall pass to
knowledge ; from their journey to their home ; from their
race to their rest ; where they shall be satisfied with the
abundance of God's house, and drink of the river of His
pleasures.

BERNARD.

BORN 1091—DIED 1157.

1. Suppose that you may be *righteous* overmuch, or *wise* overmuch, you cannot be *good* overmuch. Nowhere do I read, Be not 'good overmuch;' for no one can be better than he ought. God only seeks not to be better than Himself, because He cannot be so.

2. If, in everyday warfare, we yield, what will we do in the great conflict? If our weakness gives way before frail reeds, how shall we withstand the weapons of steel?

3. It is the devil's part to suggest; ours, not to consent. As often as we resist him, so often we overcome him; as often as we overcome him, so often we bring joy to the angels and glory to God.

4. O sons of Adam, O covetous generation, what have you to do with earthly riches, which are neither true nor yours! Gold and silver are genuine earth, red and white, which only man's folly makes, or rather reckons, precious. If they be yours, carry them with you.

5. We discover glory in the cross. To us who are saved, it is the power of God, the source of all holiness.

6. My heart is a vain heart; a vagabond and unstable heart, seeking rest, finding none. It agrees not with itself; it alters its purposes, changes its judgments, frames new thoughts, pulls down the old, then builds them up again; it wills, and wills not, never remaining the same.

7. Happy art thou, if thy heart be possessed with three fears: a fear for grace received; a greater fear for grace lost; a still greater fear to recover grace.

8. Happy is he alone, to whom the Lord imputeth not sin. To have Him propitious to me, against whom alone I have sinned, suffices for all my righteousness. If my iniquity is great, Thy grace is much greater. When my soul is troubled at the view of its sinfulness, I look at Thy mercy, and am refreshed. It is a common good; is offered to all; and he only who rejects it, is deprived of its benefits. Let him rejoice who feels himself a wretch deserving of perpetual damnation; for the grace of Jesus exceeds the number of all crimes. There is no sin greater than to despair of the forgiveness of sin; for God is kind and merciful, ready to forgive.

9. We know another Jerusalem than that in which David reigned, richer by far, more glorious by far.

10. Not in the royal city of Jerusalem was Jesus born, but in Bethlehem, which is the least among the thousands of Judah. O little Bethlehem, made glorious by the Lord, even by Him who, though great, in thee was made little! Rejoice, O Bethlehem, and through all thy streets let the festal hallelujah be sung.

11. Wonderful things I say, yet true. The Lord of hosts Himself, King of glory, shall descend to change our bodies, and make them like His body of brightness. How great will be that glory, how unutterable the exultation, when the Creator of the universe, who came lowly and hidden, to deliver souls, shall come in unveiled glory, to glorify thee, O miserable flesh!

TAULER.

BORN 1290—DIED 1361.

1. In the case of a pertinacious disputant, allow him to triumph; of a contumacious one, give way by silence; thus both parties will preserve their tranquillity.

2. Love is the shortest and swiftest way to God; nor is there any sweetness in virtue without love, for love is the essence of all virtues. Through the exercise of this love, man comes to such self-abhorrence as not only to despise himself, but to be content to be despised by others; nay, counts this contempt all joy.

3. As a sculptor is said to have indignantly exclaimed on seeing a rude block of marble, 'What godlike beauty thou hidest!' Thus God looks upon man, in whom God's own image is hidden.

4. We may begin by loving God in hope of reward; we may express ourselves concerning him in symbols; but we must throw them all away, and, much more, must we scorn all idea of reward, that we may love God only, because He is the supreme good, and contemplate His eternal nature as the substance of our own soul (that is, as the God in whom we live and move and have our being).

5. If a man truly loves God, and has no will but to do God's will, the whole force of the river Rhine may run at him, and will not disturb him nor break his peace. If we

find outward things a danger and disturbance, it comes from our appropriating to ourselves what is God's.

6. The friends of God find the truth unknown to others. Wherefore, beloved children, the masters of Paris diligently read the books and turn over the leaves; this is something; this is pretty well. But *these men* read the true living book, where all is life.

7. Know that shouldest thou let thyself be stabbed a thousand times a day, and come to life again; shouldest thou let thyself be strung to a wheel, and eat thorns and stones; with all this, thou couldest not overcome sin of thyself. But sink thyself into the deep unfathomable mercy of God, and Christ will give it thee out of his great kindness, and free goodness, and love, and compassion.

8. Wouldest thou master the flesh? Lay upon it the curb and fetters of love. With that thou wilt overcome it easiest of all, and with love thou wilt load it heaviest of all.

9. We must seek God by Himself; and this foretaste of the great, true wedding, many people would fain have, and complain that it cannot be. And if they experience no wedding when they pray, and find not God's presence in spiritual exercises, it vexes them; they say they have no experience of God; and they grow weary of their painstaking and praying. This a man should never do; for God was present though we perceived Him not. He went secretly to the wedding; and, where God is, there is the wedding; and He cannot be away from it. Where a man simply thinks of Him, and seeks Him alone, there God must, of necessity, be, either sensibly or in a hidden manner.

PETRARCH.

BORN 1304—DIED 1374.

1. If tears become any one when dying, it is him whom laughter did not become when living ; seeing he saw that which makes death a thing to be wept, ever at hand, and suspended above his head. How closely did this weeping follow upon that laughter !

2. To the eternal tribunal of the just Judge our appeal is safe. He will rescind the unjust judgment.

3. In all good studies I delighted ; but was specially given to philosophy and poetry, which even, however, I neglected in process of time, being delighted with the Holy Scriptures, in which I perceived a hidden sweetness which I once despised. Poetry I reserved as for ornamental purposes alone.

4. As truth is immortal, so a lie lasts not ; feigned things are soon discovered, as the hair that is combed and set with great diligence is ruffled with a little blast of wind. The craftiest lie cannot stand before the truth ; everything that is covered is soon uncovered ; shadows pass away ; and the native colour of things remains. No man can live long under water ; he must needs come forth and shew the face which he concealed.

5. Desire and strive to die well, which cannot be without living well. The rest commit to God, who brought you into this world unasked, but who, when you are about

to leave it, will not introduce you to His kingdom unsought.

6. Impatient of disease, do you wish for death? Foolish and proud! Allow Him who made your body to determine all things concerning it. Only the use of it, not lordship over it, have you received; and that only for a short time. Think you that you are lord of your clayey mansion? You are but a tenant. He who made all things, He is its Lord.

7. To many, liberty is servitude; to others, servitude is liberty. The yoke of care is worse than the yoke of men; yet he who has shaken off the one, bears the other patiently!

8. Where you are is of no moment, but only what you are doing there. It is not the place that ennobles you, but you the place; and this only by doing that which is great and noble.

9. You fear to die in your sins? But who is to blame but yourself? Who compelled you to sin? Who forbade you to have it washed away? Who hinders your repentance, however late? Carry not your sins away with you. There is still time; and He still lives who takes them away and blots them out, who casts them behind His back, and removes them from you as far as the east is from the west.

WICLIFFE.

BORN 1324—DIED 1384.

1. Have a remembrance of the goodness of God : how He made thee in His own likeness, and how Jesus Christ, both God and man, died so painful a death upon the cross, to buy man's soul out of hell, even with His own heart's blood, and to bring it to the bliss of heaven.

2. Bethink thee heartily of the wonderful kindness of God, who was so high and so worshipful in heaven, that He should come down so low, and be born of the maiden, and become our brother, to buy us again, by his hard passion, from our thraldom to Satan.

3. See the great kindness which God hath shewn for thee, and thereby learn thy own great unkindness; and thus thou shalt see that man is the most fallen of creatures, and the unkindest of all creatures that God ever made. It should be full sweet and delightful to us to think thus on this great kindness and this great love of Jesus Christ.

4. We are predestinated that we may obtain divine acceptance and become holy ; having received that grace through Christ's taking human nature, whereby we are rendered finally pleasing to God. And it appears that this grace, which is called the grace of predestination, or the charity of final perseverance, cannot by any means fail.

5. That shall be a dreadful doom and a fearful Doomsman. For Christ, who shall be Judge there, is now meek

as a lamb, and ready to bow to mercy; but there He will be stern as a lion to all that are damnable, and shall doom according to righteousness. Before this stern Doomsman all men and women shall yield reckoning of all their living on earth.

6. Have mind that when thou wert a child of wrath and of hell, for the sin of Adam, Christ laid his life to pledge, to bring thee out of that prison; and He gave not as ransom for thee either gold or silver, or any other jewel, but his own precious blood that ran out of his heart. This should move all Christian men to have mind of God, and to worship Him in thought, word, and deed.

7. The Father defendeth every soul that is true to Him from the power of the fiend (devil) who would overset it; and granteth it through His grace to be an heir of heaven.

8. Christ teacheth us in this prayer to ask the dreadful time of doom, in which the kingdom of God shall fully come.

CHAUCER.

BORN 1328—DIED 1400.

1. Certainly there is no sin in man so horrible, but may, in this life, be taken away, through virtue of the passion and of the death of Christ. Alas! what need men then to be despaired, sith that his mercy is so ready and large! Ask, and have.

2. For certainly, in this world, there is no wight that may be kept sufficiently without the keeping of our Lord Jesus Christ.

3. Many are the ways spiritual that lead folk to our Lord Jesus Christ, and to the reign of glory. Of which ways, there is a full noble way, which may not fail to man nor woman that through sin hath misgone from the right way of Jerusalem celestial; and this way is called Repentance.

4. O good God, well ought man to have great disdain of sin, sith that through sin he who was free from sin was made bound.

5. Sith that Jesus Christ took on him the pain of all our wickednesses, much ought sinful man to weep and bewail that, for his sins, God's Son of heaven should all this pain endure.

6. Certainly God Almighty is all good; and, therefore, either He forgiveth *all* sin, or else right nought.

7. Though no earthly man may eschew all sins, yet may

he refrain them, by the burning love that he hath to our Lord Jesus Christ.

8. Do many good works, and speak few vanities.

9. Jesus Christ is entirely all good ; in Him is none imperfection ; and, therefore, either He forgiveth *all* sin perfectly, or else, never a deal.

10. Men should remember them of the shame that is to come at the day of doom, to men that be not penitent and forgiven in this present life ; for all the creatures in earth and in hell shall see openly what has been hid in this world.

11. Full oft time I read, that no man trust in his own perfection, be he stronger than Samson, or holier than Daniel, or wiser than Solomon.

12. Thou shalt understand also that God ordained fasting ; and to fasting pertaineth four things : gifts to poor folk ; gladness of heart spiritual ; not to be angry or annoyed ; nor to grudge that he fasteth.

13. One doubt cometh of this, that he deemeth he hath sinned so greatly, and so oft, and so long lain in sin, that he shall not be saved. Against that cursed doubt he should think, that the suffering of Jesus Christ is more strong to unbind, than sin is strong to bind. As often as he falleth he may rise again ; and, though he hath lain never so long in sin, the mercy of Christ is alway ready to receive him to mercy.

14. Let men understand what is the fruit of all, after the words of Jesus Christ. It is an endless bliss of heaven. There joy hath never end ; there is no woe nor grievance ; there all harms of this present life hath passed ; there, as

there is security from the pain of hell, so there is the blissful company that rejoice evermore, every one of others' joy; there the body of man, that sometime was foul and dark, is more clear than the sun; there the body, that sometime was sick, frail, feeble, and mortal, is immortal, and strong, and whole; there is neither hunger, thirst, nor cold, but every soul replenished with the sight of the perfect knowing of God. To which life may He bring us that bought us with His precious blood. Amen.

THOMAS (A KEMPIS).

BORN 1330—DIED 1471.

1. Vanity of vanities, all is vanity, except only the love of God, and an entire devotedness to His service.

2. What have redeemed souls to do with the distinctions and subtleties of logic? He whom the Eternal Word condescends to teach is disengaged at once from the labyrinth of human opinions.

3. O God, who art the truth, make me one with Thee in everlasting love! I am often weary of reading and weary of hearing; in Thee alone is the sum of all my desires. Let all teachers be silent, let the whole creation be dumb before Thee, and do Thou only speak to my soul.

4. To place thyself lower than all mankind can do thee no hurt; but much hurt may be done by preferring thyself to a single individual.

5. We might enjoy much peace, if we did not busy our minds with what others do and say, in which we have no concern. But how is it possible for that man to dwell long in peace, who continually intermeddles in the affairs of others; who runs about seeking occasions of disquietude, and never, or but seldom, turns to God, in the retirement of a recollected spirit?

6. It is good for a man to suffer the adversity of this earthly life, for it brings him back to the sacred retirement

of the heart, where only he finds that he is an exile from his native home, and ought not to place his trust in any worldly joy.

7. It is by gradual advances, rather than impetuous efforts, that victory is obtained; rather by patient suffering, that looks to God for support, than by impatient solicitude and rigorous austerity.

8. In judging others, a man labours to no purpose; commonly errs, and easily sins; but, in examining and judging himself, he is always wisely and usefully employed.

9. If thou art not able to make thyself that which thou wishest to be, how canst thou expect to mould another in conformity to thy will?

10. If thou canst refrain from unnecessary conversation and idle visits, and suppress the desire of hearing and telling some new thing, thou wilt find not only abundant leisure, but convenient opportunity for holy and useful mediation.

11. No man can safely go abroad who does not love to stay at home; no man can safely speak who does not willingly hold his tongue; no man can safely govern that would not willingly become subject.

12. The closet, long continued in, becomes delightful; but, when seldom visited, it is beheld with reluctance, weariness, and disgust.

13. If thou hadst never gone abroad and listened to idle reports, thou hadst continued safe in the possession of peace.

14. He that loves with purity considers not the gift of the lover, but the love of the giver.

15. O Lord God, I esteem it a signal mercy that I do not possess many of those qualities and endowments which, in the eyes of men, appear glorious, and attract admiration and applause.

16. What can be more at rest than the heart that, in simplicity and singleness, regardeth only Thee?

17. We ask whether such a man be a profound scholar, or an eloquent writer; but how poor in spirit he is, how patient, how meek, how holy, how resigned, we regard as questions of no importance.

18. My God! my all! enough to say for him that understandeth; and often to say it, delightful to him that loveth.

19. How often has the growth of holiness been checked by its being too hastily known and too highly commended.

20. O my God, soften the rigour of my banishment and assuage the violence of my sorrow!

HUSS.

BORN 1376—MARTYRED 1415.

1. Truly it is a serious thing to rejoice without perturbation, and to count all joy in manifold trials. It is easy to speak of and to expound this, but to fulfil it is a serious thing. The most enduring and bravest of soldiers, though knowing that on the third day He was to rise, and by death overcome His enemies, yet after the Last Supper, was troubled in spirit, and said, My soul is exceeding sorrowful, even unto death.

2. I protest that I have never felt myself overwhelmed by persecution; that I am only borne down by my sins, and by the errors of the Christian people.

3. What are the riches of the world to me! What affliction can their loss cause me! What is it to me to lose the favour of the world, which makes us swerve from the path of Christ! What signifies infamy, which, when supported with humility, proves, purifies, and illuminates the children of God in such a manner that they shine like the bright sun in their Father's kingdom! And lastly, what is death, should this miserable life be torn from me! He who loses it in this world triumphs even over death, and finds true life in the next.

4. I do not desire to live in this corrupted age, unless I can lead to repentance myself and others, according to the will of God.

5. Pontiffs and priests, Scribes and Pharisees, Herod and Pilate, and the inhabitants of Jerusalem, condemned the Truth; they crucified and buried it; but it rose from the tomb and conquered them all, sending forth in its stead twelve preachers of the word.

6. Strengthen your hearts, dearly beloved, for the coming of our Lord Jesus Christ is nigh. Think how the Son of God, Himself God eternal, became man in order to help us. The immortal Physician came to heal our incurable sores. The all-powerful Lord came, not to trouble the dead, but to vivify the living, and redeem His elect from eternal death.

7. Mediate on those benefits which our Lord has heaped on us by His first coming, and strengthen your hearts, for His second coming is near, and with it the sentence of the great Judge, infinitely wise, infinitely just, infinitely formidable, from whom neither the great nor the learned of this world can escape; with whom will come the just, the preachers of His word, and all who have been unjustly persecuted in this world.

8. Study to avenge the insults offered to God, rather than your own. Alas! it is in this point that the whole world is mistaken, for all men are more ready to avenge their own injuries than those of God.

9. Now the saints no longer suffer anxieties and torments, but enjoy a sweet and unchangeable peace, as well as infinite joy. Peter and Paul reign already with the King of heaven; they are with the angelic choir; they behold the King of kings in His magnificence; no sorrows afflict them; they are filled with ineffable happiness.

SAVONAROLA.

BORN 1452—DIED 1498.

1. Do you wish I should preach well? Give me time to converse with my children. 'In this way,' said Savonarola, 'I have learned much, for God ofttimes speaks and expounds His revelations by these simple youths, as by pure vessels full of the Holy Spirit.'

2. What is Babylon but Rome? Babylon signifies confusion. There is not in the world greater confusion of crimes and all sorts of iniquity than at Rome. Since they have made it a dwelling for harlots, God will make it a stall for swine and horses!

3. O Lord, delay not, that the unbelievers and the wicked may not say, 'Where is the God of these men, who have so often repented and fasted?' Thou seest the bad become every day worse, and now they seem to have become incorrigible. Stretch forth, stretch forth Thy hand, Thy mighty arm! I can do no more—I think not what more to say. There is nothing left for me but to weep. I would dissolve in tears upon this pulpit. I ask not, O Lord, that thou shouldst hear us for our merits, but for Thy mercy, for the love of Thy Son. Look upon the face of Thine Anointed, have compassion on Thy sheep. Dost Thou see them here, all afflicted, all persecuted? Dost thou not love them, O my God? Didst Thou not become incarnate for them? Wert thou not crucified,

didst Thou not die for them? If I cannot prevail—if this work is too much for me, recall my soul—take me away, O Lord! release me from life. What have thy sheep done? They have done nothing. I am the guilty one; yet, O Lord, have not respect to my sins, have respect this once to Thy loving-kindness, Thy tenderness, Thy bowels of mercies, and let us feel all Thy compassion.

4. When any one begins to enjoy the Holy Spirit, he is glad to be alone, and immediately separates himself from other comforts and corporeal recreations, which would not be, if he did not feel within his heart greater consolations than those he refuses.

5. The old chaste time of the first Church has departed. Rome, polluted with all vices, rushes on towards a second fall. But to denounce her condition, is only to excite fruitless enmity. Nothing then remains, but to lament silently, and to hold fast the hope of a better future.

6. O infinite love! I have grievously sinned, and Thou, Jesus, wert stricken. I have been Thine enemy, and Thou, Jesus, for love of me, wert nailed to the cross.

7. In spiritual life we must fix our hearts on the love of Jesus Christ before everything, if we would proceed regularly in good works.

8. Would you see how one place or state is not more advantageous than another to the careless man? Judas the disciple of Christ was wicked; the school of Christ availed him not.

9. Many have been victorious in great temptations, and ruined by little ones.

10. Wonder ye that the good work has so many ene-

mies? Even Christ had constantly to contend with the Pharisees and Scribes.

11. The pillars of the church are cast down upon the earth, and evangelic doctrine is heard no more. The gold of the temple is gone; the true divine wisdom, which enlightens and gladdens the heart. The roof of the church has fallen in; in the storm and the whirlwind are swept away the devout priests and princes, who adorn the bride of Jesus. The binding lime and mortar fail. Where seest thou now-a-days true love among Christians? No more are they united in Christ Jesus—therefore no one seeks the good of the other, but each one only his own. All the walls of the Church are undermined.

12. In the primitive Church were the chalices of wood, and the prelates of gold; in our days, the prelates are of wood, and the chalices of gold.

13. We stand on the battle-field, but doubt not that we shall conquer at last, and in every way, even dying; and in death shall fight more successfully than in life.

14. This morning thought I, that I should go to heaven, but the hope is delayed. Thou, who suspectest that I perhaps have had fears, knowest thou not that faith fears nothing? He who hath faith stands where the men of the world cannot reach, where the sword and dagger of the enemy come not.

15. Oh wonderful power of hope, before whom all sorrows yield, all ready consolation comes!

16. Take away, Lord, my sins, and I am freed from all trouble. Yes! set me free, not according to my righteousness, but according to thy mercy!

ERASMUS.

BORN 1467—DIED 1536.

1. Though thou hadst gotten six hundred teachers, yet it is the Lord that doth truly and effectually teach this philosophy and wisdom.

2. Faith is the door whereby we enter into the house of God.

3. Faith purgeth the heart, and love straighteneth the crooked and corrupt will. Faith judgeth and teacheth what is to be done ; love executeth the same as the servant of faith. Faith is a gift put into man's mind, through which he does, without any doubtfulness, believe all those things to be true which God has taught and promised us. Faith is the most sure knowledge that is in the world.

4. Whom can that most meek and gentle Lamb refuse or reject, who, when the thief hanging on the cross did own Him, forthwith did bid him to the bridal feast, and, of a blaspheming sinner, made him an heir of His kingdom?

5. This life is a battle ; whether we will or not, we cannot choose but fight, either on God's side or the devil's.

6. Nothing quiets the mind of man, save only the grace of Christ.

7. The eye of faith is a simple dove's eye, reverently beholding God in the manner in which it is His pleasure to be known of us.

8. He hath come once for all. He hath once for all finished that singular and marvellous sacrifice with the commemoration of which He would have us nourished until He come again the second time, not to be then a Redeemer, but a Judge and Rewarder.

9. Christ was eternally the Son of God; but, after He was conceived by the Holy Ghost, His blessed soul was full of all heavenly grace. But, though He might thus be called twice born, once of His Father, without time, and before all time, and again of His mother, in the time appointed by God, yet are there not two sons, but only one Son. He was conceived of the substance of the virgin, that we should acknowledge the verity of His human nature.

10. Our Lord took on Him, not only the verity of man's nature, but also the miseries which accompany the nature of man fallen, those things only excepted which are not suitable to the dignity of the Person who was both God and man, or else which do exclude the fulness of grace. For neither did He receive proclivity or readiness to do sin, nor the power to sin; neither did He take unto Him error or ignorance. And those incommodities which He took, He took not of the necessity of nature, but voluntarily for our sake, to make satisfaction for our offences, and to suffer for that which we had trespassed.

11. There are three Sabbaths. The first was the Sabbath of God alone, without us. The second is ours, by His love and goodness, but imperfect here in this life. The third Sabbath is perfect in the world to come.

JACOBI DE VALENTIA. [*]

BORN 1468—DIED 1491.

1. O Lord, think not upon my sins, but think upon Thy mercy, which is greater than all my sins and transgressions.

2. The faith of the church, under both Testaments, is the same. The faith which saves us is the same that saved the ancient fathers. For, as it is the same Christ that is believed by us and by them, so it is the same faith. There is this difference only—that the mystery of the incarnation and redemption, which, we believe, is completed; to them it was future. But yet, as we believe that no one can be delivered from sin, save by the blood and passion of Christ, so did the fathers believe.

3. The sacrifice of the morning and evening lamb, of itself, brought no grace, nor did it purge away sin. But, through means of the blood of the coming Christ, thus prefigured, they received deliverance from sin who, when offering their sacrifice, believed in the blood to come. Thus it was alone their faith and hope in a coming Christ that delivered them from guilt.

4. Thus David prayed because he believed; for faith goes before all prayer.

5. As the divine Word assumed this flesh and human nature, in the unity of His person, that He might suffer in

---

[*] We translate these gems from the author's Commentary on the Psalms and Song of Solomon; a rare old Latin quarto.

it (which person is called one Christ, God and man), so this Christ assumed, and united, and espoused to Himself the whole Church and community of believers into the unity of His mystical body, that He might suffer for it. Thus Christ and the Church are called one mystical man and one mystical Christ, whose head is this true Christ, and whose body or members are the whole Church of the faithful. Thus Christ is called the Bridegroom and Head of the Church.

6. Christ is the object and the subject of all our theology, and of Holy Scripture.

7. As Christ is the dispenser of grace, so is He the giver of rewards. As God, through Christ, called and justified those whom He predestinated from eternity, so it is meet that, through Christ, He should bestow the glory, the blessedness, and the honour. Thus Christ is in all things the mediator between God and man. Seeing He is the Intercessor, the Surety, the Interpreter, so is He the Leader, the Judge, the Rewarder.

8. As Christ is the Head of the Church and of all believers, from whom flows down all virtue and all grace to all the members, so the devil is head and chief of all the wicked and unbelieving. Unbelievers are members of the devil; and as of Christ and the Church is fashioned one mystical body, so of the devil and Church, or synagogue of Satan is composed one devilish body.

9. Since His ascension, the Bridegroom has not spoken personally and familiarly to His bride, but through a medium; and this is to last till His second coming, when He will speak to us. Then will He introduce His bride

to the nuptials of glory. Then the Bride will speak personally to the Bridegroom the words of praise; and the Bridegroom shall rejoice over the Bride, without a medium, listening to her voice.

10. The first nuptials were those of redemption, and incarnation, and mystical union. To these the Bridegroom called the Bride on His first advent. The second nuptials are those of glory, to which He calls her at His second coming.

11. Delivering her from this mundane misery, He will place His church upon the mountains of the spices of celestial bliss. Make haste, my Beloved, to these mountains, and, in making haste, take me with Thee. Make haste, and I will follow!

LATIMER.

BORN 1480—DIED 1555.

1. As he is a good Augustine friar that keeps well St Augustine's rules, so he is a good Christian man that keeps well Christ's rule.

2. Christ saith, ' Come to Me.' Let us follow this word, and let us come to Him ; for the faith that hath God's word is a true faith ; but that faith which hath not God's word is a lying faith, a false faith.

3. I doubt not but that I have been laughed to scorn when I have preached that the way to get riches is to give away to the poor what we have. They have called me an old doating fool ; but what then ? We must be content to be despised with Christ in this world, that we may be glorified with Him in yonder world.

4. The love of God towards mankind passeth all natural love ; and He is ready to give unto every one that cometh to Him for help ; yea, He will give us the very Holy Ghost when we desire it.

5. Embrace Christ's cross, and Christ shall embrace you.

6. I pray you note this, we must first be made good before we can do good ; we must first be made just before our words can please God.

7. If thou art desirous to know whether thou art chosen to everlasting life, thou mayest not begin with God, for

God is too high, thou canst not comprehend Him; but begin with Christ, and learn to know Christ, and wherefore He came, namely, that He might save sinners.

8. The woman came to Him among the press of the people, desiring to touch only the hem of His garment; for she believed Christ was such a *healthful* man, that she should be sound as soon as she might touch Him. All England, yea, all the world, may take this woman for a schoolmistress, to learn by her to trust in Christ, and to seek help at His hands.

9. Faith brings Christ, and Christ brings remission of sins; but how shall we obtain faith? St Paul teaches us this, faith cometh by hearing. Then, if we will come to faith, we must hear God's word.

10. We are justified by God's free gift, and not of ourselves; but the righteousness of Christ is accounted to be our righteousness, and through the same we obtain everlasting life.

11. I never saw so little discipline as is now-a-days. Men will all be masters; they will be masters, and not disciples.

12. Mix your pleasures with the remembrance of Christ's bitter passion.

LUTHER.

BORN 1483—DIED 1546.

1. That a man may lift up his head toward heaven, he must find nothing on earth whereon to lean it.

2. That thou despairest of thyself, and doubtest of thy power, does not displease me : but this displeaseth me, that thou also despairest of the power of God.

3. Our unthankfulness for, and light esteem of, God's Word, will do more than anything to help the Pope into the saddle again.

4. He that hath Christ for his God and King, let him be assured that he hath the devil for his enemy, who will work him much sorrow, and will plague him all the days of his life.

5. No stone, nor steel, nor diamond is so hard as the impenitent heart of man.

6. They are small devils that tempt with lasciviousness and avarice; higher spirits tempt with unbelief, and despair, and heresy.

7. Thus Christ, with most sweet names, is called my law, my sin, my death, whereas in very deed he is nothing else but mere liberty, righteousness, life, and everlasting salvation.

8. Surely I could never have believed, but that I have good experience at this day, that the power of the devil is so great that he is able to make falsehood so like to truth.

9. We are mercifully called in grace, that we should be freemen under Christ, and not bondmen under Moses.

10. All our doing is to suffer God to work in us. He giveth the word, which, when we have received, by faith given from above, we are new born, and made the sons of God.

11. The difference between the offices of the law and the Gospel keepeth all Christian doctrines in their true and proper place.

12. Let who will begin and prize this thing, he shall at length find how grievous and hard a thing it is for a man that hath been occupied all his lifetime in the works of his own holiness to escape out of it, and with all his heart by faith cleave to this one Mediator. I myself have now preached the gospel almost twenty years, and have been exercised in the same daily, by reading and writing, so that I may well seem to be rid of this wicked opinion : notwithstanding I yet now and then feel the same old filth cleave to my heart. Whereby it cometh to pass that I would willingly so have to do with God, that I might bring something with myself, because of which He should for my holiness' sake give me His grace. And I can scarcely be brought to commit myself with all confidence to mere grace, which I should do : for we ought to fly only to the mercy-seat, forasmuch as God hath set it before us as a sanctuary, which must be the refuge of all them that shall be saved.

13. Ye seek peace from the world ; real peace is in Christ. Say not, Peace, peace, but, The cross, the cross.

14. That man is not justified who does many works,

but he who, without yet having done works, has much faith in Christ.

15. Christ Himself is my righteousness. I look at Him as a gift to me, in Himself; so that in Him I have all things. He says, I am the way, &c.; not, I give thee the way, &c.; as if He were working on me from without. All these things He must be *in me*, abiding, living, speaking *in me;* that I may be the righteousness of God *in Him* (2 Cor. v. 21); not in love, nor in gifts and graces which follow; but *in Him.*

16. We must make a great difference between God's word and the word of man. A man's word is a little sound which flieth into the air, and soon vanisheth; but the word of God is greater than heaven and earth, yea, it is greater than death and hell, for it is the power of God, and remaineth everlastingly. Therefore we ought diligently to learn God's word, and we must know certainly and believe that God Himself speaketh with us.

CRANMER.

BORN 1489—BURNED 1556.

1. The Holy Ghost hath so ordered and attempered the Scriptures, that in them as well publicans, fishers, and shepherds may find their edification as great doctors their erudition.

2. Our justification doth come freely by the mere mercy of God ; and of so great and free mercy, that, whereas all the world was not able of themselves to pay any part towards their ransom, it pleasured our heavenly Father, of His infinite mercy, without any our desert, to prepare for us the most precious jewels of Christ's body and blood, whereby our ransom might be fully paid, the law fulfilled, and His justice fully satisfied. So that Christ is now the righteousness of all them that only believe on Him. He for them paid their ransom by His death ; He for them fulfilled the law in His life ; so that now, in Him and by Him, every Christian man may be called a fulfiller of the law, forasmuch as that which their infirmity lacketh Christ's justice hath supplied.

3. The very sure and lively Christian faith is not only to believe all things of God which are contained in holy Scripture ; but also is an earnest trust and confidence in God, that He doth regard us and hath care of us, as the father of the child whom he doth love, and that He will be merciful to us for His only Son's sake.

4. The true faith will shew itself, and cannot long be idle; for it is written, The just shall live by faith. He neither sleepeth nor is idle, when he should wake and be well occupied.

5. Let us do good works, and thereby declare our faith to be the lively Christian faith.

6. I give warning in God's name unto all who profess Christ that they flee far from Babylon, if they will save their souls, and to beware of that great harlot the pestiferous See of Rome, that she make you not drunk with her pleasant wine. Trust not her sweet promises, nor banquet with her; for, instead of wine, she will give you sour dregs, and for meat she will feed you with rank poison. But come to our Redeemer and Saviour Christ, who refresheth all that truly come to Him, be their anguish and heaviness never so great. Give credit to Him in whose mouth was never found guile nor untruth. By Him you shall be clearly delivered from all diseases; of Him you shall have full remission. He it is that feedeth continually all that belong unto Him with His own flesh that hanged upon the cross, and giveth them drink of the blood flowing out of His side, and maketh to spring within them water that floweth unto everlasting life.

7. Faith worketh peace and quietness in our hearts and consciences. For by faith we are certified that our sins are forgiven.

8. Wherefore, good children, labour with all diligence and study, that, when Christ shall come again to judge the world, He may find you holy and obedient.

9. Christ is the true and perfect nourishment both of body and soul.

10. As the devil is the food of the wicked, whom he nourisheth in all iniquity, and bringeth up into everlasting damnation, so is Christ the very food of all them that be the lively members of His body, and them He nourisheth, feedeth, bringeth up, and cherisheth unto everlasting life.

11. Other medicines and plasters sometimes heal and sometimes heal not; but this medicine (Christ's flesh) is of that effect and strength, that it perfectly healeth all wounds and sores that it is laid unto.

12. Calling for God's grace precedeth not faith; but, contrary, faith must needs precede our invocation of God, as St Paul saith, 'How shall they call on Him in whom they have not believed?'

13. Perfect faith is nothing else but assured hope and confidence in Christ's mercy.

BALE.

BORN 1495—DIED 1563.

1. My daily desire is, in that everlasting school, to behold the eternal Son of God, both here and after this life; and not only to see the fathers, prophets, and apostles therein, but also for love of that doctrine to enjoy their blessed fellowship hereafter.

2. Doctrine without discipline maketh dissolute hearers; and, on the other hand, discipline without doctrine maketh either hypocrites or else desperate doers.

3. I am the fresh fountain which Isaiah speaketh of; most highly necessary to them that will live. Very liberal shall he find Me that seeketh Me in faith. With Me is the well of life everlasting: with My pleasant rivers shall I content your good appetites.

4. In Christ's kingdom is no outward priesthood, nor sacrifice to be made for sin. For He hath, with one oblation for all, fully satisfied for the sins of His elect number for ever.

5. This running flood, with its rivers on every side, rejoices the city of God, the habitation of the Highest. All full of quickness is it, springing into the life everlasting. Clear is this water as the pure crystal that is without spot. The nature of this water is none other but evermore to cleanse, evermore to revive, and evermore to make whole and perfect.

6. If adversity, loss of goods, detriment of fame, sickness, or any other troublous cross happeneth, it is evermore for the best to them that are faithful. Perfectly shall all these be taken away, in the regeneration, when to their glory both heaven and earth shall be blessed, and all that is cursed thrown into the lake of everlasting fire.

7. Consider how lovingly the Father doth use us ; not only *here* do we bear the name of children, but also *there* shall we be His sons indeed.

8. Of most tender mercy sent He that day-spring from above, to direct their feet in the way of His peace. And after this laborious pilgrimage, in the Sabbath of eternal quiet, shall He enlighten them thoroughly with His most glorious presence ; and with Him shall they reign for ever, in full felicity and glory continuing.

9. The proud reign of tyrants is here but for a time ; the less is it to be feared. The meek reign of the righteous continueth for ever; therefore the more is it to be sought for and desired.

10. The Bride or Congregation of the Lord, thus taught, stirred, and urged forward of His Spirit, saith in her heart, evermore, with a fervent desire, Oh come, my most delectable spouse and Lord, Jesus Christ, my health, my joy, my sweetness. Accomplish the marriage appointed from the world's beginning. Permit that prepared spouse, with her appointed number, to enter into Thy eternal tabernacle of rest.

11. Come, most merciful Saviour and Redeemer, fulfil the godly promises of this book to the eternal comfort of man. Make haste to the judgment-seat, for full deliver-

ance of the whole chosen number, that Thy servants may be where Thou art, in perfect glory and joy.

12. Oh come, most merciful Redeemer and gracious Lord Jesus Christ, to judge the universal world. Come, come, hie Thee hither apace, to separate the wheat from the chaff, and the lambs from the goats, to bring them to Thy eternal tabernacle. Woe is me that my banishment endureth so long. I dwell in the tabernacle of the sorrowful. My soul hath a thirsty desire for God, the fountain of life. Oh, when shall I come and behold His face! Like are we to these faithful servants, who wait for the return of their Lord from the wedding, very ready to open at His knocking.

M E L A N C T H O N.

BORN 1497—DIED 1560.

1. Humanity was created, and then afterwards redeemed, to be the temple of God, setting forth the glory of God.

2. God is a Being spiritual, intelligent, eternal, true, good, pure, just, merciful, free altogether, of immense power and wisdom. He is the Father eternal, who from eternity begat the Son, His image. The Son is the co-eternal image of the Father, and the Holy Spirit proceeds from the Father and the Son.

3. It is good to notice, in the baptism of Christ, the clear setting forth of the three Persons of the Godhead. The Father utters that voice, 'This is My beloved Son.' The Son is seen standing in the river; and the Holy Spirit comes down in a visible appearance.

4. Let us hold fast the distinction of the human and divine natures in Christ; and yet, at the same time, let this be known, that, because of the personal union, these propositions are true, viz., God suffered, was crucified, died. Think not that the human nature only was that which redeemed; it was the whole Son of God.

5. The Spirit is called *Spirit of Grace*, because He testifies in us that we are received into favour, and because He moves our heart to believe this.

6. The perfections of Godhead are not distinct things from the essence of Godhead. The *power of the Father*

is the Father; and the *righteousness of the Father* is the
Father; and the *righteousness of the Son* is the Son.

7. It is right to pray to the Holy Spirit, as thus: 'Holy
Spirit, who wast poured upon the apostles, who wast promised by the Redeemer, the Son of God, to kindle in us
true knowledge and worship of God, raise Thou in our
hearts true fear of God, true faith and acknowledgment
of the mercy promised in the Son by the eternal Father.
Be our *Paraclete* in all undertakings and perils, and stir
up our souls to give honour always, by true obedience,
to the Father of our Lord Jesus Christ, to His Son, our
Redeemer, and to Thee.'

8. The Law of the Ten Commandments reminds us—
1st, For what end man was made, and what was his
dignity and purity originally. For man was meant to be
what the Law describes—full of the knowledge of God;
always setting forth his honour; always obeying; ever
beholding His presence and superintending rule in all His
works; observing just order in all His actions, without
any vile lust, without any calamity, without death. It reminds us, 2d, Of present misery; for we see our nature
fallen from its first dignity; in conflict with the Law; full
of darkness and contempt of God; all disorder; full of vile
lusts of every kind. It reminds us, 3d, Of the restoration
of humanity and of eternal life; for it intimates to how
great excellency we are still called. For God repeats His
voice of the Law ever since the fall, thereby shewing that
He intends that the Law should, some time or other, be
realised as Law. Therefore, there shall be a reparation of
the human race; there shall be eternal life.

A O N I O   P A L E A R I O.

BORN 1500—DIED 1570.

1. It is not to be believed that the sin of Adam, which we have by inheritance from him, should be of more force than the righteousness of Christ, that which also we inherit by faith. It seemeth that man hath great cause to complain that (without any reason why) he is conceived and born in sin, and in the wickedness of his parents, by means of whom death reigneth over all men. But now is all our sorrow taken away; inasmuch as, by a like mean (without any occasion given on our behalf), righteousness and everlasting life are come by Jesus Christ, and by Him death is slain.

2. As Jesus Christ is stronger than Adam was, so is His righteousness more mighty than the sin of Adam. And if the sin of Adam was sufficient enough to make all men sinners and children of wrath, without any misdeed of our own, much more shall Christ's righteousness be of greater force to make us all righteous, and the children of grace, without any of our own good works.

3. Then, my dear brethren, let us embrace the righteousness of our Lord Jesus Christ, and let us make it ours by means of faith : let us assure ourselves that we be righteous, not for our own works, but through the merits of Jesus Christ : and let us live merrily, and assured that the righteousness of Jesus Christ hath utterly done away all

our unrighteousness, and made us good, righteous, and holy before God ; who, beholding us engrafted into His Son by faith, esteemeth us not now any more as the children of Adam, but as His own children, and hath made us heirs of all His riches, with His own begotten Son.

4. The godly childhood and youth of the Bridegroom hath justified the childish and youthful life of His dearly beloved bride.   For the love and union that is betwixt the soul of a true Christian, and the Bridegroom Jesus Christ, maketh all the works of either of them to be common to them both.   By reason whereof, when a man saith, Jesus Christ hath fasted, Jesus Christ hath prayed, Jesus Christ was heard of the Father, raised the dead, drave devils out of men, healed the sick, died, rose again, and ascended into heaven ; likewise, a man may say that a Christian man hath done all the self-same works ; forsomuch as the works of Christ are the works of the Christian, because He hath done them for him.   Verily, a man may say that a Christian hath been nailed to the cross, buried, raised again, is gone up into heaven, become the child of God, and made partaker of the Godhead.

5. He that cometh unto God with assuredness of this faith, believing Him, without any mistrust or doubt of His promises, and warranting himself for a certainty that God will perform all that ever He hath promised him, giveth all the glory unto God, and liveth continually in rest and endless joy, evermore praising and thanking the Lord God for choosing him to the glory of the eternal life.

6. If we will say the truth, a man can do no good works, except he first know himself to be become righteous by

faith; for, before he knoweth that, his doing of good works is rather to make himself righteous, than for the love and glory of God; and so he defileth all his works with self-love, for the love of himself and for his own profit. But he that knoweth himself to be become righteous by the merits and righteousness of Christ (which he maketh his own by faith), laboureth happily, and doth good works all only for the love and glory of Christ, and not for love of himself, nor to make himself righteous. And thereupon it cometh that the true Christian (that is, to wit, he that accounteth himself righteous by reason of Christ's righteousness) asketh not whether good works be commanded or not; but, being wholly moved and provoked with a certain violence of godly love, he offereth himself willingly to do all the works that are holy and Christian-like, and never ceaseth to do well.

7. And, therefore, may every poor sinner say, with an assured confidence, Thou, Christ, art my sin and my curse; or, rather, I am Thy sin and Thy curse; and, contrariwise, Thou art my righteousness, my blessing, and my life, my grace of God, and my heaven. And thus, if we by faith do behold this brazen serpent, Christ hanging upon the cross, we shall see the law, sin, death, the devil, and hell killed by His death; and so may, with the apostle Paul, sing that joying heart-ditty, 'Thanks be to God who hath given us victory, through our Lord Jesus Christ.

HAMILTON (PATRICK).

BORN 1503—MARTYRED 1528.

1. The law sheweth us our sin ; the Gospel sheweth us a remedy for it. The law sheweth us our condemnation ; the Gospel sheweth us our redemption. The law is the word of wrath ; the Gospel is the word of grace. The law is the word of despair ; the Gospel is the word of comfort. The law is the word of unrest ; the Gospel is the word of peace.

2. The law saith, Pay thy debt ; the Gospel saith, Christ hath paid it. The law saith, Thou art a sinner, despair, thou shalt be damned ; the Gospel saith, Thy sins are forgiven thee, be of good comfort, thou shalt be saved. The law saith, Make amends for thy sins ; the Gospel saith, Christ hath made it for thee. The law saith, Where is thy righteousness, goodness, and satisfaction ? the Gospel saith, Christ is thy righteousness, thy goodness, and satisfaction. The law saith, Thou art bound and obliged to me, to the devil, and to hell ; the Gospel saith, Christ hath delivered thee from them all.

3. He that lacketh faith trusteth not God ; he that trusteth not God, trusteth not His word ; he that trusteth not His word, holdeth Him false and a liar ; he that holdeth him false and a liar, believeth not that He may do what He promiseth ; and so he denieth that He is God. Therefore it followeth, he that lacketh faith cannot please God.

4. No man can do a greater honour to God than to count Him true.

5. Faith is a certainty or assuredness; he that hath faith well knoweth that God will fulfil His word.

6. Faith is the root of all good; unbelief is the root of all evil. Faith maketh God and man good friends; unbelief maketh them foes. Faith bringeth God and man together; unbelief sundereth them.

7. Faith sheweth us that God is a sweet Father; unbelief sheweth Him as a terrible Judge. Faith holdeth firm by the word of God; unbelief wavers here and there. Faith knoweth God; unbelief knoweth Him not. Faith only saveth us; unbelief only condemneth us. Faith extolleth God and His deeds; unbelief herself and her deeds.

8. Faith cometh of the word of God; hope cometh of faith; and charity springeth of them both.

9. What is it to say that Christ died for thee? Verily it is that thou shouldest have died perpetually, and that Christ, to deliver thee from death, died for thee, and changed thy perpetual death into His own death. For thou madest the fault, and He suffered the pain, and that for the love He had to thee, before thou wast born.

10. Thou must do good works; but beware that thou do them not to deserve any good through them. For if thou do so, thou receivest the good, not as a gift of God, but as a debt due to thee, and makest thyself fellow with God, because thou wilt take nothing of Him for nought. Therefore, do nothing to Him, but take of Him; for He is a gentle Lord, and with more glad will gives us all we need, than we can take it of Him.

BULLINGER.

BORN 1504—DIED 1574.

1. As bread nourisheth and strengtheneth man, so the body of Christ, eaten by faith, feedeth and satisfieth the soul of man, and furnisheth the whole man to all duties of godliness.   As wine is drink to the thirsty, so the blood of our Lord Jesus, drunken by faith, doth quench the thirst of the burning conscience, and filleth the hearts of the faithful with unspeakable joy.

2. I confess and acknowledge, with open mouth and sincere heart, that spiritual, divine, and quickening presence of our Lord Christ, both in the Supper and also out of the Supper, whereby He continueth to pour Himself into us, not by signs lacking life, but by His Holy Spirit, to make us partakers of all His good graces, to justify, quicken, nourish, sustain, and satisfy us ; which presence we do also feel in ourselves through faith, by the which we are sustained, nourished, and satisfied.   For Christ is the Head of the Church, and we have fellowship with Him. How should a living body be without its head ?   How should we be partakers of Christ, if we do not feel Him present, yea, living and working in us ?

3. The truest and most proper cause why sacraments be instituted under visible signs, seemeth partly to be God's goodness, and partly man's weakness.   For very hardly do we reach unto the knowledge of heavenly things, if,

without visible form, they be laid before our eyes. But they are better and more easily understood, if they be represented unto us under the figure of earthly things; that is to say, under signs familiarly known unto us. As, therefore, our bountiful and gracious Lord did covertly and darkly, nay, rather, evidently and notably, set before us the kingdom of God in parables, or dark speeches, even so by signs it pleased Him to lay before our eyes, after a sort, the very same thing, as it were in a painted table; to renew it afresh, and, by lively representation, to maintain the remembrance of the same among us.

4. The Gospel is a good and sweet word, and an assured testimony of God's grace to usward.

5. The most true Scripture doth teach us that God is, of His own inclination, naturally good, gentle, and, as Paul calleth Him, *philanthropon* (Titus iii. 4), a lover of us men; who hath sent His own Son, of His own nature, into the world for our redemption; whereupon it doth follow that God doth freely, of Himself, and for His Son's sake, love man, and not for any other cause.

6. True faith is an undoubted persuasion in the mind of the believer, even so to have the thing as his belief is, and as he is said to have it in the express word of God.

7. It is without doubt that the Son of God took true and human flesh, and in the same is consubstantial, or of the self-same substance, with us, in all points, sin excepted. One and the same Christ is, according to the disposition of His divine nature, immortal; according to the disposition of His human nature, mortal; and the self-same immortal God and mortal man is the only Saviour of the world.

K N O X   (J O H N).

BORN 1505—DIED 1572.

1. Sin was so odious and detestable in the presence of our heavenly Father, that by no other sacrifice could the same be purged, except by the blood and death of the only innocent Son of God.

2. When I deeply do consider the cause of Christ's death to have been *sin*, and sin yet to dwell in all flesh, with Paul I am compelled to sob and groan as a man under a heavy burden.

3. Albeit I never lack the presence and plain image of my own wretched infirmity ; yet seeing sin so manifestly abound in all estates, I am compelled to thunder out the threatenings of God against obstinate rebellers.

4. I sob and lament for that I cannot be quit and rid of sin.   I desire to live a more perfect life.

5. Cause have you none of desperation, albeit the devil rage never so cruelly, and albeit the flesh be never so frail, daily and hourly lusting against God's holy command-ments.   This is not the time of justice before our own eyes.   We look for that which is promised, the kingdom everlasting, prepared for us from the beginnning.

6. All England is this day called ; but ye know how mean is the number that obey the voice of the caller.

7. The member shall be correspondent and like to the Head, who in anguish of extreme dolour cried, 'My God,

my God, why hast Thou forsaken me?' Oh words most dolorous, and voice most lamentable to be heard proceeding from the mouth of the Son of God! He was no debtor to sin nor death; and yet this did he suffer, not only to make satisfaction to the justice of God, which we were never able to do, but also to put us in comfort that His suffering was not in vain, but even for our example.

8. He is our Saviour and only Mediator, the first-begotten of the dead, the sole and sovereign Prince, exalted above all powers and potentates whatsoever, that by Him we, now sore afflicted in absence of our Bridegroom, may receive immortality and glory when He shall return to restore the liberty to the sons of God.

9. Oh miserable, unthankful, and most mischievous world! what shall be thy condemnation when He that has so often gently provoked you to obey His truth, shall come in His glory to punish thy contempt!

10. Our heavenly Father, of His infinite wisdom, to hold us in continual remembrance that in this wretched world there is no rest, suffereth us to be tried with this cross, that with an unfeigned heart we may desire not only an end of our own troubles (for that shall come to us by death), but also of all the troubles of the Church of God; which shall not be before the again-coming of the Lord Jesus.

CALVIN.

BORN 1509—DIED 1564.

1. It deeply concerned us that He who was to be our Mediator—should be very God and very man. Our iniquities, like a cloud intervening between Him and us, none but a person reaching to Him could be the medium of restoring peace. The case was desperate, if the Godhead itself did not descend to us, it being impossible for us to ascend. Thus the Son of God behoved to become our Emmanuel.

2. He who was to be our Redeemer must be truly God and man. It was His to swallow up death; who but Life could do so? It was His to conquer sin; who could do so save Righteousness? It was His to put to flight the powers of the air and the world; who could do so but the mighty Power superior to both? But who possesses life, and righteousness, and the dominion of heaven, but God alone!

3. So deeply rooted in our hearts is unbelief, so prone are we to it, that, while all confess with the lips that God is faithful, no man ever believes it without an arduous struggle.

4. The goodness of God is not properly comprehended, when security does not follow as its fruit.

5. Faith has no less need of the Word than the fruit of a tree has of a living root; because, as David testifies, none can hope in God but those who know His name.

6. Every promise which God makes is evidence of His good-will.

7. Faith is the special gift of God, both in purifying the mind, so as to give it a relish for divine truth, and afterwards in establishing it therein.

8. We are naturally blind; and the word cannot penetrate our mind unless the Spirit, that eternal Teacher, by His enlightening power, make an entrance for it.

9. What the schoolmen say as to the priority of love to faith and hope, is a mere dream; since it is faith alone that first engenders love.

10. Faith includes not merely the knowledge that God is, but also, nay chiefly, a perception of his will towards us. Faith is a firm and sure knowledge of the divine favour towards us, founded on the truth of a free promise in Christ, and revealed to our minds and sealed on our hearts by the Holy Spirit.

11. Faith is a knowledge of the divine favour towards us, and a full persuasion of its truth.

12. Our faith is not true unless it enables us to appear calmly in the presence of God.

13. Faith ought to seek God, not to shun Him.

14. Therefore, let us come to a sounder mind, and however repugnant the blind and stupid longing of the flesh may be, let us desire the coming of the Lord, not in wish only, but with earnest sighs, as the most propitious of all events. He comes as a Redeemer, to deliver us from an abyss of evil and misery, and to lead us to the blessed inheritance of His life and glory.

BRADFORD.

BORN (ABOUT) 1510—MARTYRED 1555.

1. What is glory in this world but shame? Why art thou afraid to carry Christ's cross? Wilt thou come into His kingdom, and not drink of his cup?

2. Dost thou not know Rome to be Babylon? Dost thou not know that, as the old Babylon had the children of Judah in captivity, so hath this Rome the true Judah, the confessors of Christ.

3. Hath not the harlot of Babylon more costly array and rich apparel than the homely housewife of Christ? Where is the beauty of the King's daughter, the church of Christ—without or within? Doth not David say within? Can the Pope and his prelates mean honestly, who make so much of the wife, and so little of the husband? The church they magnify, but Christ they contemn.

4. Covet not earthly riches; fear not the power of man; love not this world; but long for the coming of the Lord Jesus, when your bodies shall be made like unto His glorious body.

5. Dearly beloved, remember that you are not of this world; that Satan is not your captain; that your joy and Paradise are not here; that your companions are not the multitude of worldlings. But ye are of another world. Christ is your Captain; your joy is in heaven; your companions are the fathers, patriarchs, prophets, apostles,

martyrs, virgins, confessors, and dear saints of God, who follow the Lamb whithersoever He goeth.

6. Faith must go before, and then feeling will follow.

7. Though you feel not as you would, yet doubt not, but hope beyond all hope, as Abraham did; for always, faith goeth before feeling.

8. Being assured of God's favour towards you, give yourself wholly to help and care for others; then shall you contemn this life, and desire to be at home with your good and sweet Father.

9. If you should believe or doubt for your goodness or illness' sake, which you feel or feel not, then should you make Christ Jesus, for whose sake only God is your Father, either nothing, or else but half Christ.

FOX.

BORN 1517—DIED 1587.

1. As Christ Jesus, in this earth, sought nothing but the glory only of His Father, so His Father now seeketh nothing else in heaven but the glory of His Son.

2. The devil rages ; the Turk daily winneth ground ; the Papist persecuteth ; and yet all this will not awake us to seek Christ, in whom only lieth our victory. Our covetous, voluptuous, vicious, and ambitious life, what does it declare, but either infidelity or neglecting of Christ's kingdom ! We talk of heaven, we walk not to heaven.

3. The glory of Christ is not our study, or certes, is the least part of our study. We hear of the glory of Christ, but we feel it not ; we talk of Christ, but have no experience of Him, no acquaintance with Him ; we honour Him with our lips, but our heart doth not hunger after Him.

4. Let princes learn to know this Christ ; let subjects attend upon Him ; let ancient fathers take hold of Him ; let young men embrace Him ; let the rich enlarge their treasury with this precious jewel ; and let the poor seek, as their relief, to be refreshed by Him.

5. As no man hath ever pleased the Father besides Christ, so in Him the Father is so well pleased, that for His sake, He dearly loveth all those who are of Christ.

6. Art Thou He that excellest all the children of men

in beauty? in whose lips grace was shed most plentifully? Where is that beauty of Thine? I find it not; I see it not. Fleshly eyes conceive not so great a mystery. Open Thou the eyes of my mind. Bring Thy divine light nearer to me, and give me power to look more upon Thee.

7. O noontide of fervent love and sunshine, never drawing towards eventide, shew us where Thou feedest in the midst of the day, and where Thou shroudest Thy sheep from the cold!

8. Christ was made sin for us no other way, but by imputation only; therefore we are made righteous before God no other way, but by imputation only.

9. Though the righteousness of another, which is not inherent in us, cannot render us essentially just, nothing hinders but the righteousness of another may help our righteousness, according to judicial imputation.

10. The object of that faith which justifies us, is no other thing but the person of the Son of God.

11. Love proceeds from faith, and not faith from love. Because we believe, therefore we love; but we do not believe because we love. Whence the Lord, regarding more her faith than her love, said to her, 'Thy faith'—not thy love—'hath saved thee.'

COOPER (BISHOP OF WINCHESTER).

BORN 1517—DIED 1594.

1. St Paul spake with a loud voice and a strong spirit, 'Woe be to me if I preach not the gospel!' The same was the voice of all the old fathers and godly men in the beginning. They were occupied in nothing but either in teaching and confirming truth, or in reproving and defacing falsehood and heresy; but, after six hundred years, the prelates of the church well nigh clean lost their voices.

2. In Christ's Supper ye see the Master together with the disciples, the table and the meat common to all : not so much as Judas the traitor excluded ; one loaf and one cup distributed among the whole company. Therefore when ye come together, ye must imitate the concord and equality that he then used.

3. The Lord's Supper is a remembrance of one perfect sacrifice, whereby we were once sufficiently purged from sin, and continually are revived by the same. The Lord's Supper is to be distributed in the common assembly of His people, to teach us the communion whereby we all be knit together in Christ Jesus.

4. What, I pray you, can be more contrary than, when Christ bade them drink, to take away the cup ; and when Christ bade them distribute among them, and St Paul willed one to tarry for another, until they came together, yet contrary to this (as you do), to minister and receive alone ?

5. The laws and covenants whereby we be all thus knit and joined together, are the word of God and the sacraments, used according to Christ's institution. Therefore all churches of the world have the same word of God, and the same sacraments; and by them, through faith, are graffed into one and the same body of Christ, though they be thousands of miles asunder. By the word of God our faith is instructed; by baptism we be received first into the society of Christian communion, and made members of the mystical body. By the Lord's Supper we have from time to time heavenly food ministered unto us, and, as it were, lively spirit from the head of this body Jesus Christ. He, therefore, that is baptized in India, hath the same baptism that we have; and, being graffed into the same body, hath communion with us in baptism. Likewise they that receive the Lord's Supper be fed with the same food of the body and blood of Christ that we be, and so have communion with us in that sacrament, though in place they be far off. This is the communion between Christian men.

6. As the bread of many grains is brought into one loaf, and the juice of many grapes is made wine in one cup, so the multitude of a Christian congregation, receiving together the Lord's Supper, are made members of one body, knit together in like faith and charity, and having like hope of salvation.

7. What ground shall our faith have if we leave the word of God?

SANDYS (ARCHBISHOP).

BORN 1519—DIED 1588.

1. Be thy sins never so great, fear not to come; for He that calleth thee hath stretched out His arms of mercy at length; they are wide open to receive thee; mercy is ready to all that will receive it; and to them that need it most, most ready. A comfortable lesson to all sinners.

2. A good conscience maketh a strong faith; many, by losing their hold of the one, have made shipwreck of the other.

3. Judas received the Lord's bread; but not that bread which is the Lord to the faithful receiver. The spiritual part, that which feedeth the soul, only the faithful do receive. For he cannot be partaker of the body of Christ, who is no member of Christ's body.

4. It goeth full hardly with the Church of God, when Balaam is the bishop, Judas the patron, and Magus the minister.

5. All our travail in seeking, without faith, is but a fruitless wearying of our deceived souls; for he that cometh to God must believe. And the way to believe is hearing; for by hearing cometh faith; the word is that star which guideth and directeth us to Christ.

6. We need not ask where Christ is, or what he wanteth, that we may give unto Him. He is near at hand; straying and starving in the streets, naked, cold, harbour-

less, sick, and diseased, ruthfully moaning and crying for relief. Let the pitiful cry of our Christ move our hearts to mercy.

7. As man's life is short, so is the coming of Christ at hand. Wait; for it will surely come, and will not stay. The time is short; this we know; though it be not in us to know the definite point of time, which to the angels of heaven is unrevealed. But Christ hath set down certain tokens of the end, which all are fulfilled; and, among others, He saith iniquity shall abound, charity shall wax cold, the Gospel shall be preached in all the world. Never more iniquity; never less charity; the Gospel never so liberally taught. Behold the end!

8. Let us expect the coming of the Lord. He cometh in post; the forewarnings are fulfilled; iniquity aboundeth; Christian charity is frozen; the Gospel is preached; then the end!

9. We preach Christ, and none else but Him; we know nothing, we teach nothing, we believe nothing, but Christ and Him crucified.

10. This wicked man (Popery) the Lord shall destroy with the breath of His mouth; and then shall be the end. The blast of God's trump hath made him already stagger; he hath caught such a cramp that he beginneth now to halt; his long and far-reaching arm is marvellously shortened; his coffers are waxen leaner; his falsehood is espied; many princes refuse to taste any more of his poisoned cup; he is fallen from being the head, and come almost to be the tail.

11. We are healed with His stripes; and where there is

no sore there needs no salve.   Not that we have no sin ;
but, acknowledging that we have it, it is as if we had it
not, because He is faithful to forgive it, and just to cleanse
it.

12. He that spareth a wolf spareth the blood of the
flock, saith Chrysostom.   God appointeth the magistrate
to be 'a revenger unto wrath upon him that committeth
evil.'   They who glory to have the sword rusty in the
sheath, when they would draw it out, peradventure shall
not so well be able.

13. The great devil, in these our later days, is let loose.
Antichrist rageth, and seeketh our confusion.   The wicked,
glistering world marvellously deceiveth and bewitcheth.
The flesh reigneth, and beareth sway.   The spirit is faint;
sin overfloweth ; Christ is coming in the clouds to call us
to judgment.   Therefore, be ye sober, watch and pray !

GUALTER.

BORN (ZURICH) 1519—DIED 1586.

1. Let us have Jesus Christ always set before us, as the end of all the sacred Scriptures, that in him alone we may seek all that is necessary for salvation.

2. Unless we refer everything to Christ, we shall never be able to understand the true sense of the Bible, and we shall make idols of ourselves, ascribing to our own strength and merit that which is to be sought in Jesus Christ alone.

3. The kingdom of God is only preached when Jesus Christ is preached.

4. Jesus will have ministers that engage in His work faithfully and with all their heart, and that hearken in no wise to the spirit of the age and the wisdom of the world.

5. Let the ministers of the Gospel remember that they are called the friends of the Bridegroom, a dignity infinitely superior to all the honours of this world. No one is fit for this employment, unless his heart burns with love to Jesus Christ. Hence arises their faithfulness to lead the Bride to Jesus Christ alone, and to have no other joy than to see her united to Jesus Christ, and living in tender communion with Him.

6. 'Jesus was wearied with His journey' (John iv. 6). Jesus wearied, He that created the whole of this vast universe by His almighty power! How strange is this! but it was not without reason that Jesus was wearied. It

was for thee, O man, that He was wearied. He who is the true God, took on Himself our flesh and blood, with all our infirmities. He was made like unto us in all things, sin only excepted, that He might be a faithful and compassionate High Priest.

7. By faith we embrace Jesus Christ, and are so united with Him, that we are in Him and He in us. As He was pleased to take upon Himself all our miseries, and make them His own, so by faith He is made ours; His obedience is ours, His innocence, His righteousness, His satisfaction, His holiness ; nay, all that He hath is ours.

8. Jesus Christ says of him that believeth, that he *hath*, not that he *shall* have, eternal life. For faith, laying hold on Jesus Christ as present, receives all that is offered us in Him, so that those who believe have eternal life already, though, as to the body, they are still mortal.

9. Faith is not a vain opinion, but a certain and full assurance, which God Himself brings forth in our hearts, and preserves by His Spirit. Therefore it produces such wonderful effects, as surpasses the human understanding.

10. The Church of Jesus Christ is a stranger here below, and has on earth no fixed abode ; her dwelling and her home are in heaven. When Christ is, to all appearance, banished from every part of this world, it is then that the knowledge of Him is spread far and wide ; and the Church never prospers better than when her enemies suppose that there is hardly a spot left on which she can set her foot. It is in this state of poverty and contempt that the divine power of Jesus Christ manifests itself in the church.

CHEMNITZ.

BORN 1522—DIED 1586.

1. He might easily have created a new human nature to take upon Himself; a nature which should have been more rich and glorious than it had been in Adam before the fall. But He chose rather to take our nature in the womb of the blessed Virgin; this nature which, on account of the frailty, weakness, and misery with which it is laden by reason of sin, is called *flesh*.

2. The fulness of grace in which God desires to embrace man, He has deposited in the eternal Word, in order that there it might be sought and there received.

3. As the motion of the air is now violent, now gentle, now not perceived at all, so the regenerated must know that the presence and operating power of the Spirit is not measured by their *perception* of spiritual movements.

4. It is a beautiful name here given to the ministers of the word, *friends of the Bridegroom*. For, as a bridegroom employs confidential friends to sue for him his bride, so also does Christ employ His servants to propose to poor sinners spiritual betrothment with Him, and by discovering their sins, and setting before them His atonement, shall win them unto Him, in order that thus the chosen bride may be conducted to the Bridegroom. And even after the bride is betrothed to the Bridegroom, it is the Bridegroom's will that His friend should be present at the

marriage, that she who is espoused to one husband may be
presented as a chaste virgin, and may maintain her con-
jugal fidelity.   At all times does the Son of God thus employ His servants' labours in the Church, whether it be to
conduct the bride to the Bridegroom, or to see that the
betrothed keep her fidelity, or, if she break it, to bring her
back again to the marriage-bond.   Those who do this are
the friends of the Bridegroom.   Thus ministers are re-
minded of their true calling, and that it should be their
highest joy to win many souls to Christ, and to lead them
to Him.   For he who is indeed the friend of the Bridegroom can experience no greater joy than that of hearing
the Bridegroom's voice, as He receives His bride and
unites her for ever with Himself, and gives her fellowship
with Himself in all that he is and has.

5. Christ, in suffering persecution, emptied Himself of
His power ; He stooped down to the deepest lowliness, in
order that we may be able, with His weakness, to comfort
ourselves.

6. Attend to the order in which the words are placed.
Christ places the exhortation in the middle, *Sin no more*
(John v. 14).   But He supports the exhortation both ways
by powerful reasons.   In front, by the consideration of the
received benefit, *Behold, thou art made whole.*   Behind,
by the threat of a heavier punishment in case of sin, *lest a
worse thing come upon thee.*

7. It is through the word that Christ deals with us ; it
is through the word that He offers Himself and His blessings to us, and imparts Himself to our souls.

BUCHOLTZER.

BORN 1529—DIED 1584.

1. In Paul I observe five gloryings : (1.) He glories in weakness ; (2.) in the cross of Christ ; (3.) in a good conscience ; (4.) in afflictions ; (5.) in the hope of eternal life.

2. A Christian is one who speaks and does what the devil hates ; one who glorifies God, the author of his life and salvation.

3. Many kiss Christ ; few love Him ; it is one thing to love and another to kiss.

4. To rejoice in God is the height of all blessedness on earth.

5. If you would live in the world, learn to despise and to be despised.

6. This I have for refuge and defence in my troubles ; converse with God, with my true friends, and with my silent teachers (books).

7. In the Churches men's words breed more controversies than the words of God ; and we contend more about Apollos and Peter and Paul than about Christ. Hold fast what is divine ; give up what is human.

8. Poets have never disturbed states ; orators often.

9. A good man will do what he can, though he cannot do all that he would desire.

10. I have discovered a middle condition between

being and not being, namely, *becoming*. I am becoming
what I am not ; and when I shall cease to be, then I
shall be.

11. When God calls, always would I answer with
Abraham, Here I am ; but most joyfully would I thus
answer, if He would at length call me out of these narrow
abodes into the boundlessness of a blessed immortality ;
nothing do I long for so much as the hour of my peaceful
death.   I wonder that it has been so long deferred, and
that this feeble body, like a frail pitcher, has not been
sooner broken.

12. After this battle we shall triumph as conquerors,
with our Standard-bearer, in life eternal.   I have long believed in Christ ; and I long for the end of faith, that I
may no more *believe* in Him, but *see* Him in whom I have
believed ; that I may taste how sweet the Lord is, that I
may touch with my hands my Lord and my God.   There
I shall be called Abraham, because Abraham rejoiced to
see the day of Christ.   I have experienced that in this life
sin is all and in all ; I shall experience another life, where
the Lord is all and in all.

TRELCATIUS (OF LEYDEN).

BORN 1542—DIED 1602.

1. Of all things here there is nothing immortal; but everything marcheth by little and little to corruption and decay.

2. The points of God's eternal decree are man's bounds, the which he hath no sooner touched but he dies.

3. What care, waywardness, passions, troubles, hinder the action of a true life?

4. What is the present but the twinkling of an eye, a moment which flies away as suddenly as can be spoken? Whatsoever is past is dead to us, as if it had never been; whatsoever is to come is as if it should not be. The hours pass, so do the days and years; what is past returns no more; neither can we divine what is to come; who can assure us that the moment after this shall remain to be added to the former? This which we call life, what is it else but a very point, a moment?

5. Thou canst not comprehend this depth of time without time, which we call eternity; in like sort thou canst not conceive rightly the shortness of thy life.

6. Let the assurance of God's decree make us resolve and attend His will and ordinance, in all events, in every place, at all times, and at every moment; laying our care on Him who hath numbered all our days.

7. The counsel of God is a power too wise and a wisdom too powerful to resist either by force or policy.

8. Let this brevity put us in mind, on the one side, of the justice of God in the punishment of our sins ; on the other, of His mercy, for that it hath pleased Him to convert this punishment into a blessing and an expectation (as sure as it is short) of that eternal and immortal life ; for seeing that sin hath banished us from that celestial paradise, and that this world is, as it were, the place of our exile, what sweeter comfort can' we receive than a short and speedy end of our banishment, and a sudden recall into our heavenly country?

9. As the perfection of nature in its integrity was to live and not to die, so the imperfection of corrupted nature is to die, and that soon.

10. Shall we not esteem the days of this life very short, if we compare them with the eternal Sabbath, which shall not only give an end to all our labours, but also change our six days into eternity?

11. Shall we, who are Christians, be so delicate, not only to take pleasure in this garment (the flesh), but also like children to cry and weep when it is spoiled, if a thorn take hold of it, or any one in passing hath rent it? The flesh is not the wedding garment, but the righteousness of our Lord Jesus Christ, which we put on by believing in Him ; for that is the garment of our eldest brother, wherewith we must be clothed if we will be partakers of the blessings of our heavenly Father, as Jacob, putting on the garment of his elder brother Esau, received the blessing of his father Isaac.

12. The exchange is dangerous, to lose the infinite for that which is momentary, the eternal for the temporal, heaven for earth, this glory so surpassing excellent for a shadow of inconstant pleasure.

13. What is then this duty of watching, seeing this life is but a watch of the night? To watch for with a burning affection, a constant patience, and a most certain assurance, the coming of the morning and most glorious appearing of our sun. Shall not we, who are watchmen in this world, sigh under the toils of this night, after the coming of that final day of our deliverance?

14. Let that voice which cries at midnight, Behold, the Bridegroom cometh, sound continually in our ears and awaken us.

15. Let our conversation be as of burgesses of heaven, and that our hearts be where our treasure is, that is, Jesus Christ.

16. We have been chosen from all eternity, and shall be glorified in all eternity.

17. We must not measure the life according to the time, but according to the actions.

18. Let us aspire with a holy desire and firm hope to the enjoying of this eternal life; sighing under the vanity and shortness of this frail and earthly life. Jesus Christ saith, For certain I come soon: let us, with the church, answer with holy affection, Come, Lord Jesus, come quickly.

DENT (ARTHUR).

BORN (?)—DIED 1607.

1. Most men now-a-days have nothing to spare for Christ, nothing for His church, nothing for the poor children of God and needy members of Christ. Christ is little beholden to them.

2. Men are sick of the golden dropsy; the more they have, the more they desire. The love of money increaseth as money itself increaseth.

3. Why should we hang down our heads? Why do we not pluck up good hearts and be of good cheer? God is our father, our best friend, our daily benefactor; He keepeth us at his own cost and charges; He grudgeth us nothing; He thinketh nothing too much for us; He loveth us most dearly; He is most chary and tender over us; He cannot endure the wind should blow upon us; He will have us want nothing that is good for us; if we will eat gold, we shall have it. Let us, therefore, rejoice and be merry; for heaven is ours, earth is ours, God is ours, Christ is ours, all is ours. The world clap their hands and crow long before it be day, saying, All is theirs; but the children of God may say, and say truly, All is ours.

4. Mark and consider what a man may do, yea, what *one* man may do; what an Abraham may do; what a Moses may do; what an Elijah may do; what a Daniel, what a Samuel, what a Job, what a Noah may do! Some

one man, by reason of his high favour with the Eternal, is able sometimes to do more for a land by his prayers and tears, than many prudent men by their counsel, or valiant men by their swords. Yea, it doth evidently appear, in the sacred volume of the Holy Ghost, that some one poor preacher, being full of the spirit and power of Elijah, doth more in his study either for offence or defence, either for the turning away of wrath or the procuring of mercy, than a camp-royal even four thousand strong.

5. Now-a-days we have many hedge-breakers, few hedge-makers; many openers of gaps, few stoppers; many makers of breaches to let in the flood of God's wrath upon us, but very few to make up the breach and let down the sluices, that the gushing stream of God's vengeance may be stayed.

6. We ought to be as sure of our salvation as of any other thing that God hath promised, or which we are bound to believe.

7. Is not the doctrine of the assurance of salvation a most comfortable doctrine? Yes, doubtless, for except a man be persuaded of the favour of God, and the forgiveness of sins, and consequently of his salvation, what comfort can he have in anything? Besides this, the persuasion of God's love toward us is the root of our love and cheerful obedience towards Him.

8. The doctrine of the Papist, which would have men always doubt and fear, is a servile sort, is most hellish and uncomfortable. For as long as a man holds that, what encouragement can he have to serve God? What love to His majesty? What hope in the promises? What comfort in trouble? What patience in adversity?

RALEIGH (SIR WALTER).

BORN 1552—DIED 1618.

1. The law sheweth the way of righteousness by works, the gospel by faith; the law woundeth, the gospel healeth; the law terrifieth, the gospel allureth; Moses accuseth, Christ defendeth; Moses condemneth, Christ pardoneth; the one restraineth the hand, the other the mind. Christ came to save the world, which the law had condemned; and as Moses was but a servant, and Christ a son, so the greatest benefit was reserved to be bought by the worthiest person; for the law made nothing perfect, but was an introduction of a better hope.

2. He that hath pity on another man's sorrow, shall be free from it himself; and he that delighteth in, and scorneth the misery of another, shall one time or another fall into it himself.

3. Speaking much is a sign of vanity; for he that is lavish in words, is a niggard in deeds. Restrain thy anger; hearken much and speak little; for the tongue is the instrument of the greatest good and the greatest evil that is done in the world.

4. Jest not at those that are simple, but remember how much thou art bound to God, who hath made thee wiser.

5. When once we come in sight of the port of death, to which all winds drive us, and when, by letting fall that fatal anchor, which can never be weighed again, the navi-

gation of this life takes end; then it is that our own cogitations return again, and pay us to the uttermost for all the pleasing passages of our lives past.

6. God is He, from whom to depart is to die; to whom to repair is to revive; and in whom to dwell is life for ever. Be not, then, of the number of those that begin not to live till they be ready to die.

7. O eloquent, just, and mighty Death! Whom none could advise, thou hast persuaded; what none hath dared, thou hast done; and whom all the world hath flattered, thou only hast cast out of the world and despised. Thou hast drawn together all the far-stretched greatness, all the pride, cruelty, and ambition of man, and covered it all over with those two narrow words, *Hic jacet*.

8. There is not the smallest accident, which may seem unto man as falling out by chance, and of no consequence, but that the same is caused by God, to effect something else by; yea, and oftentimes to effect things of the greatest worldly importance, either presently, or in many years after, when the occasions are either not considered or forgotten.

9. The father provideth for his children; beasts, and birds, and all living things, for their young ones. If providence be found in *second* fathers, much more in the *first* and universal; and if there be a natural, loving care in men and beasts, much more in God, who hath formed this nature, and whose divine love was the beginning, and is the bond of the universal.

10. Although religion, and the truth thereof, be in every man's mouth, yea, in the discourse of every woman, what

is it other than a universal dissimulation? We profess
that we know God, but by works we deny Him; for beati-
tude doth not consist in the knowledge of divine things, but
in a divine life, for the devils *know* them better than man.

11. The service of God is the path leading us to perfect
happiness, and hath in it a true, though not complete,
felicity; yielding such abundance of joy to the conscience,
as doth easily countervail all afflictions whatsoever; though,
indeed, those brambles that sometimes tear the skin of
such as walk in this blessed way, do commonly lay hold
upon them, at such time as they sit down to take their
ease, and make them wish themselves at their journey's
end, in presence of their Lord, in whose presence is the
fulness of joy.

HOOKER (RICHARD).

BORN 1554—DIED 1600.

1. Regard not who it is which speaketh, but weigh only what is spoken.

2. There will come a time when three words, uttered with charity and meekness, shall receive a far more blessed reward than three thousand volumes written with disdainful sharpness of wit.

3. The manner of men's writings must not alienate our hearts from the truth, if it appear they have the truth.

4. Think ye are men : deem it not impossible for you to err ; sift impartially your own hearts, whether it be force of reason, or vehemency of affection, which hath bred, and still doth feed, these opinions in you. If truth do anywhere manifest itself, seek not to smother it with glozing delusion ; acknowledge the greatness thereof, and think it your best victory when the same doth prevail over you.

5. Dangerous it were for the feeble brain of man to wade far into the doings of the Most High ; whom, although to know be life, and joy to make mention of His name, yet our soundest knowledge is to know that we know Him not as indeed He is, neither can know Him ; and our safest eloquence concerning Him is our silence, when we confess, without confession, that His glory is inexplicable, His greatness above our capacity and reach. He is above,

and we upon earth; therefore it behoveth our words to be wary and few.

6. All those venerable books of Scripture, those sacred volumes of Holy Writ, are with such absolute perfection framed, that in them there neither wanteth anything, the lack whereof might deprive us of life, nor anything in such wise aboundeth, that, as being superfluous, unfruitful, and altogether needless, we should think it no loss or danger at all, if we did want it.

7. The general end both of Old and New Testaments is one; the difference between them consisting in this, that the Old did make wise by teaching salvation through Christ that should come, the New by teaching that Christ the Saviour is come; and that Jesus, whom the Jews did crucify, and whom God did raise from the dead, is He.

8. There be two kinds of Christian righteousness, the one without us, which we have by imputation; the other in us, which consisteth of faith, hope, and charity, and other Christian virtues; and St James doth prove that Abraham had not only the one, because the thing believed was imputed unto him for righteousness, but also the other, because he offered up his son. God giveth us both the one justice and the other: the one, by accepting us for righteous in Christ; the other, by working Christian righteousness in us.

9. Longer than it holdeth the foundation whereof we have spoken, faith neither justifieth, nor is; but ceaseth to be faith, when it ceaseth to believe that Jesus Christ is the only Saviour of the world.

ROLLOCK.

BORN 1555—DIED 1598.

1. In faith we stand not passively, but, being moved by the H⌄ly Ghost, we work ourselves; as being stirred up to believe, we believe; and, in a word, we work with God's Spirit working in us.

2. It is not so much our faith apprehending, as Christ Himself, and God's mercy apprehended in Him, that is the cause wherefore God performeth the promise of His covenant unto us, to our justification and salvation.

3. Do you mean that the prophetical and apostolical Scripture ought to be now in as great account with us of the lively voice of God Himself, and of extraordinary men as in times past? I mean so; and in this kind was revelation alone I willingly rest, as in that which came by inspiration from God, so long until I shall hear, at His glorious coming, that lively and most sweet voice of Christ my Saviour.

4. Paul, in the eighth chapter to the Romans, uses these arguments against those wicked men that cannot sigh for heaven. He takes his argument from the elements, the senseless and dumb creatures, which sob and groan for the revelation of the sons of God, and travail for that time as a woman in her birth.

5. O miserable man! the earth shall condemn thee. The floor thou sittest on is sighing, and would fain have

that carcase of thine to heaven. The waters, the air, the heavens, are all sighing for that last deliverance, the glory whereof appertains to thee; and yet thou art laughing! Alas, what shall betide thee!

6. The soul cannot have so great joy as if the soul and body were together; but still, the soul, when separate, has greater joy in heaven than soul and body can have together in this earth.

7. Ever walking, a pilgrim must not sit down. Thou art a pilgrim upon thy journey toward another country; thou must not sit down; for otherwise thou shalt never come to thy journey's end.

8. Therefore love Jesus, and thou shalt get part with Him. Well is the soul that can love the Lord Jesus.

9. Therefore it is that the godly in this life hope still for the coming of Jesus Christ; till they be set with Him in that inheritance purchased for us by His blood.

PERKINS (WILLIAM).

BORN 1558—DIED 1602.

1. Search the Scripture and see what is sin, and what is not sin in every action; this done, carry in thy heart a constant and resolute purpose not to sin in anything.

2. Shew thyself to be a member of Christ and a servant of God, not only in the general calling of a Christian, but also in the particular calling wherein thou art placed. It is not enough for a magistrate to be a Christian man; he must also be a Christian magistrate. It is not enough for the master of a family to be a Christian man, or a Christian in the church; he must also be a Christian in his family, and in the trade which he followeth daily.

3. Labour to be displeased with thyself, and labour to feel that thou standest in need of every drop of the blood of Christ to heal and cleanse thee.

4. If thou be demanded what, in thine estimation, is the vilest of the creatures upon earth, thine heart and conscience may answer with a loud voice, *I, even I, by reason of mine own sins;* and again, if thou be demanded what is the best thing in the world for thee, thy heart and conscience may answer again, with a strong and loud cry, *One drop of the blood of Christ to wash away my sins!*

5. The most comely garment that ever we can wear is the robe of Christ's righteousness.

6. Hence we learn that the doctrine of the Church of Rome, and of all others which hold that men cannot be assured of their salvation by faith, is wicked and damnable; for hereby they cut off a part of Christ's prophetical office, whereof the dignity doth consist in assuring a man particularly of the truth of God's promises unto himself.

7. Justifying faith, in regard to its nature, is always one and the same; and the essential property thereof is to apprehend Christ, with His benefits, and to assure the very conscience thereof.

8. Faith doth not justify in respect of itself, because it is an action or a virtue, or because it is strong, lively, and perfect, but in respect of the object thereof, Christ crucified, whom faith apprehendeth, as He is set forth unto us in the word and sacraments. It is Christ that is the author and matter of our justification; and it is He that applieth the same unto us. As for faith, it is but an instrument to apprehend and receive that which Christ, for His part, offereth and giveth. Therefore, if faith err not in its proper object, but follow the promise of God, though it doth but weakly apprehend, it is true faith, and justifieth.

9. A man must first believe in Christ, and then followeth repentance; and for new obedience, it is not a part of repentance, but a fruit thereof.

10. These are the days of grace, but how long they will last God only knoweth.

11. The daily persuasion of the speedy coming of Christ is of notable use; for, first, it will daunt the most desperate wretch that is, and make him tremble in himself, and restrain him from many sins. And if a man belong to

God, and be yet a loose liver, this persuasion will rouse him out of his sins and make him turn to God; for who would not seek to save his soul, if he were persuaded that Christ is now coming to give him his final reward? Secondly, if a man have grace and do believe, this persuasion is a notable means to make him constant in every good duty, both of piety to God and of charity towards his brethren. Thirdly, this serveth to comfort any person that is in affliction; for, when he shall believe that which Christ hath said, *I come shortly*, he cannot but think but that his deliverance is at hand; for at His coming He bringeth perfect redemption to all His elect.

HUME (ALEXANDER).

BORN 1560—DIED 1609.

1. Beware thou justifie not thyself in heart; for thou knawest that thou cannot abstaine fra sinne, nor cannot be saued without the meere mercie of God, shewn in the righteous merits of Jesus Christ.

2. Travaile to be familiar and acquainted with thy God, be prayer and meditation, and walk with Him.

3. Remember that nothing can come unto thee bot by God's prouidence and permission: why, then, suld thou beare onie thing impatiently, seeing it is the Lord's work?

4. The Lord is able to doo exceeding aboundantlie aboue all that we aske or think: why suld thou, then, be carefull or avaritious?

5. Studie earnestly to be temperate of thy mouth; for intemperance hurts the memorie and the judgment, smores the spirituall gift, makes the heart fat and sensuall, banishes heauenlie thoughts and meditations, and makes men unable for any gude exercise.

6. Be continuallie occupied ather in the Lord's service, or in thine awin vocation, for the neglecting theirof wounds the conscience.

7. Gif the Lord haue given thee any reasonable maintenance of thy awin, haunt not meikle the tables of other men.

8. Refrain thy tunge from cursed speaking, fraward or filthy speaking, whereby the conscience is wonderfullie wounded, and the Spirit of Christ that dwells in us sair greeued.

9. Crave of God a large and liberall heart; for a gnewous (*i.e.*, gnawing) and pinching heart, in matters of small importance, is odious.

10. Endeuour thyself to have thy mind stabill in thy prayer and meditation, and suffer not the samin to be interrupted with vaine thoughts or naughtie actions.

11. Be not bitter, fraward, earnest, or offended for trifles. . . . If thou be a pastour or a teacher, wherever thou cummis, let thy secret purpose be be to conqueis sum to Christ.

12. Whereuer thou art iniured, or heirs words vttered to thy reproch or griefe, incontinent perswade thyselfe that it proceids fra God, and that He has stirred up the speaker or iniurer against thee. Therefore, consider if thou be iustly quarrelled, and then take it as a chastisement for thy sin. But if thou be falsely and uniustly quarrelled, then think it is done by God to try thy faith and patience, wherein thou suld reioyce and receaue comfort.

13. Quhen thou art in perplexitie, and knawis not quhat to choose, intrenche thyselfe, and flee to the throne of grace to seeke resolution.

14. Thinke not that thou, by thy industrie, convoy (*i.e.* prudence), or diligence, art able to accomplish onye gude thing; therefore, craue the Lord's blessing to thy affairs, and wait patiently upon Him.

15. Walk with grauitie, integritie, and with ane upright

heart in all thy actions; and not craftely, feircely, or wil-fully, bot without fretting, murmuring, or upbraiding.

16. Be silent and modest, and not light, revealing thy griefe, imperfection, and weakenes to euerie man, lest thou be despised. But poure out thy griefes before the Lord, and lament thine estait to Him.

17. Be benevolent till all men, and patient towards all; suffering euerie thing patiently for Christ's sake, and after His example.

18. Although thy prayer appeare to be without effect, yet cease not from praying; for, if thy petition be lawfull, and that thou submit the granting thereof unfeinedly to the will of God, be sure that at length thou sall ather get thy desire, or else contentment, as though thou had gotten it.

B A C O N (L O R D).

BORN 1561—DIED 1626.

1. Virtue is like precious odours, most fragrant when they are incensed or crushed; for prosperity doth best discover vice, but adversity doth best discover virtue.

2. The Scripture exhorteth us to possess our souls in patience. Whosoever is out of patience is out of possession of his soul.

3. Men must know, that in this theatre of man's life, it is reserved only for God and angels to be lookers on.

4. A man's life is not to be trifled away; it is to be offered up and sacrificed to honourable services, public merits, good causes, and noble adventures.

5. A cripple on the right way may beat a racer on the wrong one. Nay, the fleeter and better the racer is, who hath once missed his way, the further he leaveth it behind.

6. There is no man that imparteth his joys to his friends but he joyeth the more; and no man that imparteth his griefs to his friend, but he grieveth the less.

7. Fame is like a river that beareth up things light and swollen, and drowns things weighty and solid.

8. Great riches have sold more men than they have bought.

9. The first creature of God, in the works of the days, was the light of the sense; the last was the light of the reason; and His Sabbath work, ever since, is the illumination of His Spirit.

10. Clear and round dealing is the honour of man's nature.

11. The mislayer of a stone is to blame ; but it is the unjust judge that is the capital remover of landmarks. One foul sentence doth more hurt than many foul examples.

12. I can find no space of ground that lieth vacant and unsown in the matter of divinity ; so diligent have men been, either in sowing of good seed or in sowing of tares.

13. It is not St Augustine's, nor St Ambrose's works, that will make so wise a divine as ecclesiastical history, thoroughly read and observed.

14. Divine prophecies being of the nature of their Author, with whom a thousand years are as but one day, are not fulfilled punctually at once, but have springing and germanent accomplishment through many ages, though the height of fulness of them may refer to some one age.

15. Earnest writing must not hastily be condemned ; for men cannot contend coldly, and without affection, about things which they hold dear and precious.

16. The harmony of a science, supporting each part the other, is, and ought to be, the true and brief confutation and suppression of all the smaller sort of objections.

17. The night was even now ; but that name is lost ; it is now not *late*, but *early*.   Mine eyes begin to discharge their watch, and compound with this fleshly weakness for a time of perpetual rest ; and I shall presently be as happy as though I had died the first hour I was born.   Believe it, the sweetest Canticle is *Nunc Dimittis*,— Now lettest Thou Thy servant depart in peace.

ABBOT (ARCHBISHOP).

BORN 1562—DIED 1633.

1. To be blind and have no guide, and yet to walk there, where treading awry is the stumbling into hell; to be hungry and to famish; to suck, but on dry breasts; this is the evil of all evils!

2. The tempter would insinuate to Jonah that he was but one man. What! One man to a multitude; a single person to a whole kingdom! Yea; but Jonah might have heard, that the day was when those that were with Elisha and his servant were more in number than all the enemies which were against them. Where God is, and His angels, there man is not alone.

3. It shall be but a bad shift for the miscreants of the earth to cry, in the day of vengeance, to the mountains and to the rocks, 'Fall on us.'

4. In these most perilous times, in which Satan frets and rages; in which Papism is a little weakened, but Atheism waxes strong, and the sins of men cry loud; but, on the other side, pity waxes thin, and charity grows cold; this should be a lively motion to the Spirit of God in us, that with alacrity we may go forward to the building up of God's house, and not be wearied in well doing, or withdraw ourselves from the work.

5. Surely God looks for much, of them whom He has singled out to be messengers of His glory.

6. Shall many smart for one? Here is a question. But learn here God's hatred to sin; learn here His deep and endless wisdom. His wisdom shines in this, that oftentimes, with one man, He strikes the many, for reasons which, in themselves, are very different; being evermore well-known to His majesty, but secret to us, the party principal He punishes; to the next He teaches obedience; the patience of the third He will have to be tried; and so forward with the rest; in all He seeks His glory; His honour in the wicked, His true fear in the good. If all these be whipped at once, He does no wrong to any.

7. It is better to fear too much than to presume but a little. Our God is of fearful majesty.

8. Let us fear the Lord for His love, and love Him for His mercy; let us not provoke Him to strike us, because otherwise He cannot awake us; but let us watch to Him that His anger may sleep to us.

9. The *glass* is bright but brittle; it cannot endure the hammer; the *gold* is another kind of metal; do you melt it, or do you rub it, or do you beat it, it shineth still the more orient. So it is with our faith: it does not fear the touch-stone.

10. My heart oftentimes doth ache, and my very soul doth tremble, to think what guides be over souls in many places; I say over the souls of men, which are the most precious substances that God hath made under the heaven, and for the ransoming of which Christ Jesus came down from His glory.

11. Justice called for a death; take My death, saith the Saviour, let one die for the people, the head for all

the members. The King of men and angels had this choice put to Him, that either Himself or His, the mystical head or body, should undergo a death; He took the turn upon Himself, and so wrought a reconcilement from His Father toward His Church. To procure our peace, He plucked wars upon Himself; and what we should have borne, His humanity did sustain with a lovely change of our parts, for the unrighteous sinneth and the righteous man is punished. This brought a way to the wandering; this brought life to the dying and safety to the perishing; for His loss was our gain, and His impoverishing our enriching.

12. This it is which holdeth us when we are living; this it is which helpeth us when we are dying. A God become man! The celestial made terrestrial! Our Judge become our Jesus!

13. When he appointeth salvation, then everything in His time shall work unto salvation, but it must be in His time. He draweth the unwilling to Him, the broken He bindeth up, the lost He seeketh out; He toucheth with remorse that which was before as adamant; the hardest heart he doth mollify. He that ordaineth glory to any will give him grace to attain it; He who is the Life is the way leading to that life; He who giveth the one granteth the other: when He determineth the end, then also He offereth the means to apprehend that end.

SUTTON (CHRISTOPHER).

BORN 1565—DIED 1629.

1. To meditate of the life of Him by whom we have eternal life, is the very life of life.

2. Ought we not often in soul to go with the wise men to Bethlehem, by the direction of the star of grace, and there fall down and worship the little King, there offer the gold of charity, the frankincense of devotion, the myrrh of penitency, and return, not by cruel Herod or by troubled Jerusalem, but another way, a better way, unto our long and happy home !

3. Merciful Lord, to compare our coldness with their fervency, our negligence with their industry, our faint love with their burning charity, we shall find such odds, as we may sorrow to see our own defects in this case. Calling to mind the learning of the ancient fathers, we may think they did nothing but read ; seeing their works, that they did nothing but write ; considering their devotion, that they did nothing but pray.

4. Farewell, glory of the world, for in thy delights promises are made and never kept ; in thy vineyard men labour, but are never rewarded. Farewell world, which callest the rash, valiant ; proud, seemly ; covetous, good husbands ; the babbler, eloquent ; the wanton, youthful. Farewell world, which deceivest all that trust in thee ; which dost promise to the ambitious honour ; to the

greedy, rewards; to the covetous, riches; to the young, time. Farewell, I say, vainglory, which, because thou art not of God, failest all.

5. Happy honour, when Jesus calleth from tears to joy. How dry and hard art thou without Jesus! How foolish and vain if thou covetest anything without Jesus! Is not this greater loss than if thou hadst lost the whole world? What can the world bestow without Jesus? To be without Jesus is a grievous hell, and to be with Jesus is a sweet paradise. If Jesus be with thee, no enemy can hurt thee; if Jesus be from thee, no friend can help. He is most poor that liveth without Jesus, and he is most rich who is with Jesus.

6. To deny our goods, our friends, yea, our very pleasures, is very much; and yet, to follow Christ we must go a step further; that is, to wit, we must deny even our very selves. It is not only required that we deny that which is ours, but even *ut nos* that we deny ourselves also.

7. It is a hard saying, 'Take up thy cross': it will be harder, 'Depart, ye cursed'! Christ hath many lovers of His kingdom, but few lovers of his cross; many that follow Him to the breaking of bread, few to the drinking of His cup.

8. The head doth not rise without the body: the head is risen, the body therefore shall rise. So the resurrection of Christ is the cause of our resurrection; and He rising we all rise.

9. Let us follow the Lamb whithersoever He goeth, at least whither we are able to go. Let us follow Him

suffering, by mortifying the flesh: let us follow Him
rising, by newness of life; but most joyfully of all, let
us follow Him ascending, by setting our affections on
heavenly things, or things above.

10. A remembrance of Christ's second coming unto
judgment ought to incite every well-minded Christian
to study his soul. Let him call to mind that the great
Lord of heaven and earth, whom we have all this while
proposed unto ourselves (according to His humanity)
the best pattern for imitation of living, even Christ
Jesus, He is gone into a far country, and hath committed His goods unto us His servants, willing us all
to watch, because He will return at an hour we think
not of.

11. Concerning Christ's coming to judgment, we are
to observe, out of the Evangelist, the things going before,
things accompanying His coming, and things that follow
after; they are so many heralds sent before to proclaim
the command of the King, which are these, that we shall
hear of false prophets, wars, and rumours of wars, famines,
pestilences, earthquakes, the abounding of iniquity, wax-
ing cold of charity, and such like. These signs shew
before that the time is near: for the things that do
accompany His coming, they are the darkening of the
sun, the moon losing her light, the falling of the stars of
heaven, the trouble of the powers of heaven.

12. When this μικρόκοσμος, or little world, Man, suffereth
his last agony; when his sense is troubled, and the
whole body distressed (it is a sign that he is upon his
dissolving), how much more shall this be done in the

greater world, where these things are seen? The things following after, are the separating of the sheep and goats; the appointing to the left and right hand: the two sentences of judgment, Go, you cursed! and, Come, ye blessed! the visible appearing of the King of glory. Then Pilate shall not need to ask, Art Thou a King? but he shall see it, that He is a King of kings, and Lord of lords. Again, as we know the signs of old age, but not the year, month, week, nor day, when the aged shall depart; so, the world to be dissolved we know by God's word, and the signs precedent; but when, we know not.

LINDSAY (DAVID).

BORN (ABOUT) 1570—DIED 1627.

1. Let man behold that unspeakable love wherewith God hath loved him, and that rare account his God maketh of him in that shining glass of the creation of the world.

2. Sin is a monstrous foul thing, defiling everything it toucheth, so that our holy God can, upon no condition, join with it.

3. Let none beside thy God, teaching thee by His written word, be thy master and leader on earth, if thou wouldest walk hereafter with Him.

4. Let all sick in soul because of sin, to whose ears the sound of the sweet name of that great Physician, JESUS, is come, by the means of the Gospel seek to Him for medicine, whom they cannot find but in His word.

5. That white shining lily, Jesus, is not to be found but among pricking thorns.

6. Sweet wise Jesus will cross thee first, if He be to crown thee afterwards.

7. While thou livest here, desire not to live, but *to* that God and *for* that God who made thee and sent thee hither.

8. Let man consider how dearly sweet Jesus hath loved him.

9. Honourable, precious, and forcible beyond measure,

is that clean and cleansing blood of Jesus, blessed for evermore.

10. Clean Jesus will not wash thee in His clean, cleansing blood, to the end that thou may prove a swine but a swan; a filthy dog, but a clean turtle-dove; and so not a bond-slave to sin and Satan, but a free king to God, His and thy Father.

11. He whom blessed Jesus hath made a son unto God, to *serve* His Majesty for a while, shall also be made by Jesus a king unto God, to *reign* with Him for ever.

12. Seek not that which is God's but God Himself.

13. No person nor thing can possibly content the sight, the smell, the taste, the touch, of that royal eagle, the true Christian, beside that blessed Jesus, who sometime was dead, but is alive, blessed for evermore.

14. All men should so live in the world, that they may amend the world.

15. O Lord God! when shall the loose Christians of this last age be enlightened and quickened in soul by Thy majesty? In mercy look on their dead souls!

16. But how shall you love this Jesus, O my soul? Lend thine ears unto Jesus; cast thine eyes upon Jesus; and out of that love wherewith He hath loved thee, learn thou, I pray thee, how to love again.

HALL (BISHOP).

BORN 1574—DIED 1656.

1. I am glad of your sorrow; and should weep for you, if you did not thus mourn. Your sorrow is, that you cannot enough grieve for your sins. Let me tell you that the angels themselves sing this lamentation; neither doth the earth afford any so sweet music, in the ears of God. This heaviness is the way to joy. Worldly sorrow is worthy of pity, because it leadeth to death; but this deserves nothing but envy and gratulation.

2. Think how little the world can do for you, and what it doth how deceitfully; what stings there are with its honey; what farewell succeeds its welcome. When this Jael brings you milk in the one hand, know, she hath a nail in the other.

3. Cares are a heavy load, and uneasy: these must be laid down at the bottom of this hill, if we ever look to attain the top. Thou art loaded with household cares, perhaps public; I bid thee not cast them away: even these have their season, which thou canst not omit without impiety: I bid thee lay them down at thy closet door, when thou attemptest this work. Let them in with thee— thou shalt find them troublesome companions, ever distracting thee from thy best errand. Thou wouldest think of heaven; thy barn comes in thy way, or perhaps thy 'count-book, or thy coffers; or, it may be, thy mind is

beforehand travelling upon the morrow's journey. So, while thou thinkest of many things, thou thinkest of nothing; while thou wouldest go many ways, thou standest still.

4. There is nothing, but man, that respecteth greatness: not God, not nature, not disease, not death, not judgment. Not God: He is no accepter of persons. Not nature: we see the sons of princes born as naked as the poorest ; and the poor child as fair, well favoured, strong, witty, as the heir of nobles. Not disease, death, judgment : they sicken alike, die alike, fare alike after death. There is nothing, besides natural men, of whom goodness is not respected. I will honour greatness in others ; but, for myself, I will esteem a dram of goodness worth a whole world of greatness.

5. If I die, the world shall miss me but a little ; I shall miss it less. Not it me, because it hath such store of better men ; not I it, because it hath so much ill, and I shall have so much happiness.

6. With men it is a good rule, to try first, and then to trust ; with God it is contrary. I will first trust Him, as most wise, omnipotent, merciful, and try Him afterwards. I know it is as impossible for Him to deceive me, as not to be.

7. Every man hath a heaven and a hell. Earth is a wicked man's heaven ; his hell is to come. On the contrary, the godly have their hell upon earth, where they are vexed with temptations and afflictions, by Satan and his accomplices ; their heaven is above, in endless happiness. If it be ill with me on earth, it is well my torment

is so short and so easy; I will not be so covetous as to hope for two heavens.

8. Good prayers never came weeping home: I am sure I shall receive, either what I ask, or what I should ask.

9. I never loved those Salamanders that are never well but when they are in the fire of contention. I will rather suffer a thousand wrongs than offer one; I will suffer a hundred, rather than return one; I will suffer many, ere I complain of one, and endeavour to right it by contending. I have ever found, that to strive with my superior is furious; with my equal, doubtful; my inferior, sordid and base; with any, full of unquietness.

10. I would rather confess my ignorance than falsely profess knowledge. It is no shame not to know all things; but it is a just shame to overreach anything.

11. Every sickness is a little death. I will be content to die oft, that I may die once well.

12. Some children are of that nature, that they are never well but while the rod is over them; such am I to God. Let Him beat me, so He amend me; let Him take all away from me, so He give me Himself.

DAVENANT (BISHOP).

BORN 1576—DIED 1641.

1. In justification we are liberated from the chains of our sins, so far as they bound us for condemnation, yea, even so far as they held us under the dominion of Satan; and this suffices for its being truly said that the chains of our sins are broken asunder by the grace of God; for the remains thereof, abiding in us, have not the nature of a chain, but are themselves enchained by the grace now predominant over them, and treading them, as it were, under foot.

2. As original righteousness comprehended the spiritual light of the mind, so original sin implies the densest mental darkness.

3. We acknowledge that God *infuses* a righteousness, in the very act of justifying; but we deny that the sentence of God, in justifying, has respect to this as the cause by which man is constituted justified.

4. The perfect obedience of Christ, the Mediator, is the formal cause of our justification.

5. The justification of believers does not rest on this, that they have in themselves a quality of new righteousness, which they would venture to subject to a legal examination of the strict judgment of God; but that, by and through the merits of the Redeemer, in whom they believe, they are not to undergo such judgments, but are

dealt with as if they had in themselves exact legal right-eousness.

6. The obedience of Christ, whereby He fulfilled the law, is so imputed to His mystical members, that, in consideration of it, they stand guiltless before God, justified and accepted to everlasting life.

7. God, by His decree, transferred the fulfilling of the law to Christ, the God-man, and willed that that obedience and righteousness which Christ performed, in our flesh, should become ours by imputation. The Apostle most clearly teaches that Christ was made subject to the law, not for himself, but for us; whence it will follow, that the fruit of His obedience redounds to us; which is the same as that the righteousness of Christ, or His perfect fulfilling of the law, is imputed to us.

8. Christ not only made satisfaction for us by under-going the penalty of the cross, but also by taking upon Himself the burden of the law.

9. The blood of Christ washes and reconciles to God, not the righteous and those who are fulfilling the law, but sinners and the transgressors of the law.

10. How will he obtain peace by faith, who is uncertain whether he possesses faith or not? Faith resembles a great light, which makes itself visible as well as other things.

11. The Romanists admit that there is an assurance of *hope*, of the remission of sins, &c., but assent not to there being an assurance of *faith*. It is vain to make a distinction between the assurance of *hope* and the assurance of *faith*, seing the *hope* of salvation cannot fluctuate in the

justified man, unless his faith in Christ fluctuates at the
same time; nor can faith remain assured, except where
hope maintains the same certainty.

12. Such is the efficacy of the promises of the Gospel,
that, as soon as any one receives them by a living faith,
and applies them to himself, he straightway derives from
thence firm and solid consolation. But how can the promise of the forgiveness of sins yield to the believer solid
comfort, while he remains uncertain whether he has faith
or not? . . . Faith wrought by the Spirit apprehends the
forgiveness of sins, and the paternal love of God towards
us. This faith, in laying hold of the free love of God
towards us, does not make men reckless and easy; but the
want of this assurance is the cause why men wallow in
earthly lusts. 'Men do not' (says Bernard) 'repay the
love of God with a return of love, unless as the Spirit reveals to them, through faith, the eternal purpose of God
respecting their future salvation.'

SIBBES.

BORN 1577—DIED 1635.

1. When we come to be religious, we lose not our pleasure, but translate it. Before we fed on common notions, but now we live on holy truths.

2. The whole life of a Christian should be nothing but praises to God.

3. Is it not an unreasonable speech for a man at midnight to say, It will never be day? It is as unreasonable for a man in trouble to say, O Lord, I shall never get free; it will be always thus!

4. Having given up ourselves to God, let us comfort our souls that God is our God. When riches, and men, and our lives fail, yet God is ours. We are now God's Davids, God's Pauls, God's Abrahams. We have an everlasting being with Him, as one with Jesus Christ his Son.

5. God takes it unkindly if we weep too much for the loss of a wife, or child, or friend, or for any cross in this life; for it is a sign that we do not fetch our comfort from Him. Nay, though our weeping be for sin, we must keep moderation, with one eye looking on our sins, and the other on God's mercy in Christ. If, therefore, the best grief should be moderated, how much more the other!

6. That is spiritual knowledge which alters the *relish* of the soul; for we must know there is a bitter opposition in our nature against all saving truths; especially, there is a

contrariety between our nature and that doctrine which teaches us we must deny ourselves and be saved by another. The soul must relish before it can digest.

7. When thou art disappointed with men, retire to God and to his promises; and build upon this, that the Lord will not be wanting in anything to do thee good.

8. Faith makes us kings, because thereby we marry the King of heaven. The church is the queen of heaven, and Christ is the king of heaven.

9. If we have a time of sinning, God will have a time of punishing.

10. If the touch of Christ in his abasement upon earth drew virtue from Him, certain it is that faith cannot touch Christ in heaven but it will draw a quieting virtue from Him which will in some measure stop the issues of an unquiet spirit.

11. Sin is not so sweet in the committing as it is heavy and bitter in the reckoning.

12. He wants no company that hath Christ for his companion.

13. Most of our disquietness in our calling is that we trouble ourselves about God's work Trust God and be doing, and let Him alone with the rest.

14. God is never nearer his church than when trouble is near.

15. Every Christian may truly say, God loves me better than I do myself.

16. God hath two sanctuaries; he hath two heavens: the heaven of heavens and a broken spirit.

DICKSON (DAVID).

BORN 1583—DIED 1663.

1. The invincible grace of God, working regeneration and conversion, does not destroy the freedom of man's will, but makes it truly free, and perfects it.

2. Grow in the estimation of Christ's righteousness.

3. Let no man complain of wrong done to man's free will, when God stops its way to hell; wisely, powerfully, graciously and sweetly moveth it to choose the way of life ; but rather let men beware to take the glory of actual conversion from God, and either give it wholly to their idol of free-will, or make it sharer of the glory of regeneration with God.

4. That man who, daily, in the sense of his sinfulness and poverty, fleeth unto Jesus Christ, that he may be justified by His righteousness, and endeavoureth, by faith in Him, to bring forth the fruits of new obedience, and doth not put confidence in his works, when he hath done them, but rejoiceth in Jesus Christ, the Fountain of holiness and blessedness,—that man is a new creature.

5. Let us beware of laying any sort of merit upon our daily exercise of faith and sorrow for sin ; otherwise we shall be found offerers unto God of satisfaction from us, and not suitors of remission of sins from God.

6. Be comforted in that Lord who gathereth the ragged and scattered desires of supplicants, and taketh away the iniquity of the service of His clients, as our High Priest,

bearing (in His appearing for us), as it were, in His forehead, holiness to the Lord.

7. God is worthy to be credited, upon His word without a pawn; yea, when His dispensation seemeth contrary to His promise.

8. Christ's obedience, even to the death of the cross, did begin in His emptying Himself to take on our nature and the shape of a servant, and did run on till His resurrection and ascension. As for His sufferings in the end of His life, both in soul and body, they were the completing of His formerly begun obedience; but were not His only obedience for us, or His only suffering for us.

9. Man, by the law of nature, is bound to give credit to God when He speaketh; and bound to trust in God when He offereth Himself as a Friend and a Father to him; and when God bids him seek His face, he is bound to obey Him, and seek His face.

10. There remaineth for making of the covenant (of reconciliation), but that the hearer do honestly answer, 'The offer and condition pleaseth me well; I consent to be reconciled.'

11. The more poor and empty a man is in his own eyes, he ought to draw the more near unto the riches of grace in Christ.

12. We need not be afraid lest any person go, or be sent, too soon unto Christ, and that the teacher of this doctrine be supposed to foster presumption, and to offer untimeous consolation.

MEDE (JOSEPH).

BORN 1586   DIED 1638.

1. The Christian as well as the Jew, after six days spent in his own works, is to sanctify the seventh, that he may profess himself thereby a servant of God, the Creator of heaven and earth, as well as the Jew. For the *quotum* the Jew and Christian agree ; but in designation of the day they differ. For the Christian chooseth for his holy day that which, with the Jew, was the first day of the week, and calls it the Lord's day, that he might thereby profess himself a servant of that God who, on the morning of that day, vanquished Satan, the spiritual Pharaoh, and redeemed us from our spiritual thraldom by raising Jesus Christ our Lord from the dead; begetting us, instead of an earthly Canaan, to an inheritance incorruptible in the heavens. The Christian, by the day he hallows, professes himself a Christian. The Jew and Christian make their designation of their day on like ground : the Jews, the memorial day of their deliverance from the temporal Egypt and temporal Pharaoh ; the Christians, the memorial day of their deliverance from the spiritual Egypt and spiritual Pharaoh.

2. It would be uncomely for a man to wear a veil, .that is, a woman's habit ; so was it uncomely for a woman to be without a veil, that is, in the guise and dress of a man (1 Cor. xi. 10) ; and howsoever the devils of the Gentiles

took pleasure in uncomeliness, yet the God they worshipped, and His holy angels who were present at their devotions, loved a comely accommodation, agreeable to nature and custom, in such as worshipped Him.

3. Whence comes that unchristian, or, indeed, atheistical language, 'A base priest; a paltry priest! it would never have grieved me had any other served me thus; but to be served thus by a base priest, who can endure it?' Tell me in good earnest, is this to honour a priest or a prophet in the name of a prophet (Matt. x. 41); or not rather, point blank unto it, to reproach and dishonour him under that reverend name, that is, to despise and reproach the calling itself? For how can a man honour that condition, the name whereof he thinks to be a reproach? Is any man wont to say, 'A base lord, a base gentleman, a base Christian'? No. And why? Because these are terms and titles of honour. Judge, then, by this, what account they make of God's *ambre*, who turn the very title of their calling into a name of reproach; and what reward, by proportion, they are like to merit at Christ's hand. Not a *prophet's*, I am sure; and whether a *Christian's* or not, themselves may judge.

4. By reason of sin, heaven and earth, God and man, were at enmity; but by Christ this is taken away, and man, by forgiveness of sin, restored unto peace and favour with God. And as, by this nativity, God and man became one person, so, by this conjunction, heaven and earth, angels and men, become one fellowship, one city and kingdom of God.

5. The way whereby the blessed Seed should vanquish

Satan, and redeem His elect out of his power and jurisdiction, was by becoming a sacrifice for sin, so to cancel the title whereby the devil held the world in thraldom.

6. I will not look upon any other cause or occasion of my misery, of my cross or calamity ; but look unto my *sin*, and give glory to God, who sent the hand which hath done all this unto me.

7. Wouldest thou have comfort in thy misery? wouldest thou have joy in all thy sorrows ? wouldest thou find rest in the greatest troubles of thy life ? wouldest thou welcome the Lord Jesus at His coming ?   Oh labour, then, to make thy election sure.   Never cease till thou hast gotten the seal and earnest of thy salvation ; renounce all kind of peace till thou hast found the peace of conscience ; discard all joy till thou feelest the joy of the Holy Ghost. Do this, and there is no calamity so great but thou mayest undergo it ; no burden so heavy but thou mayest easily bear it.   Do this, and thou shalt live in the fear, die in the favour, and rise in the power of God the Father, and help to make up the heavenly concert, singing, with the saints and angels, Hallelujah, Hallelujah, glory, and honour, and praise be unto the Lamb, and to Him that sitteth upon the throne, for evermore !

QUARLES (FRANCIS).

BORN 1592—DIED 1644.

1. The gate of heaven is strait; canst thou hope to enter without breaking? The bubble that would pass the flood-gates must first dissolve.

2. Think not that a pleasure which God had threatened; nor that a blessing which heaven hath cursed.

3. My soul, how hast thou profaned that day thy God hath sanctified! how hast thou encroached on that which Heaven hath set apart! If thy impatience cannot act a Sabbath twelve hours, what happiness canst thou expect in a perpetual Sabbath? Is six days too little for thyself, and two hours too much for thy God?

4. Art thou in bondage? O my soul, here is freedom; art thou dejected? here is comfort; art thou pursued? here is a refuge; art thou overburdened? here is rest; art thou condemned? here is a pardon.

5. Lord, I am sick, I fly to Him as my Physician; I am a trespasser, I fly to Him my Advocate; I am a suitor, I fly to Him my Mediator; I am a delinquent, I fly to Him my Sanctuary; I am a sinner, I fly to Him my Saviour.

6. O sweet Jesus, pierce the marrow of my soul with the shafts of Thy love, that it may burn and melt, and languish with the only desire of Thee. Let it always desire Thee, and seek Thee, and find Thee, and sweetly

rest in Thee. Be Thou in all my thoughts, in all my words, in all my actions; that both my thoughts, my words, and my actions being sanctified by Thee here, I may be glorified by Thee hereafter.

7. If thy sins fear the hand of justice, behold thy Sanctuary; if thy offences tremble before the Judge, behold thy Advocate; if thy creditor threaten a prison, behold thy bail. Behold the Lamb of God that hath taken thy sins from thee: behold the Blessed of heaven and earth that hath prepared a kingdom for thee. Be ravished, O my soul! Oh bless the name of Elohim! Oh bless the name of our Emmanuel, with praises and eternal hallelujahs!

8. Thinkest thou, my soul, to be made happy by the smiles of earth, or unhappy by her frowns? When she fawns upon thee, she deludes thee; when she kisses thee, she betrays thee. She brings the butter in a lordly dish, and bears a hammer in her deadly hand. Trust not her flattery, O my soul, nor let her malice move thee. Her music is thy magic; her sweetness is thy snare; she is the highway to eternal death. If thou love her, thou hast begun thy journey; if thou honour her, thou mendest thy pace; if thou obey her, thou art at thy journey's end. When she distastes thee, Christ relishes in thee; when she afflicts thee, God instructs thee; when she locks her gates against thee, heaven opens for thee; when she disdains thee, God honours thee; when she forsakes thee, He owns thee; when she persecutes thee, He crowns thee. Why art thou then disquieted, my soul, and why is thy spirit troubled within thee? Trust thou

in Him by faith: if thou want comfort, fly to Him by prayer.

9. How dost thou wrong the God of mercy, how slight the God of truth! He that hears the cry of ravens, and feeds them with a gracious hand, will He be deaf to thee? He that robes the lilies of the field, that neither sue nor care to be apparelled, will He deny thee those graces He hath commanded thee to ask? Art thou hungry? He is the bread of life. Art thou thirsty? He is the water of life? Art thou naked? fly to Him, and He will give thee the righteousness of His own Son. Build upon His promise, who is truth itself; rely upon His mercy, who is goodness itself. Art thou a prodigal? yet remember thou art a son. Is He offended? He will not forget He is a Father. Come, therefore, with a filial boldness, and He will grant thy heart's desire.

MESTREZAT (A FRENCH DIVINE).

BORN 1592—DIED 1657.

1. The law said, 'This do, and live;' but the Gospel says, Do this, because God hath freely given thee life. This makes our obedience not servile but filial, springing from gratitude and love.

2. It was fitting that the Redeemer of the human race should be the same who had been its Creator, since it did not require less power to restore life to man, than to impart it at the beginning.

3. To join in one person the Creator with the creature, the Infinite with the finite, the Eternal with a being brought forth in time, far surpasses all the wonders of creation.

4. Fear not, O mortals, to draw nigh unto God; in Him you have your nature; no longer will He be a consuming fire to you, seeing He yet retains your flesh.

5. It behoved our Lord Jesus Christ to be made to us everlasting life by His death. Though He is the source of life, yet He could not have restored life to us without having first died.

6. What is there, O believers, that should disturb your joy and peace, since the blood of God is your ransom?

7. Faith is the hand by which we lay hold on Jesus. By faith, we are not only permitted to put the finger into

the print of the nails, and to thrust the hand into His side, but the very soul finds refuge in His wounds.

8. Faith justifies us, not by its merit or worth; for in this way we should be justified by our works, or by faith as by a work; but it justifies us by referring us to Jesus Christ, and by the oneness which it establishes between Him and us.

9. The feeling which we have in our souls, of the expiation of sin by the blood of Jesus Christ, is that inward witness, that white stone with the new name written on it, which no man knoweth saving he that receiveth it.

10. Believers have to engage with enemies, already vanquished by Jesus Christ, their Head; so that their combat is nothing more than a continued application of the victory which He has obtained for them.

11. Believers, under the old covenant, waited for the coming of Christ in the flesh, to atone for sin by the sacrifice of Himself. The Christian Church is now in expectation of His Second coming, of which the angels said to the disciples, 'This same Jesus shall so come as ye have seen Him go into heaven.'

12. Christ is the Head of the church and the Saviour of the body. Hence it appears that to stand unconfounded before Him in the day of judgment, nothing is necessary but to be found in Him. Since Christ Himself is ordained to be the Judge of quick and dead, the sentence which He shall pronounce will not be to the hurt of His members, who are a part of Himself. The Apostle, therefore, says, that He shall come to be glorified in His saints; and, for this reason, the church, which is the

whole body of believers, is represented as hastening His coming, saying, 'Even so come, Lord Jesus.'

13. When believers are on their deathbeds, and apparently deprived of all their faculties, then the Holy Spirit can and does act upon them, by energies and operations altogether inexplicable, as He acted upon the babe in the womb of Elizabeth.

14. Though Christ is no more in this world, He is still God with us, by the indissoluble union of our nature with His. Wherever He is, He hath us with Him, in that nature which He hath united to His Godhead. Thus, since the birth of the Son of God, God is ever with men.

HERBERT (GEORGE).

BORN 1593—DIED 1632.

1. I can never do too much for Him that hath done so much for me. And I will labour to be like my Saviour, by making humility lovely in the eyes of all men, and by following the merciful and meek example of my dear Jesus.

2. I beseech you to be cheerful, and comfort yourself with the God of all comfort, who is not willing to behold any sorrow, but for sin.

3. As the earth is but a point in respect of the heavens, so are earthly troubles compared to heavenly joys.

4. I never find, Blessed be the rich ; or, Blessed be the noble ; but, Blessed be the meek, blessed be the poor, blessed be the mourners. And yet, O God, most carry themselves, as if they not only not desired, but even feared to be blessed.

5. God intends your soul to be a sacred temple for Himself to dwell in, and will not allow any room there for such an inmate as grief, or allow that any sadness shall be His competitor.

6. We live in an age that hath more need of good examples than precepts.

7. I would not willingly pass one day of my life without comforting a sad soul or shewing mercy.

8. The parson's yea is yea, and nay, nay ; and his

apparel plain, but reverend and clean, without spots, or dust, or smell; the purity of his mind breaking out and dilating itself even to his body, clothes, and habitation.

9. What an admirable Epistle is the second to the Corinthians! How full of affections! He joys and he is sorry, he grieves and he glories. Never was there such care of a flock expressed, save in the great Shepherd of the fold, who first shed tears over Jerusalem, and afterwards blood.

10. Man would sit down at this world; God bids him sell it, and purchase a better.

11. A prophecy is a wonder sent to posterity, lest they complain of want of wonders. It is a letter sealed and sent, which to the bearer is but paper, but to the receiver and opener is full of power.

12. Oh make Thy word a swift word, passing from the ear to the heart, and from the heart to the life and conversation.

13. Difficulties are so far from cooling Christians that they whet them.

GOODWIN (THOMAS).

BORN 1599—DIED 1679.

1. Seek to be pardoned, but above all seek to be beloved.

2. They only are wise who are wise unto salvation.

3. Surely that which hath long ago satisfied God Himself for the sins of many thousands now in heaven, may well serve to satisfy the heart and conscience of any sinner now upon earth.

4. Is Christ God's Beloved, with and in whom He is well pleased? And is He not thy Beloved? What is the matter? Is thy narrow soul more curious about an object of love than God Himself is? Oh let Him be to each of us our Beloved! If He be God's Beloved, He may well be thine. Is He able to satisfy God's best thoughts, and is He not able to satisfy thee, poor creature? God Himself is satisfied, and at rest in Him. Says Christ, 'I was daily His delight'; and wouldst thou be happier than God is? Is He God's Beloved, in whom He is well pleased, and wilt thou be pleased with anything but Christ?

5. Let thy soul be set on the highest mount that any creature was ever set upon, and enlarged to take in the most spacious prospect, both of sin, and misery, and difficulties of being saved, that ever yet any poor soul did find within itself; yea, join to these all the hindrances and

objections that the heart of man can invent against itself and salvation ; lift up thine eyes and look to the utmost thou canst see ; yet Christ, by His intercession, is able to save thee beyond the horizon and utmost compass of thy thoughts, even 'to the uttermost.'

6. Why do men leave Christ for the pleasures of the world ? Because these are real things to them. Therefore God comes and weighs down the reality of the things of this world, by the reality of the things of the world to come.

7. To go to God upon the freeness of His grace and promises, and to refer our will to His, and cast ourselves into those everlasting arms, is as if a man should leave his own standing, and cast himself into the arms of a mighty giant that stands upon another pinnacle—one whom he has often wronged—and he himself has no hands to lay hold of him by, but must depend on his catching him ;— here is the greatest trust, the greatest self-denial that can be. Thus the heart throws itself out of all possibilities, and submits to the free grace of God in Christ ; and this is done in believing.

CALAMY (EDMUND).

BORN 1600—DIED 1666.

1. Miserable is that man whose heart is too hard to pray.

2. Strive to be good in all concerns ; to be good subjects, good governors, good dealers, good husbands, good masters, and good neighbours : so will God love you and bless you, and the rest respect you.

3. If thou risest from a low estate to a great one, it is but like stepping from a boat or barge into a ship ; thy dangers continue, for thou art still upon the sea.

4. Make the Lord's day the market-day for thy soul ; let the whole day be spent in prayer, repetitions, or meditations; lay aside the affairs of the other part of the week ; let the sermon thou hast heard be converted into prayer. Shall God allow thee six days, and wilt not thou afford Him one ?

5. The sinner is always grinding at the devil's mill ; and the devil is no less busy in supplying the hopper, lest his mill should stand still.

6. The first that named God's name in Scripture was the devil, and he likewise confessed our Saviour to be the Son of God ; however, he was the devil notwithstanding that.

7. Our God is a living God, and loves not dull and drowsy saints : we must not only serve Him in this life, but we must have life in our service.

8. The cap and the knee are but outward ceremonies ; but he that avoids iniquity is the best Christian.

9. In your repentance, remember church-sins, sermon-sins, sacrament-sins, lest the Church give you up to Satan for your sins.

10. For know, God is a guest that requires the upper rooms, that is, the head and the heart.

11. Pray often ; for prayer is a shield to the soul, a sacrifice to God, and a scourge to Satan.

12. Let your acquaintance be few and good ; cousins, country-men, and school-fellows, are spenders of money and time.

13. If thou hast an estate, and wouldest improve it, be charitable to the poor : scattered seeds increase, but those that are hoarded die.

HALE (SIR MATTHEW).

BORN 1600—DIED 1675.

1. If we do but seriously believe the truth of the gospel, and the truth of the life to come, the best things of this world will seem of small moment; and the worst things this world can inflict will seem but of small moment; and the worst things this world can inflict will appear too light to provoke us to impatience or discontent. He that hath everlasting glory in prospect, will have a mind full of contentment in the darkest condition here.

2. Our home, our country, is heaven, where there are no sorrows, nor fears, nor troubles: this world is the place of our travel and pilgrimage, and, at the best, our inn.

3. In my Father's house there are mansions, many mansions, instead of my inn; and my Saviour Himself hath not disdained to be my harbinger. He is gone before me to prepare a place for me. I will therefore content myself with the inconveniences of my short journey, for my accommodations will be admirable when I come to my home, that heavenly Jerusalem, which is the place of my rest and happiness.

4. Weigh and consider your words before you speak them, and do not talk at random.

5. I would not have you meddle with any recreations, pastimes, or ordinary work of your calling, from Saturday night, at eight of the clock, till Monday morning. For,

though I am not apt to think that Saturday night is part of the Christian Sabbath, yet it is fit then to prepare the heart for it.

6. I have been acquainted somewhat with men and books, and have had long experience in learning and in the world ; there is no book like the Bible for excellence, learning, wisdom, and use; and it is want of understanding in them that think or speak otherwise.

7. Be frugal of your time ; it is one of the best jewels we have.

8. This is the great art of Christian chemistry, to convert those acts that are natural and civil into acts truly religious; whereby the whole course of this life is a service to Almighty God, and an uninterrupted state of religion which is the best and noblest, and most universal redemption of His time.

9. Remember that this is the very elixir, the very hell of hell to the damned spirits, that they had once a time wherein they might have procured everlasting rest and glory ; but they foolishly and vainly mis-spent that time and season, which is now not to be recovered.

10. The happiness of mankind is not to be found in this life ; it is a flower that grows in the garden of eternity, and to be expected in its full fruition only in that life which is to come.

CRISP.

BORN 1600—DIED 1642.

1. The iniquities of us all, the Lord hath laid upon Christ; they cannot lie upon Christ and upon us too; if they be reckoned to Christ, they are not reckoned to him that doth receive Christ.

2. 'I spread my skirt over thee;' mark it, I pray you. Not a scanty skirt to cover some of this filth, but a broad skirt, a large skirt, a white raiment, as Christ calls it Himself. There is such a covering of Christ that He casts upon a person to cover his nakedness.

3. Our sins are so translated to Christ, that God reckons Christ the very sinner; nay, God reckons all our sins to be His, and makes Him to be sin for us, and we are made the righteousness of God in Him.

4. God neither looks to anything in the creature to win Him to shew kindness, nor yet to anything in the creature to debar Him; neither righteousness in men persuades God to pardon sin, nor unrighteousness in men hinders Him from giving this pardon: it is only and simply for his own sake that He doth it unto men.

5. Had not Christ made a full satisfaction to the Father, He Himself must have perished under those sins that He did bear; but in that He went through the thing, and paid the full price, as He carried them away from us, so He laid them down from Himself. So that now Christ is freed from sin, and we are freed from sin in Him.

6. Our standing is not founded upon the subduing of our sins, but upon that foundation that never fails, and that is Christ Himself.

7. Christ is He that justifies the ungodly; Christ is He that is the peace-maker; our peace depends upon Christ alone. Beloved, if you will fetch your peace from anything in the world but Christ, you will fetch it from where it is not.

8. Christ is the fountain of peace and life; and men forget that peace is to be had in Christ, when they would have peace out of righteousness of their own, out of their enlargements or out of their humiliations. These are broken cisterns, and what peace is there in them? Is there not sinfulness in them? and if there be sinfulness in them, where, then, is their peace? Sin speaks nothing but war to the soul. Let me tell you, beloved, you that look for peace from the subduing of your sins, what peace can it afford you, in case there be any defects of subduing of your sins? There can be no peace.

9. None but Christ! none but Christ! While your own acts proclaim nothing but war, Christ alone and His blood proclaim nothing but peace.

10. I have not said that God is not offended with the sins that believers commit; but God stands not offended with the persons of believers for the sins committed by them.

11. The anger of God for sin hath spent itself upon the person of Christ; and having so spent itself, there remains none of it to light upon the person of a believer.

12. 'This is My beloved Son, in whom I am well

pleased.' He doth not say *with* whom I am well pleased, but *in* whom I am well pleased, that is, in whom I am well pleased with you.

13. Men are mistaken, who think that the law makes them see their own vileness; a gracious sight of our vileness is the work of Christ alone.

14. Christ is a free way; Christ is a near way; Christ is a firm way; there is no need of sinking; Christ is a pleasant way; 'all Thy ways are pleasantness;' Christ is a safe way; there is a continual guard in that way; Christ is an easy way to hit; 'wayfaring men, though fools, shall not err therein;' Christ is a spacious way; 'Thou hast set my feet in a large room.'

RUTHERFORD (SAMUEL).

BORN 1600—DIED 1661.

1. Honour God, and shame the roaring lion.

2. Faith is exceedingly charitable, and believeth no evil of God.

3. Sigh and long for the dawning of that morning, and the breaking of that day of the coming of the Son of Man, when the shadows shall flee away.

4. Persuade yourself the King is coming; read His letter sent before Him, 'Behold, I come quickly.' Wait with the wearied night-watch for the breaking of the eastern sky, and think that ye have not a morrow.

5. Ye may have, for the seeking, three always in your company, the Father, Son, and Holy Spirit.

6. Surely it cannot be long till day. Nay, hear Him say, Behold I come, my dear Bride; think it not long. I shall be at you at once. I hear you, and am coming. Amen; even so come, Lord Jesus, come quickly, for the prisoners of hope are looking out at the prison windows, to see if they can behold the King's ambassador coming with the King's warrant and the keys.

7. O thrice fools are we, who, like new-born princes weeping in the cradle, know not that there is a kingdom before them!

8. Our fair morning is at hand; the day-star is near the rising, and we are not many miles from home.

9. Home! and stay not! For the sun is fallen low, and hides the tops of the mountains, and the shadows are stretched out in great length. Linger not by the way.

10. It is better to weep with Jerusalem in the forenoon, than with Babylon after noon, or near the end of the day. Our day of laughter and rejoicing is coming.

11. The day is near the dawning; the sky is riving; our Beloved will be on us ere we be aware.

12. If ye were not strangers here, the dogs of the world would not bark at you.

13. The back of your winter night is broken. Look to the East, the day-sky is breaking. Think not that Christ loseth time, or lingereth unsuitably. O fair, fair and sweet morning!

14. I am come to love a rumbling and raging devil best. Seeing we must have a devil to hold the saints waking, I wish a cumbersome devil, rather than a secure and sleeping one.

15. I know not a thing worth the buying but heaven.

16. I want nothing but a further revelation of the beauty of the unknown Son of God.

17. O what owe I to the file, to the hammer, to the furnace of my Lord Jesus!

18. How many a poor professor's candle is blown out, and never lighted again!

19. It is now nigh the Bridegroom's entering into His chamber, let us awake and go in with Him.

20. My faith hath no bed to sleep upon but Omnipotency.

CRADOCK (WALTER.)

BORN (ABOUT) 1600—DIED 1660.

1. There are but three ways to fulfil the law: either in my own person here; or to suffer for ever in hell; or to believe in and receive another that may do it for me.

2. I beseech you stand not trifling, and dallying, and whining; going to this preacher saying, What shall I do, sir? and to that Christian, What course shall I take? as though there were many ways, and you had choice of things. What shouldest thou do but study Christ thoroughly, and roundly make a work of it, or else thou wilt be damned.

3. This is the misery of most Christians, that they mislay their justification. They lay it partly upon their faith, and partly upon their holiness. And this is the reason that, when a poor soul is tempted to some sin, he loseth his faith, his assurance, and his peace of conscience; because he grounds his saintship and justification upon his holiness.

4. I am a just man only by the righteousness that is in Christ; the law is perfectly fulfilled for me by Jesus Christ, and not partly by Him and partly by me.

5. Be not cheated of the Gospel; it is a precious pearl.

6. Christ crucified, and the outpouring of the Spirit of God,—these are the two pillars of our religion.

7. The Gospel is a more simple, plain thing than most men in the world conceive. It is a simple story concerning Christ crucified. When the apostles preach Christ they tell a simple story of a Man born of the Virgin Mary, apprehended of the Jews; that He bare the sins of His people; that He was put to death; and that He rose again for our justification. The simplest people most commonly understand·the Gospel of Jesus Christ best.

8. The knowledge of Christ crucified is the height, and depth, and breadth, and length, of all knowledge; that is, it is all knowledge to know Christ crucified in the simplicity of the Gospel. The apostle opposeth not philosophy to philosophy, or science to science; but he saith, 'Ye are complete in Christ.'

9. It is a more glorious truth than we have judged it to be, that poor saints are one with Christ. The Lord Jesus is anointed, and so are they; we have the same unction with Christ; we have the same name with Christ; we have the same offices with Christ; we have the same love of God with Christ; we have the same Spirit with Christ; and the same kingdom with Christ. The Church is the fulness of Jesus Christ. Christ is not properly a Christ without His members. We have a share in all His actions; we are one with Him in His graces, in His life, and death, and resurrection, and ascension. There is nothing that Christ is or hath, but we are one with Him in it.

10. You are not justified by your own personal good, nor unjustified by your personal evils; you are not one jot the more just when you have done all the good you

can, and not one jot the less just for all the weaknesses and frailties that a saint can fall into ; because your justification is built only upon Christ, and upon what He did and suffered. My justification is built upon the death of Christ and His resurrection ; He hath fulfilled the law, and He hath paid the debt, and He is out of prison, and the Father is satisfied ; He is my justification ; and, believing this, I am happy.

11. The Son of man hath two days : one which every wicked man shall see, when He shall judge the world ; the other the day of grace, wherein He offereth Himself to thee, with life and salvation by His death.

TRAPP.

BORN 1602—DIED 1669.

1. Truth is the daughter of time; it will not always lie hid.

2. Crosses come thick;—be patient!

3. Let us labour to be like unto angels, 'strengthened with all might,' walking about the world as conquerors, able to do all things through Christ who strengtheneth us.

4. Let no man envy others their better parts or places, since they have them on no other condition but to be put upon greater temptations, hotter services. If we could wish another man's honour, when we feel the weight of his cares, as David once did of Saul's armour, we should be glad to be in our own coat.

5. We know not what we lose by making haste, and not holding up our hands, as Moses did, to the going down of the sun. If God have begun to enlarge us, He will in due time do it to the full, if we should not be in straits sometimes.

6. David saw the features of his friend Jonathan in lame Mephibosheth, and therefore loved him. He forgave Nabal at Abigail's intercession, and was pacified towards Absalom at Joab's. Pharaoh favoured Jacob's house for Joseph's sake; shall not God do as much more for Jesus' sake? Joseph was well pleased with his brethren when they brought Benjamin. Bring but the

child Jesus in our arms, as Simeon did, and He cannot but smile upon us. Were He never so much displeased before, yet, upon the sight of this His well-beloved Son, in whom He is well pleased, all shall be calm and quiet as the sea was when once Jonah was cast into it.

7. Endure hardness. Never dream of a delicacy. Think not to find God in the gardens of Egypt, whom Moses found not but in the burning bush. Many love Canaan, but loathe the wilderness; commend the country, but look upon the conquest as impossible: would sit in the seat of honour with Zebedee's children, but not drink the cup of affliction.

8. No wearing the crown, but by bearing the cross first. Christ Himself was not glorified, till first crucified.

9. That is one way (affliction) by which the Lord Christ doth purge His people, and separate between the son whom He loves and the sin which He hates. We may observe in this the difference between Christ and the tempter. Christ hath His fan in His hand, and He fanneth us; the devil hath a sieve in his hand, and he sifteth us. Now, a fan casteth out the worst, and keepeth in the best; a sieve keepeth in the worst, and casteth out the best. So Christ and His trials purgeth chaff and corruption out of us, and nourisheth and increaseth his graces in us. Contrariwise the devil, what evil soever is in us, he confirmeth it; what faith or good thing soever, he weakeneth it.

10. When faith heals the conscience, and grace husheth the affections, and composeth all within, what should ail such a man not to be perpetually merry.

CARYL.

BORN 1602—DIED 1672.

1. The reason why God is trusted so little, is because He is so little known. We say of some men, 'They are better known than trusted;' and if we knew some men more, we should trust them less: but the truth is, God is always trusted as much as he is known; and if we knew Him more, we would trust Him more: every discovery of God shews somewhat which renders Him more worthy of our trust.

2. How can we believe that God heareth us, when we do not hear ourselves? or that He should be mindful to grant what we ask, when we do not mind what we are asking.

3. As every sin has the more need of pardon by how much the greater it is, so God will have the more glory in pardoning it by how much the greater it is.

4. The saints are described in the present state by this periphrasis, 'Such as love the appearing of Christ,' as if they loved nothing else. What, then, will Christ be to them when He shall appear? They who love Christ, whom they have not seen, how much more shall they love Christ when they see Him!

5. Mercy covereth those iniquities which we confess, and those which we conceal shall be discovered by justice.

6. The heart is the place where Christ and the thoughts

of heaven should lodge. All below heaven should be below our hearts.

7. The Scripture is much in shewing how much God makes of holy prayers.

8. We are never safe but where God sets us, or while God holds us in His hand.

9. He doth not say, the word was a light unto his eyes, but a light unto his feet.   The word is a light to the eyes: that is, it shineth to the understanding ; yet the word is sometimes a light unto our feet when it is not a light unto our eyes ; that is, God will have us to go where we cannot see our way.

10. Our hiding from the wrath of God, is in the love of God.

11. These few days are all the working days that ever we shall have.   Let this be a spur to diligence and to duty.   In heaven there is nothing but rest ; and in hell, though there be no rest, yet there is no labour.   In hell there is nothing but wages, and in heaven there is nothing but reward; our whole work lies in the few days which are on this side both.

12. All the motions of man are aberrations, when he moves without or against the counsel of God.

13. God sleeps not at the prayer of those who are awake in prayer.

14. They who separate from whatsoever is unholy, have Him nearest them, who is altogether holy.

LEIGH (EDWARD).

BORN 1603—DIED 1671.

1. There is but one true, proper, and genuine sense of Scripture, viz., the literal or grammatical, whether it arise from the words properly taken, or figuratively understood, or both.

2. By Christ's passion is understood all His humiliation, all the miseries, infirmities, sorrows, torments, both in soul and body, to which Christ, from His birth, to the hour of His death, was obnoxious for our sakes.

3. The serpent of brass, being without a sting, signified Christ, who was without sin.

4. The whole gospel concerneth Christ. The doctrine of the apostles was a long story concerning Christ, His Person, and the end of His coming.

5. Christ performeth expiation by the offering of His own self once for all to the Father; as in all the sufferings of His life, so in the last and worst of all, in the garden and on the tree.

6. Christ rules in heaven by His power, in the church by His grace, in hell by His justice.

7. Adam's disobedience is universal, not in power alone, but in act too; it maketh all sinners. The obedience of Christ hath a potential universality, and is sufficient to make all righteous; but actually it justifies the faithful only.

8. The burnt-offering was for all sins in general, a sacri-

fice all burnt to ashes, except the skin and entrails. Here a goat as well as a sheep might be offered. Now, a goat is, by Christ, used as an emblem of a wicked man, to shew both that Christ was reputed as a sinner for us, though in Himself He was righteous, and we in Him accepted as righteous, though in ourselves sinners. The blood was to be sprinkled on the altar, to signify that the merit of the sufferings all came from the Godhead of Christ, and from thence is all the acceptation of our services.

9. Christ is risen! why do not I rise with Him from all looseness, vanity, and wickedness? Christ has ascended and taken His place in heaven! why do I not cast off all earthly, base affections, and lift up my soul, and aspire to that high place?

10. Let us long for His appearance, and thirst after the great day when He shall come to judge the quick and dead. What good wife would not often long for the coming of her absent husband?

11. It is the righteousness of Christ imputed to us, and accepted for us, by which we are judged righteous. There is no appearing before God without the righteousness of Christ. We are sinners by the imputation of Adam's sin, and we are righteous by the imputation of Christ's righteousness.

12. We are bound to love and desire the last coming of Christ, which we cannot do until we are certified of His love. We are bound to rejoice in God, and that always, even in tribulation ; which no understanding can conceive to be possible, unless the soul be assured of life eternal.

BROWNE (SIR THOMAS).

BORN 1605—DIED 1682.

1. 'Tis too late to be ambitious. The great mutations of the world are acted, or time may be too short for our designs.

2. To be nameless in worthy deeds exceeds an infamous history. The Canaanitish woman lives more happily without a name than Herodias with one. And who would not rather have been the penitent thief than Pilate?

3. Many that feared to die shall groan that they can die but once: the dismal state is the second and living death, when life puts despair on the damned; when men shall wish the coverings of the mountains, not of monuments, and annihilations shall be courted.

4. Many would have thought it an happiness to have had their lot of life in some notable conjunctures of ages past; but the uncertainty of future times hath tempted few to make a part in ages to come. And surely he that hath taken the true altitude of things, and rightly calculated the degenerate state of this age, is not likely to envy those that shall live in the next; much less three or four hundred years hence, when no man can comfortably imagine what face the world will carry; and, therefore, every age makes a step unto the end of all things: and the Scripture affords so hard a character of the last times, quiet minds will be content with their generations,

and rather bless ages past, than be ambitious of those to come.

5. Fear not to be undone by mercy; for, since he who hath pity on the poor lendeth unto the Almighty Rewarder, charity becomes pious usury, Christian liberality the most thriving industry.   He who thus casts his bread upon the waters shall surely find it again; for though it falleth to the bottom, it sinks but like the axe of the prophet, to rise again unto him.

6. Trust not to the omnipotency of gold, and say not unto it, Thou art my confidence.   A slave unto mammon makes no servant unto God.

7. Moses broke the tables without breaking of the law; but where charity is broken, the law itself is shattered; which cannot be whole without love, which is the fulfilling of it.

8. Measure not thyself by thy morning shadow, but by the extent of thy grave.

9. When God forsakes us, Satan also leaves us ; for such offenders he looks upon as sure and sealed up, and his temptations then needless unto them.

10. There is but One who died salvifically (to procure salvation) for us, and able to say unto death, Hitherto shalt thou go, and no farther; only one enlivening death, which makes gardens of graves, and that which was sown in corruption to arise and flourish in glory; when death itself shall die, and living shall have no period; when life, not death, shall be the wages of sin; when the second death shall prove a miserable life, and destruction shall be courted.

MILTON.

BORN 1608—DIED 1674.

1. Pomp and ostentation of reading is admired among the vulgar; but, doubtless, in matters of religion, he is learnedest who is plainest.

2. Who is there that measures wisdom by simplicity, strength by suffering, dignity by lowliness? Who is there that counts it first to be last, something to be nothing, and reckons himself of great command in that he is a servant?

3. It had been a small mastery for Him to have drawn out His legions into array, and flanked them with His thunder; therefore He sent foolishness to confute wisdom, weakness to bind strength, despisedness to vanquish pride; and this is the great mystery of the gospel, made good in Christ Himself, who, as He testifies, came not to be ministered to, but to minister; and must be fulfilled in all His ministers till His second coming.

4. Come, O Thou that hast the seven stars in Thy right hand, appoint Thy chosen priests, according to their orders and courses of old, to minister before Thee, and duly to press and pour out the consecrated oil into Thy holy and ever-burning lamps.

5. Give me the liberty to know, to utter, and to argue, freely according to conscience, above all liberties.

6. We boast our light; but if we look not wisely on the

sun itself, it smites us into darkness. The light which we have gained was given us, not to be ever staring on, but by it to discover onward things more remote from our knowledge.

7. Many a man lives a burden to the earth; but a good book is the precious life-blood of a master-spirit, embalmed and treasured up on purpose to a life beyond life.

8. Revolutions of ages do not often recover the loss of a rejected truth, for the want of which whole nations fare the worse.

9. We reverence the martyrs, but rely only upon the Scriptures.

10. Let us not dally with God when He offers us a full blessing, to take as much of it as we think will serve our ends, and turn Him back the rest upon His hands, lest in His anger He snatch all from us again.

11. The very essence of truth is plainness and bright-ness; the darkness and crookedness are our own.

12. Right truly it may be said that Antichrist is Mam-mon's son.

13. England and Scotland, dearest brothers both in nature and in Christ.

14. This most mild, though withal dreadful and inviol-able prerogative of Christ's diadem . . . seeks not to bereave or destroy the body, but seeks to save the soul by humbling the body; not by imprisonment or pecuniary mulct, much less by stripes, or bonds, or disinheritances; but, by fatherly admonishment and Christian rebuke, to

cast it into godly sorrow, whose end is joy and ingenuous bashfulness to sin.

15. Did God take such delight in measuring out the pillars, arches, and doors of a material temple? Was He so punctual and circumspect in lavers, altars, and sacrifices, soon after to be abrogated? Should not He rather now, by His own prescribed discipline, have cast His line and level upon the soul of man, which is His rational temple, and, by the divine square and compass thereof, form and regenerate in us the lovely shapes of virtues and graces, the sooner to edify and accomplish that immortal stature of Christ's body, which is His church, in all her glorious lineaments and proportions.

*FISHER (EDWARD).**

BORN (ABOUT) 1610.

1. The very truth is, our father Adam, falling from God, did, by his fall, dash him and us all in pieces, that there was no whole part left either in him or us.

2. The law of faith is as much as to say the *covenant of grace*, or the gospel, which signifieth good, merry, glad, and joyful tidings, that God before all time purposed, and in time promised, and in the fulness of time performed, the sending of His Son Jesus Christ into the world to help and deliver fallen mankind.

3. It is as easy for faith to apprehend righteousness to come, as it is to apprehend righteousness that is past. Wherefore, as Christ's birth, obedience, and death were, in the Old Testament, as effectual to save sinners as now they are; so all the faithful forefathers did partake of the same grace with us, by believing in the same Jesus Christ; and so were justified by His righteousness.

4. The covenant of grace terminates only on Christ and His righteousness.   God will have none to have a hand in the justification and salvation of a sinner but Christ only.   Christ will either be a whole Saviour or no Saviour; He will either save you alone, or not save you at all.

---

* These Gems are from Fisher's well-known work, the 'Marrow of Modern Divinity,' published in 1645.

5. Whosoever goeth about to please God with works going before faith, goeth about to please God with sin.

6. The obedience of Christ being imputed unto believers by God, for their righteousness, it doth put them into the same estate and case, touching righteousness unto life, as if they had perfectly performed the perfect obedience of the covenant of works.

7. I beseech you, be persuaded that here you are to work nothing, here you are to do nothing, here you are to render, nothing to God; but only to receive the treasure, which is Jesus Christ, and apprehend Him in your heart by faith, although you be never so great a sinner; so shall you obtain forgiveness of sins, righteousness, and eternal happiness, not as an *agent*, but as a *patient;* not by *doing*, but by *receiving*.

8. God the Father, as He is in His Son Jesus Christ, moved with nothing but His free love to mankind lost, hath made a deed of gift and grant unto them all, that whosoever of them all shall believe in this His Son, shall not perish, but have eternal life. And hence it was that Jesus Christ Himself said unto His disciples, Preach the gospel to every creature under heaven; that is, Go and tell every man that there is good news for him.

9. If you would be acceptable to God, and be made His dear child, then by faith cleave unto His beloved Son Christ, and hang about His neck, yea, and creep into His bosom; so shall the love and favour of God be as deeply insinuated into you as it is into Christ Himself.

10. I know no other God, neither will I know any other

God, besides this God that came down from heaven, and clothed Himself with my flesh.

11. The greater any man's sins are, either in number or nature, the more haste he should make to come to Christ.

12. Godly humiliation proceeds from the love of God, their good Father, and so from hatred of that sin which hath displeased Him; and this cannot be without faith. Sorrow and grief for displeasing God argue the love of God; and it is impossible we should ever love God, till, by faith, we know ourselves loved of God. Although repentance goes not before, as an antecedent of faith, yet it follows, as a consequent. For, when a man believes the love of God to him in Christ, then he loves God, because He loved him first; and that love constrains him to humble himself at the Lord's footstool.

13. If you, or any man, shall exempt yourselves from being under the law of the ten commandments, as they are the law of Christ, I tell you truly, it is a shrewd sign you are not yet in Christ.

14. I would have you close with Christ in the promise, without making any question whether you are in the faith or no; for there is an assurance which ariseth from the exercise of faith by a direct act; and that is when a man, by faith, lays hold on Christ, and concludes assurance from thence.

LOCKYER.

BORN 1612—DIED 1684.

1. Christians, you are honoured to be baptized with Christ's baptism; to pledge your dear Saviour in His own cup. Count not, call not honour misery. The wine in your cup is red indeed, but without dregs to you. Christ's drinking first hath sweetened it well to saints.

2. Hearts dead and unstirred when Christ speaks, have certainly stopped their ears against the charmer. This soul is prisoner to a perverse will; there is no damnable prison but this; he is resolved that nothing shall sway that is holy; that his heart shall rule truth, and not truth his heart; which will damn a man if he had a thousand souls. This man hath the plague in his heart, and hath shut up himself, that none may come at him; no, not the King of glory, not words of glory. Write, 'Lord, have mercy on this man's door,' upon his forehead, for he will die in his sin; all the world cannot save him. Whom truth cannot stir, nothing can; whom glorious words of truth cannot stir, nothing shall; the man is stretched out for dead; I am now ringing his knell. Does any dead soul hear me?

3. At what height you sin, sinners, at that height you will perish.

4. A hypocrite has least of heaven of any man, and most of hell.

5. A man climbs up to heights in grace by hanging much upon God.

6. Some duties have their termination, joy hath none; 'tis an *alway* work, an everlasting duty. 'Tis not to cease when goods cease, when honours cease; no, 'tis not to cease when all contents cease; 'tis to last summer, winter, spring, fall, day, and night. Joy is the nightingale grace in the soul; it is to sing all the night long let the night be never so long, never so dark; ' Rejoice evermore.'

7. The great heaven at a distance makes a little heaven at present.

8. A little guilt is heavier than a great deal of misery; than all the afflictions of this world.

9. How tender is God of the felicity of man! He does much to destroy his sin, but nothing to destroy his joy.

10. The worst that God does to a Christian is to make him a heaven, and to increase it.

11. God is a vexing God to the heart of an earthly man; he wakes, sleeps, eats, talks, laughs, with a sad, restless soul. He sleeps, but his conscience wakes; he rises, but his heart is down; his soul is in a deep consumption, far gone from God.

12. I see love hath a long arm and a full hand : mercy to thousands; and from generation to generation.

13. All earthly cisterns are cracked; what folly is it to seek for all in that which will drop out all! All is lost when the world is made all; death is in the pot when you are taken with the broth; the birthright is gone when affection is so strong to the pottage. Ah, wretch! thou hast lost thy soul to gain the world!

14. Bestow love upon Christ when you will, He will meet you ; or what love you will, he will out-love you. Promise to yourselves what you will in Christ, you shall find it, and more ; make a God of Christ, you shall find Him so ; make Him all, and you shall find him all, more than all the world beside.

15. No evil carries the heart so totally from God as evil joy. A merry devil jostles Christ out of all.

16. Thankfulness is a making everything that is good, cry, Abba, Father, to God.

17. God makes His glory pass by us, and we let it pass.

18. Will hell ever give up her dead to heaven?

19. The world gives no certificate to saints ; and saints give no certificate to the world : he that gets a certificate from both—Lord ! what is he ? A saint or a worldling?

20. Electing love hath a still, sweet, calling voice. This is the way, saith love ; there is no way in comparison with this, saith the beloved. .

PEARSON (BISHOP).

BORN 1612—DIED 1686.

1. There is one degree of sonship founded on creation, and that is the lowest, as belonging unto all, both good and bad; another degree above that there is, grounded upon regeneration or adoption, belonging only to the truly faithful in this life; and a third, above the rest, founded on the resurrection or collation of the eternal inheritance and the similitude of God, appertaining to the saints alone in the world to come.

2. Is it not this Jesus in whom the love of God is demonstrated to us, and that in so high a degree as is not expressible by the pen of man? Is it not He who shewed His own love to us far beyond all possibility of parallel? Shall thus the Father shew His love to the Son? Shall thus the Son shew His love in Himself? And shall we no way study a requital; or is there any proper return of love but love?

3. Jesus, as the first-begotten of God, was by right a priest, and being anointed unto that office, performed every function, by way of oblation, intercession, and benediction.

4. Our belief in Christ as the eternal Son of God is necessary to raise us unto a thankful acknowledgment of the infinite love of God, in the sending of His only-begotten Son into the world to die for sinners.

5. To derogate any way from the person and nature of our Saviour before He suffered, is so far to undervalue the love of God, and consequently to come short of that acknowledgment and thanksgiving which is due unto Him for it. If the sending of Christ into the world were the highest act of the love of God which could be expressed; if we be obliged unto a return of thankfulness of some way correspondent to such infinite love ; if such a return can never be made without a true sense of that infinity, and a sense of that infinity of love cannot consist without an apprehension of an infinite dignity of nature in the person sent ; then it is absolutely necessary to believe that Christ is so the only-begotten of the Father, as to be the same substance with Him, of glory equal, of majesty co-eternal.

6. Our High Priest is gone up unto the Holy of holies not made with hands, there to make an atonement for us; therefore, as the people of Israel stood without the tabernacle, expecting the return of Aaron, so must we look unto the heavens, and expect Christ from thence.

7. If Christ were not life, the dead could never live ; if He were not resurrection, they could never rise.

8. This belief (in eternal punishment) is necessary to teach us to make a fit estimate of the price of Christ's blood, to value sufficiently the work of our redemption, to acknowledge and admire the love of God to us in Christ.

LEIGHTON.

BORN 1613—DIED 1684.

1. The stones appointed for the glorious temple above, are hewn, and polished, and prepared for it here, as the stones were wrought and prepared in the mountains for building the temple at Jerusalem.

2. All the peace and favour of the world cannot calm a troubled heart; but where this peace is which Christ gives, all the trouble and disquiet of the world cannot disturb it.

3. All outward distress, to a mind at peace, is but as the rattling of the hail upon the tiles to him that sits within at a sumptuous feast.

4. What are our lame praises in comparison of His love? Nothing, and less than nothing; but love will stammer rather than be dumb.

5. Faith looks above all, both what the soul hath and what it wants; and answers all fears with this almighty power upon which it rests.

6. Oh, if we considered that solemn day, how light should we set by the opinions of men, and all hardships that can befall us! How easily should we digest dispraise and dishonour here, provided we be found in Him, and so partakers of praise, and glory, and honour, in that day of His appearing.

7. It is the eye of the new creature, that quick-sighted

eye, which pierces all the visible heavens, and sees above them,—which looks to the things which are not seen.

8. The more the soul looks upon Christ, the more it loves ; and still, the more it loves, the more it delights to look upon Him.

9. Believe, and you shall love ; believe much, and you shall love much.

10. The childish world is hunting shadows, gaping and hoping after they know not what. But the believer can say, I know whom I have trusted.

11. To ask a believer, How know you the Scripture to be divine? is the same as to ask him, How know you light to be light?

12. The firmest thing in this inferior world, is a believing soul.

13. That nature which He stooped below them to take on, He hath carried up and raised above them ; the very earth, the flesh of man, being exalted, in His person, above all those heavenly spirits, who are of so excellent a nature, and from the beginning of the world have been clothed with such transcendent glory. A parcel of clay is made so bright, and set so high, as to outshine those bright flaming spirits, those stars of the morning ; that flesh being united to the Fountain of light, the blessed Deity, in the person of the Son.

14. A sad bed is that which the most have to go to, after· they have wearied themselves all the day, all their life, in a chase of vanity !

15. The conscience must be washed in blood ere it can be clean ; all our pains will not cleanse it ; floods of tears

will not do it ; it is blood, blood alone, that can purge the conscience from dead works.

16. I know of no heart's ease but to believe ; to honour thy God, in resting on His word.

17. Faith hath this privilege, never to be ashamed ; it takes sanctuary in God, and sits and sings under the shadow of His wings.

18. Thou art never bidden believe in thyself ; no, that is countermanded as faith's great enemy.

19. He is wise that hath learned to speak little with others, and much with himself and with God.

20. What are the breasts of most of us, but so many nests of foolish hopes and fears intermixed, which entertain us day and night, and steal away our precious hours from us, that might be laid out so gainfully upon the wise and sweet hopes of eternity, and upon the blessed and assured hope of the coming of our beloved Saviour.

TAYLOR (JEREMY).

BORN 1613—DIED 1667.

1. Faith is the root of all blessings. Believe, and you shall be saved. Believe, and you must needs be sanctified. Believe, and you cannot choose but be comforted.

2. Throw all the miserable comforts of the world out of doors for rubbish, and cast yourself upon the strength of God, and upon that alone.

3. Deep disputings will yield but shallow comforts.

4. Mark the rain that falls from above ; the same shower that drops out of one cloud increaseth sundry plants in a garden, and severally, according to the condition of every plant. In one stalk it makes a rose ; in another a violet ; diverse in a third ; and sweet in all. So the Spirit works its multifarious effects in several complexions, and all according to the increase of God.

5. Sweet Saviour! should any of Thy servants love Thee better than I ? Should any of Thy disciples be more obedient than I ? No, Lord ; for none of Thine are so much indebted to Thy passion, because none had so many sins to be forgiven. How amiable are Thy commandments, O Lord of hosts ! My soul thirsteth to be the nearest of them that stand before the living God. Lord, let me love Thee as Peter did ; Lord, let me love Thee more than these.

6. Every furrow in the book of Psalms is sown with

such seeds (cxxxv. 3; cxlvii. 1). I know nothing more constant to expel the sadness of the world, than to sound out the praises of God as with a trumpet; and when the heart is cast down, this will make it rebound from earth to heaven.

7. God is not extreme to mark what is done amiss in every convulsion of faith, as Psalm xxxi. 22.

8. I give God thanks, that every blessing of worldly comfort that I prayed for, the longer I was kept from it; and the more I prayed for it, I found it greater in the end.

9. What! Art thou, Moses, more merciful than God (Ps. cvi. 23)? Art thou more merciful to the people than He who saves us from all evil? No. Thou art infinitely short of the loving-kindness of the Lord; but He puts thy charity to the proof, to see what vehement entreaties thou wouldest make for the deliverance of the nation.

10. What comfortable orators (pleaders) are the mighty saints of God! What a safeguard it is to us all that they live among us.

11. The worthy servants of the Lord may prevail much one by one; others of the common rank had need to meet by hundreds and by thousands in great congregations, that every single man's prayer may be a drop in a shower; that while every man prays for all, all may pray for every man.

12. All that have a care to walk with God, fill their vessels more largely as soon as they rise, before they begin the work of the day, and before they lie down again at night; which is to observe what the Lord appointed in

the Levitical ministry—a morning and an evening lamb to lay upon the altar. So with them that are not stark irreligious; prayer is the key to open the day, and the bolt to shut in the night. But as the skies drop the early dew and the evening dew upon the grass, yet it would not spring and grow green by that constant and double falling of the dew, unless some great showers at certain seasons did supply the rest; so the customary devotion of prayer twice a-day is the falling of the early and latter dew; but if you will increase and flourish in the works of grace, empty the great clouds sometimes, and let them fall in a full shower of prayer; choose out the seasons in your own discretion, when prayer shall overflow, like Jordan in the time of harvest.

BAXTER.

BORN 1615—DIED 1691.

1. None of thy enemies are asleep; and yet wilt thou sleep in the thickest of thy foes?   Is the battle a sleeping time, or the race a sleeping time, when heaven or hell must be the end?

2. It is not a forgotten Christ that comforteth the soul, but a Christ believed in and used to that end?

3. He knoweth the meaning of the Spirit's groan.

4. You come not to the school of Christ to be idle. Knowledge droppeth not into the dreamer's mouth.

5. None so successfully serveth Satan as a false or bribed minister of Christ.

6. To love a small sin is a great sin.

7. Unworded groans come oft from the Spirit of God, and God understandeth and accepteth them.

8. There is more of the success of prayer to be believed than to be felt.   If God hath promised to hear, He doth hear, and we must believe it whether we feel it or not.

9. A religion that tendeth but to grief, hath too much in it of the malice of the enemy to be of God.   No tears are desirable but those that tend to clear the eyes from the filth of sin, that they may see better the loveliness of God.

10. Come home, my soul, my wandering, tired, grieved soul!   Love where thy love shall not be lost.   Love Him that will not reject thee, nor deceive thee, nor requite thee

with injuries as the world doth. Despair not of entertainment though the world deny it thee. The peaceable region is above. Retire to the harbour if thou wouldest be free from storms. God will receive thee when the world doth cast thee off.

11. Many would be damned if God did not keep them from digesting their own errors.

12. Oh what heads, what hearts, have all those men who, standing on the verge of an endless world, can think they have any time to spare.

13. The devil tempteth many millions of souls with the offers of the kingdom of heaven itself.

14. We owe greater love to angels than to men, because they are better, nearer God, liker to Him, and more demonstrate His glory.

15. How vain is the judgment of man! How contrary is it frequently to the truth! With what caution must history be read! And oh how desirable is the great day of God, when all human censure shall be justly censured!

16. I have marvelled at some wordy preachers. With how little matter they can handsomely fill up an hour!

17. He is not sincere who desireth not to be perfect.

18. To repent is the best way to peace. I am elected to repent.

19. A swearer warranteth you to suspect him for a liar.

20. Is this a world for a holy soul to be in love with?

21. Oh hasten Thy appearance, and come with Thy holy, glorious angels! Hast thou not said, Behold, I come quickly? Even so, come Lord! and let the great marriage-day of the Lamb make haste!

O W E N.

BORN 1616—DIED 1683.

1. The more eminent in any season are the real effusions of the Holy Spirit upon ministers of the gospel and disciples of Christ, the more diligence and watchfulness against delusions are necessary. For, on such opportunities it is, when the use and reputation of spiritual gifts is eminent, that Satan doth lay hold to intrude his own deceitful suggestions.

2. There is nothing excellent among men, whether it be absolutely extraordinary, or whether it consist in an eminent improvement of those principles and abilities, but it is ascribed to the Holy Spirit of God as the immediate operator and efficient cause. Of old He was all; now some would have him nothing.

3. The chiefest privilege of the church of old was but to hear tidings of the things which we enjoy.

4. It was not His merely enduring the penalty of the law that was the means of our deliverance, but the voluntarily giving Himself up to be a sacrifice in those holy acts of obedience, was that upon which, in an especial manner, God was reconciled to us.

5. Great opportunities for service neglected, and great gifts not improved, are oftentimes the occasion of plunging the soul into great depths.

6. It is easy to follow a multitude to do evil. Would

any one have thought it possible that such and such professors, in our days, should have fallen into ways of self, of flesh, and of the world? To play at cards, dice, revel, dance? To neglect family and closet duties? To be proud, haughty, ambitious, worldly, covetous, oppressive? Or that they should be turned away after foolish, vain, ridiculous opinions, deserting the gospel of Christ.

7. Do not deceive yourselves; it is not an indifferent thing whether you will come to Christ upon his invitations or not; a thing which you may put off from one occasion into another. Your present refusal of it is as high an act of enmity against God as your nature is capable of.

8. God made not man to be at perpetual quarrel with Him, nor to fill the world with tokens of His displeasure because of sin. This men saw of old by the light of nature; but what it was that opened the floodgates unto all that evil then, they could not tell. The springs of it indeed they searched after: but with more vanity and disappointment than they who sought for the sources of the Nile.

9. But although the persons are designed and allowed unto Him from eternity, who were to receive this grace at His hands, yet as to the manner and the circumstances of His dispensing and communicating these blessings, they are wholly committed unto His sovereign will and wisdom. Hence, some He calls at one time, some at another; some in the morning that they may glorify grace in working all the day; some in the evening of their lives, that

they may exalt pardoning mercy to eternity. On some He bestows much grace, that He may render them useful in the strength of it; on others less, that He may keep them humble, in a sense of their wants. Some He makes rich in light, others in love; some in faith, and others in patience, that they may all peculiarly praise Him, and set out the fulness of His stores. And hereby He glorifies every grace of His Spirit by making it shine eminently in one or other; as faith in Abraham and Peter, love in David and John, patience in Job; and He renders His subjects useful to one another, in that they have opportunities, upon the defects and fulness of each other, to exercise all their graces. And so He renders His whole mystical body comely and uniform, keeping every member in humility and dependence, while it sees its own wants in some graces that others excel in; and so the joints and bands having nourishment ministered and knit together, increaseth with the increase of God.

10. Oh in how many vanities doth vain man place his glory.

11. In all ages, men coming out of great trials have been most useful to others; for God doth not exercise any of His own but with some special view to His own glory.

BROOKS (THOMAS).

BORN (ABOUT) 1620—DIED 1680.

1. God puts a great deal of honour upon suffering saints. To suffer for Christ is honourable ; God will not put this honour upon every one, He puts this honour only upon those that are vessels of honour ; by grace God makes men vessels of silver and vessels of gold, and then casts them into the fire to melt and suffer for His name, and a higher glory He cannot put upon them on this side glory.

2. A believer's dying day is his resting day : it is a resting day from sin, sorrow, afflictions, temptations, desertions, dissensions, vexations, oppositions, and persecutions. This world was never made to be the saints' rest : arise, for this is not your resting-place ; they are like Noah's dove, they cannot rest but in the Ark.

3. The very suffering condition of the people of God is, at the present, a glorious condition, for the Spirit of Glory rests upon them.

4. Suffering for Christ and religion, is the most gainful kind of merchandise. Christ is a noble, a liberal paymaster, and no small things can fall from so great a hand as His is.

5. God's covenant is grounded upon God's free grace ; and, therefore, in recompensing their obedience, God hath a respect to His own mercy and not to their merits. God is a God of mercy, and His covenant with His people is a covenant of mercy.

6. Christ, for our sakes, hath taken all our spiritual maladies upon Him, to make satisfaction for them, and, as our Surety, to pay the debt that we had run into.

7. It pleased our Lord Jesus Christ to put Himself under our guilt; and, therefore, it pleased the Father to wound Him, bruise Him, and chastise Him.

8. The singular pleasure that God the Father takes in the work of our redemption, is a wonderful demonstration of His love and affection to us.

9. Christ takes a singular pleasure in the work of our redemption, and doth herein, as it were, refresh Himself with the fruits of His own labour.

10. All the temporal, spiritual, and eternal deliverances which we enjoy, swim to us through the blood of that covenant, that has passed between the Father and the Son.

11. If Christians are not very much upon their watch, their very callings and offices may prove a very great snare to their souls.

12. Joy in the Holy Ghost will make its nest nowhere, but in a holy soul. A man will have no more comfort from God, than he makes conscience of sinning against God. A conscience good in point of integrity, will be good also in point of tranquillity.

13. If God be so faithful and just to forgive us all our sins, we must be so faithful and just as to turn from all our sins.

14. Surely He, who hath spoken so much for His saints, whilst He was on earth, and who hath continually interceded for them since He went to heaven, wont speak anything against them in the great day.

WILCOX (THOMAS).

BORN 1622—DIED 1687.

1. Apply what thou wilt besides the blood of Christ, it will poison the sore. Thou wilt find that sin was never mortified truly, if thou hast not seen Christ bleeding for thee upon the cross. Nothing can kill it but a sight of Christ's righteousness. Nature can afford no balsam fit for soul-cure. Healing from duty, and not from Christ, is the most desperate disease. Poor ragged nature, with all its highest improvements, can never spin a garment fine enough (without spot) to cover the soul's nakedness. Nothing can do it but Christ's perfect righteousness.

2. When thou believest, and comest to Christ, thou must leave behind thee thine own righteousness,—all thy holiness, sanctification, duties, tears, humblings, &c., —and bring nothing but thy sins, thy wants, and miseries, else Christ is not fit for thee, nor thou for Christ. Christ will be a perfect Redeemer and Mediator, and thou must be an undone sinner, or Christ and thou will never agree. It is the hardest thing in the world to take Christ alone for righteousness; that is, to acknowledge Him Christ.

3. Thou thinkest it easy to believe. Was thy faith ever tried with an hour of temptation, and a thorough sight of sin? Was it ever put to resist Satan, and to

feel the wrath of God lying upon thy conscience? When thou wert apprehensive of hell and the grave, then did God shew thee Christ, a ransom, a righteousness, &c. Then couldst thou say, 'Oh, I see grace enough in Christ!' If so, thou mayest say that which is the greatest word in the world—I BELIEVE. Untried faith is uncertain faith.

4. To accept Christ's righteousness alone, His blood alone for salvation, is the sum of the Gospel. When the soul, in all duties and distresses, can say, 'Nothing but Christ; Christ alone for righteousness, justification, sanctification, redemption (1 Cor. i. 30); not humblings, not duties, not graces;' then the soul has got above the reach of the billows.

5. When a sense of guilt is raised up, take heed of getting it allayed any way but by Christ's blood; all other ways tend to harden the conscience. Make Christ thy peace (Eph. ii. 14), not thy duties, thy tears, &c. Thou mayest oppose Christ by duties as well as by sins. Look at Christ, and then do as much as thou wilt.

6. In the highest commands consider Christ, not as an exactor to require, but as a debtor, an undertaker, to work in thee and for thee. If thou hast looked at thy resolutions, endeavours, workings, duties, qualifications, more than at the merits of Christ, it will cost thee dear.

7. Nature would do anything to be saved, rather than go to Christ, or close with Christ, and owe all to Him.

8. Thou sayest, I cannot believe, I cannot repent. But Christ is exalted a Prince and a Saviour, to *give* repentance and remission of sins (Acts v. 31). Hast

thou nought but sin and misery? Go to Christ with all thy impenitency and unbelief, to get faith and repentance from Him. This will be very acceptable to Him.

9. Many call Christ Saviour; few know Him to be so. To see grace and salvation in Christ, is the greatest sight in the world.

10. A Christless, formal profession is the blackest sight next to hell.

11. Judge not Christ's love by providences, but by promises.

12. Treasure up manifestations of Christ's love; they make the heart low for Christ, too high for sin.

PASCAL.

BORN 1623—DIED 1661.

1. It were to be wished that the enemies of religion would at least learn what it is before they oppose it.

2. Nothing betrays so much weakness of understanding as not to perceive the misery of man *without God.* Nothing is a surer token of extreme baseness of spirit than not to wish for the reality of eternal promises. No man is so truly a coward as he that acts the brave against heaven.

3. Under the Jewish economy truth appeared only in figure; in heaven it is without veil; in the church it is veiled, but discerned by its correspondence to the figure. As the figure was first built upon the truth, so the truth is now distinguishable by the figure.

4. When the Scriptures speak of the Messiah as great and glorious, it is evident they refer to His judging the world, and not to His redeeming it.

5. How delightful it is to behold with the eye of faith, Darius, Cyrus, Alexander, the Romans, Pompey, and Herod, all conspiring, without knowing it, to promote the glory of the gospel.

6. He is the true God to us men; that is, to miserable and sinful creatures; He is the centre of all and the object of all. He who knows not Him knows nothing either in the order of the world or in himself. For not only do we know nothing of God but by Jesus Christ, but

we know nothing of ourselves also, but by Jesus Christ alone.

7. A little thing comforts us, because a little thing afflicts us.

8. Many err the more dangerously, because they take a truth as the foundation of their error. This mistake lies. not in the believing a falsehood, but in regarding one truth to the exclusion of another.

9. I see no greater difficulty in believing the resurrection of the dead, or the conception of the Virgin, than the creation of the world. Is it less easy to reproduce an human body than it was to produce it at first?

10. The history of the church ought in propriety to be called the history of truth.

11. If our condition were really happy, we should have no occasion to divert ourselves from thinking of it.

12. His sacrifice continued through His life, and was completed by His death.

13. O Lord, open my heart; enter into this rebellious place that my sins have possessed. They hold it in subjection; do Thou enter, as into the strong man's house; but first bind the strong and powerful enemy, who is the tyrant over it, and take to Thyself the treasures which are there. Lord, take my affections, which the world has robbed me of: spoil Thou the world of this treasure; or rather, resume it to Thyself, for to Thee it belongs; it is a tribute I owe Thee, for Thine own image is stamped upon it.

BINNING.

BORN 1625—DIED 1654.

1. Let others be wise to their own destruction; let them establish their own imaginations for the word of God, and rule of their faith; hold you fast what you have received, and contend earnestly for it; add nothing, and diminish nothing. Let this lamp shine till the day dawn, till the morning of the resurrection, and walk ye in the light of it, and do not kindle any other sparkles, else ye shall lie down in the grave in sorrow, and rise in sorrow.

2. Therefore the gospel opens the door of salvation in Christ, the law is behind us with fire and sword, and destruction pursuing us; and all for this end, that sinners may come to Him and have life.

3. To believe in Christ is simply this: I, whatsoever I be, ungodly, wretched, polluted, desperate, am willing to have Jesus Christ for my Saviour. I have no other help or hope if it be not in Him.

4. Now, I know no more effectual way to increase love to Jesus Christ than to believe His love. Christ Jesus is the author and finisher both of faith and love; and we love Him because He first loved us.

5. Faith in Jesus Christ is the soul's flight into the city of refuge.

6. He that is in earnest about this question, 'How shall I be saved?' should not spend the time in reflecting

on, and examination of himself, till he find something promising in himself, but, from discovered sin and misery, pass straightway over to the grace and mercy of Christ, without any intervening search of something in himself to warrant him to come.

7. My conscience challengeth and writeth bitter things against me, yet I have an answer in that blood that speaketh better things than Abel's.

8. Heaven is a land of peace, and all things are there in full age; here all are in minority, it is but yet night; but, when the day shall break up, and the shadows fly away, and the Prince of peace shall appear and be revealed, He shall bring peace and grace both with Him, and both perfect.

9. Ofttimes we make our liberty and access to God the ground of our acceptation; and, according to the ebbings and flowings of our inherent righteousness, so doth the faith and confidence of justification ebb and flow. Christians, this ought not to be; in so doing, you make your own righteousness your righteousness before God; for, when the want of satisfaction in your duties maketh you question your interest so often, is not the satisfaction of your minds in such duties made the ground of your pleading interest? Give you liberty and access, you can believe anything; remove it, and you can believe nothing. Certainly this is a sandy foundation.

BATES.

BORN 1625—DIED 1699.

1. As the whole race of mankind was virtually in Adam's loins, so it was presumed to give virtual consent to what he did. When he broke, all suffered shipwreck. He broke the first link in the chain whereby mankind was united to God, and all the parts necessarily separated from Him.

2. By assuming our nature, the only gain Christ purchased to Himself was to be made capable of loss for the accomplishing of our salvation.

3. Though the death of Christ was the highest provocation of God's displeasure, and brought the greatest guilt upon the Jews, yet, in respect of the end, namely, the salvation of men, it was the most grateful offering to Him, 'a sacrifice of a sweet-smelling savour.'

4. It was excellently said by Pherecides, that God transformed Himself into love when He made the world ; but with greater reason it is said by the apostle, 'God is love,' when He redeemed it. It was love that took our nature ; it was love that stooped to the form of a servant, and led a poor, despised life here below ; it was love that endured a death neither easy nor honourable, most unworthy of the glory of the divine and the innocency of the human nature. Love chose to die on the cross, that we might live in heaven, rather than to enjoy that blessedness, and leave mankind in misery.

5. The love of God is the most powerful persuasive to repentance. Real repentance is the consequent of faith, and always in proportion to it. The law can never work true repentance in a sinner. Despair hardens.

6. The degrees of wrath shall be in proportion to the riches of neglected goodness. The refusing life from Christ makes us guilty of His death. And when He shall come in His glory, what vengeance will be the portion of those who despised the majesty of His person, the mystery of His compassions and sufferings! Those that lived and died in the darkness of heathenism shall have a cooler climate in hell than those who neglected the great salvation.

7. The civil law determines that a tree transplanted from one soil to another, and taking root there, belongs to the owner of that ground, in regard that, receiving nourishment from a new earth, it becomes, as it were, another tree, though there be the same individual root, the same body and the same soul of vegetation, as before. Thus the human nature, taken from the common mass of mankind, and transplanted by personal union into the divine, is to be reckoned as entirely belonging to the divine ; and the actions proceeding from it are not merely human, but are raised above their natural worth, and become meritorious. One hour of Christ's life glorified God more than an eternity spent by angels and men, and in the praises of Him.

8. The last glass of time was turned up at the revelation of the Gospel by the Son of God ; and now the last sands are running : when it is out, it shall never be turned more.

FLAVEL.

BORN 1627—DIED 1691.

1. As the old, so the new creation begins in light; the opening of the eyes is the first work of the Spirit.

2. In the studying of Christ it is as in the planting of a newly discovered country; at first, men sit down by the seaside, upon the skirts and borders of the land, and there they dwell; but by degrees they search farther and farther into the heart of the country. Ah, the best of us are yet but upon the border of this vast continent!

3. The *condemnation* was Thine, that the *justification* might be mine; the *agony* Thine, that the *victory* might be mine; the *pain* was Thine, and the *ease* mine; the *stripes* Thine, and the *healing balm* issuing from them were mine; the *vinegar* and *gall* were Thine, that the *honey* and *sweet* issuing from them might be mine; the *curse* was Thine, that the *blessing* might be mine; the *crown of thorns* was Thine, that the *crown of glory* might be mine; the *death* was Thine, the *life* purchased by it mine; Thou paidst the *price*, that I might enjoy the *inheritance.*

4. Souls are very dear. He that paid for them found them so; yet how cheaply do sinners sell their souls, as if they were but low-priced commodities. But you that sell your souls cheap will buy repentance dear.

5. One heaven cannot bear two suns, nor one soul two kings; when Christ takes the throne, sin quits it.

6. If thy dearest friends intrude unseasonably between thee and thy God, it is neither rude nor unmannerly to bid them give place to better company.

7. The devil knoweth that he hath a foul cause to manage, and therefore will get the fairest hand he can to manage it, with the less suspicion.

8. O soul, of all the false signs of grace, none more dangerous than those that most resemble true ones, and never doth the devil more surely destroy than when transformed into an angel of light. What if these meltings of thy heart be but a power of nature? What if this act be more beholden to a good temper of body than a gracious change of spirit for those things?

9. The world affords not a sadder sight than a poor Christless soul shivering upon the-brink of eternity. To see the poor soul that now begins to awake out of its long dream, at its entrance into the world of realities, shrinking back into the body and crying, *Oh I cannot, I dare not die!* And then the tears run down. Lord, what will become of me, and what shall be my eternal lot. This truly is as sad a sight as the world affords.

10. Religion is no fancy, as the atheistical world would persuade us ; and this evidently appears in the uniform effects of it upon the hearts of all men, in all nations of the world that are truly religious ; all their desires, like so many needles touched by one loadstone, move toward Christ, and all meet together in one and the same blessed object, Christ.

11. He that lives by faith shall never die by fear. The more you trust God, the less you will torment yourselves.

B U N Y A N.

BORN 1628—DIED 1688.

1. The doctrine of the Trinity! you ask me what that is. I answer, It is that doctrine that sheweth us the love of God the Father in giving His Son; the love of God the Son in giving Himself; and the love of the Lord the Spirit in His work of regenerating us, that we may be made able to lay hold of the love of the Father by His Son.

2. Peace in a sinful course is one of the greatest of curses.

3. The sinner, when his conscience is fallen asleep, will lie, like the smith's dog, at the foot of the anvil, though the fire-sparks fly in his face.

4. Blush, sinner, blush! Oh, that thou hadst grace to blush!

5. Oh that I was one skilful in lamentation, and had but a yearning heart toward thee, how would I pity thee, how would I bemoan thee! Poor soul, lost soul, dying soul, what a hard heart have I that I cannot mourn for thee! If thou shouldest lose but a limb, a child, or a friend, it would not be so much; but, poor man, it is thy soul! If it was to lie in hell but for a day, but for a year, nay, ten thousand years, it would be nothing; but oh it is for ever! Oh this cutting ever!

6. Let the law be with thee, not as it comes from Moses, but from Christ; for, though thou art set free from the law as a covenant of life, yet thou still art under

the law to Christ; and it is to be received by thee as out of His hand, to be a rule for thy conversation in the world.

7. O Thou loving One, O Thou blessed One, Thou deservest to have me all. Thou hast paid for me ten thousand times more than I am worth.

8. It was not my good frame of heart that made my righteousness better, nor yet my bad frame that made my righteousness worse; for my righteousness was Jesus Christ Himself, the same yesterday, to-day, and for ever.

9. He that has lost his soul has lost himself! He is, as I may say, now out of his own hands; he hast lost himself, his soul-self, his own self, his whole self, by sin and wrath, and hell hath found him.

10. The angels now wait on God and serve Him; the Son of God is now a minister, and waiteth upon His service in heaven. Some saints have been employed about service for God after they have been in heaven; and why we should be idle spectators, when we come thither, I see not reason to believe.

11. All the visions were rich, but this the richest, that the floor of the house shall be covered with gold. The floor and street are walking places, and how rich will our steps be then. Gold! gold! all will be gold and golden perfections when we come into the Holy Place.

12. Alas! we are a company of worn-out Christians. Our moon is in the wane; we are much more black than white, more dark than light; grace in the most of us is sore decayed.

CHARNOCK.

BORN 1628—DIED 1680.

1. Many times we serve God as languidly as if we were afraid He would accept us, and pray as coldly as if we were unwilling He should hear us.

2. We would amplify His mercy and contract His justice; we would have His power enlarged to supply our wants, and straitened when it goes about to revenge our crimes. We would have Him wise to defeat our crimes, but not to disappoint our unworthy projects; we would have Him all eye to regard our indigence, and blind not to discern our guilt.

3. Man would make anything his end and happiness rather than God.

4. Were it possible to see the picture of God according to the fancies of men, it would be the most monstrous of beings; such a God as never was nor can be.

5. What is the reason that the heart of man is more unwilling to embrace the Gospel than to acknowledge the equity of the law? Because there is more of God's nature and perfection evident in the Gospel than in the law; because there is more reliance on God, and distance from self, commanded in the Gospel.

6. Well, then, what awakenings and elevations of faith and love have we? what strong outflowings of our love to Him? what indignation against sin? what admirations

of redeeming grace? How straitly have we clasped our faith about the cross and throne of Christ! Do we, in hearing, hang upon the lips of Christ; in prayer, take hold of God, and will not let Him go! Do we act more by a soaring love than by a drooping fear?

7. Without eternity, what were God's perfections, but glorious yet withering flowers, a great but decaying beauty?

8. Custom dips men in as durable a dye as nature.

9. Convictions are the first rude draught of the divine image on our spirits.

10. Our spiritual extraction from Him is pretended, unless we do things worthy of so illustrious a birth, and becoming the honour of so great a Father.

11. The last time is not called a time of destitution, but of restitution: and that of all things. The disorder of the creature, arising from the venom of man's transgression; the fierceness of the creatures, one against another, shall vanish. The world shall be nothing but an universal smile; nature shall put on triumphant vestments.

12. The Church grows by tears, and withers by smiles. God's vine thrives the better for pruning.

13. Unsanctified wisdom is the devil's greatest tool.

14. The earlier the new birth, the weightier will be the glory in the kingdom of God. Young ones regenerated, and enabled to bear head against the temptations of their violent natures, shall have crowns set with more jewels; they shall have an abundant entrance.

15. There is such a thing as the new birth; believest thou this? It is necessary to be had; believest thou this? God only can work it; believest thou this?

FLEMING (ROBERT).

BORN 1630—DIED 1694.

1. In the worst of times, there is still more cause to complain of an evil heart than of an evil world.

2. Bold sinning doth afterwards make faint believing.

3. None are more ready to shrink, in a day of trouble, than those who at a distance seem most daring.

4. How sweet is his smile in whose countenance heaven lieth.

5. One minute sooner than God's time would not be His people's mercy.

6. Oh, how marvellous a contrivance is there, when the blessed majesty of God finds an argument in Himself, when man had none wherewithal to plead. The Son was found in the form of a servant, and became our nearest kinsman, to redeem the inheritance! His people's standing is ensured by another's strength than their own; not on their apprehending, but their being apprehended.

7. Is it not strange that multitudes in these times profess the truth, and yet hate it, and were never drawn with the cords of love? How very many have courted the name of Christian, and have wooed the shadow of religion, who never knew the truth thereof.

8. Oh, what an excellent interpreter is experience! Taste and see! Thus the Christian getteth a view of spiritual things, which the most piercing eye of unsancti-

fied schoolmen cannot reach. It cannot be found in books; men will not meet with it in a theory of choicest notions; it confoundeth the wise and the disputer of this world, while the meanest and most simple Christian often knoweth more than those of greatest parts.

9. How strange is formality in such a business as prayer! Sad that many times this should be rather a piece of invention than a matter of earnest pleading with the Lord; not so much the breathings of the soul after Him, as the expressing what should be our desires! Oh! to what class can such a piece of atheism be reduced, as appears in our nearest approaches to God! Should we look on prayer as a duty, and not consider it as a singular enjoyment also, without which earth would have a near appearance of hell, if we could not thus solace the soul in God, and get a vent under its greatest pressures.

10. Oh, prayer, prayer! what thoughts should we have of it, if the truth thereof were believed! I think that man who is sure of the being and faithfulness of God, and of the reality of prayer, needs not be solicitous with what face the world looks on him.

11. Oh, what rare mercies lie often hid under dire providences, even while they are at our hand, and are not seen, from the frowardness of an embittered spirit, that will not let its own eyes see the advantage of such a case; but, as if they did well to be angry against God, will quarrel more His crossing their humour than observe His tenderness in promoting their good, and cry against Him, because He will not undo them.

12. I must say that, if the characters of godliness,

which the Scripture hath laid down, were seriously pon-
dered, there never was an age wherein more professors are
like to come short of heaven, and be found in a delusion
about their state, than this.

13. How few among the throng of professed Pro-
testants, know what it is to have the Bible for the security
of the Protestant interest, and thus quiet their souls,
though all the foundations seem to shake, because they
know the cause is God's, and He is faithful when He has
promised.

14. Outward things do never yield less than when we
press them most; and when we are eager in the pursuit of
the world, our spirits are bruised with many perturbations;
so that we must say, that that which keepeth us from
enjoying God doth also hinder the comfortable enjoyment
of ourselves.

H O W E .

BORN 1630—DIED 1705.

1. If all that I am and have be from Him, I cannot surely owe Him less than all.

2. As to religion, it is all one whether we make nothing to be God or everything ; whether we allow of no God to be worshipped, or leave none to worship Him.

3. God is in good earnest, and intends no mockery or deceit in His offer of peace.

4. Though none can *claim* mercy, all may *forfeit* it.

5. The soul hath its clothing, its vestment of life, upon as cheap terms as the lilies theirs ; it doth neither toil nor spin for it.

6. When our eye shall take in the discovery of divine glory, how sweet and satisfying a pleasure shall arise from that grateful mixture of reverent love, humble joy, modest confidence, meek courage, a prostrate magnanimity, a triumphant veneration ; a soul shrinking before the divine glory into nothing, yet not contenting itself with any less enjoyment than of Him who is all in all.

7. The womb of grace knows no maimed defective births.

8. So far from doating on that popular idol liberty, I hardly think it possible for any kind of obedience to be more painful than an unrestrained liberty.

9. How many visits from heaven are lost to us when we are, as it were, between sleeping and waking.

10. The seal is fair and excellent, but the impression is languid or not visible. We think to be saved by an empty name, and glory in the *appearance* of that, the life and power whereof we hate and deride. 'Tis a reproach with us not to be called a Christian, and a greater reproach to be one !

11. With what compassionate tears should the state of mankind be lamented by all that understand the work of a soul.

12. It is not fatal necessity, but a wilful choice that has made thee miserable.

13. Wherefore doth God discover His own heart to thee, but to melt, and win, and transform thine.

14. Who sees not that a man is more wicked according as his *will* is more wickedly bent.

15. How often do Christians meet and not a word of heaven ! O heavy, carnal hearts ! Our home and eternal blessedness appear to be forgotten among us.

16. There cannot be a greater participation of the misery of hell beforehand than a discontented spirit, perpetually restless and weary of itself; nor of the blessedness of heaven than in a well-pleased, satisfied, contented frame of spirit.

17. Can the love of God live and grow in an unquiet, angry, uncharitable breast ?

18. To converse with the holy is the way to be holy ; with heaven, the way to be heavenly ; with God, the way to be godlike.

19. Let the weary, wandering soul bethink itself and retire to God. He will not mock thee with shadows as the world hath done.

20. Their measured hour is almost out; an immense eternity is coming on upon them; and lo, they stand as men who cannot find their hands!

21. What is the whole of our life here but a dream? What is the entire scene of this sensible world but a vision of the night, where each man walks in a vain show?

22. God was made in the likeness of man, to make man after the likeness of God; He partook with us of the human nature, that we might partake with Him of the divine; He assumed our flesh in order to impart to us His Spirit.

23. When the whole soul shall seat itself in the eye; when it shall be, as it were, all eye, wholly intent upon vision, what joy shall it taste! How shall it, as it were, prey upon glory, as the eye of the eagle upon the beams of the sun. We read of thirsty ears; here will be thirsty eyes, a soul ready to drink in glory at the eye!

GRAY (ANDREW).

BORN 1634—DIED 1656.

1. One of the most soul-enriching exercises that a Christian can fall upon, is to wait for returns of prayer. There shall never be a word that he speaks to God, but he shall know what worth it is of. A Christian not waiting for the returns of prayer, doth obstruct many precious returns. Know this, if we had been waiting for answers to our prayers, there are many sweet returns from God which we would have had, in comparison of what we now have.

2. It is much to pray, as though we prayed not ; to use the means, as though we used them not ; to pray, and not to trust to our prayers.

3. A Christian should watch before prayer, in prayer, and after prayer. It is not certain that a Christian will be serious the first ten words he speaks to God, and yet ere the end he will be dead as a stone ?

4. Ere long the praying Christian shall be the praising Christian. We should long for that day when Christ shall say, Come up hither, and I will give thee a new name : thy name while thou wast below upon earth was a praying and a complaining Christian ; but now I will give thee a new name : thy name shall now be a praising Christian.

5. There is no rod which a Christian can bear worse than the rod which strikes at the root of his predominant

idols; so a proud man can bear any cross better than reproach, and a worldly-minded man can bear any cross better than poverty.

6. This is the house of complaints, heaven is the house of praise; this is the house of sorrow, heaven is the house of joy; this is the house of our pilgrimage, heaven is the house of our abode; this is the house of our misery, heaven is the house of our eternal solace, when there shall be no end of our joy and rejoicing. Wait, then, for behold He cometh with ten thousand of His saints.

7. Here there is much repining and fretting at God's dispensations; but believe it, the day is approaching when ye shall write upon the posts of the doors of heaven, He hath done all things well.

8. Love puts a tie upon the omnipotency of God to be forthcoming to His people. If a Christian have Christ's heart, he shall also have His hands; if a Christian be beloved of Christ, He will give him the precious out-lettings of His power to help him to overcome the strong enemies that meet him in the way; love and compassion in Christ makes Him give His hands to us when we are straitened.

9. A Christian who does not observe his victories, wants many excellent songs.

10. We must not expect two heavens; it is enough if we possess one. We must not travel to heaven through a bed of roses; it is not much that we go to heaven in a fiery chariot, having afflictions and calamities our companions all the way. When our feet shall stand upon the threshold

of the door of our everlasting rest, then our chains shall fall from our hands, and our fetters from our feet, and we shall lift up our heads with joy.

11. Do not say thy wound is incurable, and thy stroke grievous; but comfort thyself with this, that there is balm in Gilead, and a Physician there. Let thy case be never so broken, bring it to Christ and He will heal it; commit it to the Advocate that never lost a cause. Oh how many broken and desperate-like cases has Christ pleaded in heaven! Believe this, He can invent things for the clearing of our cause that we never could invent ourselves!

QUESNEL (PASQUIER).

BORN 1634—DIED 1719.

1. Jesus clothes Himself with us and our sins, that He may clothe us with Himself and His righteousness.

2. Every one flies from tears, and seeks after joy; and yet true joy must be the fruit of tears.

3. The only way to render perishing goods eternal, to secure stately furniture from moths, the richest metals from rust, and precious stones from thieves, is to transmit them to heaven by charity.

4. It is peculiar to God alone that He need only *will* what He intends to perform. His power is His will.

5. How terrible to the devil is the word of Jesus Christ!

6. Great tempest, great calm; God proportions the comfort to the affliction.

7. To call persons to the ministry belongs only to Him who can give power over the unclean spirit of sin, and over the diseases of the soul.

8. The church, or Christ entire, has the Incarnate Word for its head, and all the saints for members.

9. O my Saviour, how dost thou confound the pride and vanity of men, in relation to their genealogies, by having Thine composed of a long line of sinners!

10. A man ought to preach only that which he has learned from God, in the secret exercise of prayer, and of meditation on the Scriptures.

11. My God is my life; I die not but when I lose Him.

12. How sweet is it to have our dependence on God, who comes to meet us, in order to solicit us to come to Him !

13. The majesty of God is so great as to have a God-man for His servant.

14. There are few who conceive how instrumental the tongue is to salvation or condemnation.   We count words as nothing ; and yet eternity depends upon them.

15. That man wrongs the truth who submits to the caprice of its enemies in the manner of proving it.

16. The garner of God is heaven ; it is the bosom of God Himself.   Thither His elect, who are His wheat, are carried, after having been bruised and ground by persecutions in this world, in order to become His bread in eternity, as He will also be eternally theirs.

17. All the difference between a good Jew (of old) and a good Christian consists in this,—the one waited for the first coming of Christ in the weakness of mortal flesh, the other waits for His second coming in the majesty of immortal glory.

JANEWAY (JAMES).

BORN 1636—DIED 1674.

1. Faith goes to the borders of the promised land, to the very top of Pisgah, and upon Mount Nebo ; it sends love into heaven, to dwell there with the Lord for ever.

2. Let your hearts be early and late with God.

3. The cross of Christ is the Christian's crown ; the reproach of Christ is the Christian's riches ; and the shame of Christ is his glory.

4. If I had the wings of a dove, I would fly from the winds, the storms, and tempests of this wicked world, and rest myself in the bosom of my Father.

5. God gives this world oftentimes to His greatest enemies ; He gives glory in another world to none but His friends and children.

6. They think they make a very wise bargain, when they sell their conscience, God, and heaven, for a little of that which some call riches.

7. Oh that I could but bring down the price of sublunary things, and raise the things of that other world to their true worth !

8. How can they look for heaven when they die, that thought it not worth their minding whilst they lived ?

9. Not every one that wears Christ's livery shall have His wages.

10. How many seeming saints shall gain nothing at death, but a thorough knowledge of their own folly !

11. He that counts nothing worth the having, except Christ, and for Christ, cannot be miserable, when he is lodged safe in His embraces.

12. God is oftentimes better, but never worse, than His word. The running Christian shall at last obtain the prize, and the crown He fights for he shall wear.

13. O ye foolish world, condemn not these spiritual wise merchants, till you know what their returns are, when their burden is delivered.

14. How will the heavens echo of joy, when the Bride,, the Lamb's wife, shall come to dwell with her Husband for ever !

15. I see now, it is not for nothing that the virgins did love Him.

16. This Porter opens the door, and lets the saint's soul into that palace, where all the favourites of that great Prince reside.

17. If you would be better satisfied what the beatifical vision means, my request is, that you would live holily, and go and see.

18. They that die in sin must be buried in hell.

19. Who would be afraid of everlasting rest ?

20. It is our trifling with God that makes the thought of appearing before Him so dreadful.

21. How can you live within a few inches of death, and look the king of terror in the face every day, without some well grounded evidence of your interest in God's love ?

MARSHALL.

BORN 1638—DIED 1680.

1. His resurrection was our resurrection to the life of holiness, as Adam's fall was our fall into spiritual death.

2. We have in Christ a full reconciliation with God, and an advancement into higher favour with Him, than the first Adam had in the state of innocency; because the righteousness that Christ wrought out for us by His obedience unto death, is imputed to us for our justification—which is called the righteousness of God, because it is wrought by One that is God as well as man.

3. Any the least change of our hearts and lives from sin to holiness before our receiving of Christ and His salvation by faith, is not at all necessary according to the terms of the gospel, nor required in the word of God. Christ would have the vilest sinners come to Him for salvation immediately, without delaying the time to prepare themselves for Him. When the wicked jailor inquired what he must do to be saved, Paul directed him forthwith to believe on Christ, with a promise that in so doing he should be saved; and straightway he and all his were baptized (Acts xvi. 30, 33). Paul doth not tell him that he must reform his heart and life first, though he was in a very nasty pickle at that

time, having but a little before fastened Paul and Silas
in the stocks, and newly attempted an horrid wilful self-
murder.

4. Christ would have us to believe on Him that justifieth the ungodly; and, therefore, He doth not require us
to be godly before we believe (Rom. iv. 5). He came
as a physician for the sick, and doth not expect that they
should recover their health in the least degree before they
come to Him (Matt. ix. 12).

5. We are to know, that Christ requireth repentance
first as the end to be aimed at, and faith in the next
place, as the only means of attaining to it; and though
the end be first in intention, yet the means are first in
practice and execution, though both be absolutely necessary to salvation. For what is repentance, but an hearty
turning from sin to God and His service? and what way
is there to turn to God, but through Christ, 'who is the
way, the truth, and the life; without whom none cometh
to the Father?' (John xiv. 6). And what way is there of
coming to Christ but by faith? Therefore, if we would
turn to God in the right way, we must first come to Christ
by faith; and faith must go before repentance, as the
great instrument afforded us by the grace of God for the
effectual performance of it. Repentance is indeed a duty
which sinners owe naturally to God; but the great question is, How shall sinners be able to perform it? This
question is resolved on by the gospel of Christ, Repent
and believe. The way to repent is, to begin with believing.

6. The first right holy thoughts thou canst have of God,

are thoughts of His grace and mercy to thy soul in Christ, which are included in the grace of faith. Get these thoughts first by believing in Christ, and they will breed in thee love to God, and all good thoughts of Him, and free thee from blasphemous and murmuring thoughts by degrees; for 'love thinks no evil' (1 Cor. xiii. 5).

7. True humiliation for sin is either a part or fruit of faith; for, on believing, 'we shall remember our own evil ways.' Godly sorrow for sin is wrought in us by believing in the pardoning grace of God; as it is found by experience, that a pardon from a prince will sometimes sooner draw tears from a stubborn malefactor, than the fear of a halter will.

8. It is a true saying, That believers should not act *for* life, but *from* life. They must act as those that are not procuring life by their works, but as such who have already received and derived life from Christ, and act from the power and virtue received from Him.

BEVERIDGE (BISHOP).

BORN 1638—DIED 1707.

1. I cannot obey what God hath commanded me unless I first believe what He hath taught me. And they are both equally difficult, as they are necessary. Indeed, of the two, I think it is harder to lay the sure foundation of faith, than to build the superstructure of obedience upon it, for it seems next to impossible for one that believes every truth, not to obey every command written in the word of God.

2. How glorious, how transcendently glorious must He needs be, who is the Being of all beings, the perfection of all perfections, the very glory of all glories, the eternal God!

3. Man can suffer but he cannot satisfy; God can satisfy but He cannot suffer; Christ, being God and man, can suffer and satisfy too; and so is perfectly fit both to suffer for man, and to make satisfaction unto God, to reconcile God to man, and man to God.

4. Christ by his life and death merited so much for us, because the same person that so lived and died was God as well as man; and every action that He did, and every passion that He suffered, was done and suffered by Him that was God as well as mankind. Hence it is that Christ, of all the persons in the world, is so fit, yea, only fit to be my Redeemer, Mediator, and Surety; because He alone

is both God and man in one person. If He was not man, He could not undertake that office; if He was not God, He could not perform it; if He was not man, He could not be capable of being bound for me; if He was not God, He would not be able to pay my debt.

5. Christ lay three days in the tomb, that I might believe He was not alive but dead; He rose the third day, that I might believe He is not dead but lives.

6. Christ is in heaven, not as a private person, but as the Head and Saviour of His church, and as I believe that Christ is there for me, so I am there in Him, for where the head is there must the members be; I am as really there in Him my representative now, as I shall be in my own person hereafter.

7. I believe that Christ did purchase this inheritance for me from eternity, whereupon I was even then chosen and elected unto it; and had by this means a place in heaven before I had any being upon earth.

8. How is it possible that I should be justified by good works, when I can do no good works at all, before I be first justified! My works cannot be accepted as good until my person be so.

9. It is not in the power of any person to merit anything from God; but such an one who is absolutely co-essential with Him, and so depends not upon Him, either for His existence or actions.

10. I very much wonder how any man can presume to exclude the active obedience of Christ from our justification before God; as if what Christ did in the flesh was only of duty, not at all of merit; or, as if it was for Himself and not for us.

11. I cannot look upon Christ as having made full satisfaction to God's justice for me, unless he had performed the obedience I owe to God's law, as well as borne the punishment that is due to my sins.

12. Though it is the death of Christ, by which I believe my sins are pardoned, yet it is the life of Christ by which I believe my person is accepted. His passion God accounts as suffered by me, and therefore I shall not die for sin; His obedience God accounts as performed by me, and therefore I shall live with Him.

FRASER (JAMES, OF BREA).

BORN 1639—DIED 1698.

1. The soul, in conversion, closeth chiefly with the Person of Christ.

2. Legal terrors in themselves tend to evil, though God accidentally drives good in them.

3. A backslider ordinarily goeth a great length ere he recover.

4. A fiery temptation may be suspended and calmed ; but until it be cured by the word, it will return again.

5. A carnal generation of professors is greatly abominable to the Lord, and are great plagues in the earth, especially to young beginners.

6. A man's whole life is but a conversion; and the Lord, after every kind of backsliding, draws often in the same way as at the first conversion ; yea, and deals with them as they may seem never to have been converted before.

7. 'Tis easy to let a man see that he is not converted, that he cannot save himself; but 'tis hard persuading him that he can do nothing, not so much as to be thankful for the least mercy.

8. 'Tis the frequency and constancy of God's waterings that doth good, rather than any measure of a particular fit or visitation ; and from this more love may be gathered.

9. There may be wearying, and loading, and real humiliation, though there be no terrors on the soul. Sense

of a dead, hard heart, is an effectual means to draw to Christ; yea, more effectual than any other, because it is the dead, miserable, and naked that God speaks to.

10. If faith fetches all from Christ, then it brings nothing to Christ but deadness, blindness, and sinfulness. Come to Him for grace to prize Him.

11. The whole life of man is a continued conversion to God, in which he is perpetually burdened under a sense of sin, and draws nearer and nearer to God with more fervent faith and love.

12. There may be a real closing with Christ, and yet felt deadness and hardness. A sick faith is a living faith.

13. I was put out of conceit with legal terrors; for I thought they were good, and only esteemed them happy that were under them. They came, but I found they did me ill; and unless the Lord had guided me thus, I think I should have died doating after them.

14. Seldom do mercies good when there is too much peremptoriness in asking them.

15. Prosperity, ease, and the desires of the soul, send leanness to the soul; the evils of the world are much better than the good thereof.

16. Assurance of faith, though it do not firstly flow from holiness, yet is ever proportionable to holy walking.

17. Unbelief is more heinous than the sin of Sodom.

18. When God afflicts, it is in earnest, and not in jest.

19. There is no greater curse than for a man to get his will and desires in the world.

20. God's love is more seen in comforting and strengthening under trouble, than in delivering from it.

BURGESS (ANTHONY).

ABOUT 1640.

1. Let not the troubled heart say, Where is my perfect repenting? where is my perfect obedience? but rather ask, Where is God's forgiving? where is God's not imputing? How hardly is the soul drawn off from resting in itself! It is not *thy* doing, but *God's* doing. Thou must consider not what do I, but what God doth. Do not, then, look for Christ in the grave, when He is risen. Do not pore into thyself for this treasure, when it is to be looked for from heaven. Duties, graces will say, This is not in me.

2. What quietness can a man have till he know what judgment the Lord hath of him?

3. Who would not think that, while God's goodness in the Scripture is thus unfolded, there should not be a dejected, unbelieving Christian in the world? Shall our sin abound to condemnation, more than His grace to justification? Because sin is too strong for us, is it therefore too much for the grace of God also?

4. God putteth no bounds to His mercy, whereas He doth set some to His anger.

5. As it is hypocrisy to make our sins less than they are, so it is unbelief to diminish His grace. The sins of all the world, if they were thy sins, were but a drop of water to His mercy.

6. Was not David, in his fall, like a tree in winter?

The moisture of grace was within, yet nothing did outwardly appear.

7. I will have no such free grace as shall take away godly sorrow.

8. Do not think that justification giveth thee such a *quietus est*, that new sins daily committed by thee should be no matter of humiliation or confession. Our Saviour's command is, that we should desire this forgiveness as often as we do our daily bread.

9. At the last day, all these fears, diffidence, and darkness, will be quite removed out of our hearts. There shall be no more disturbance in our souls, than there can be corruption in the highest heavens. We shall then have such a gourd as no worm can devour. Our souls shall not then know the meaning of sitting in darkness, and wanting God's favour. There will then be no complaints, Why hath the Lord forsaken me? Well may God's children be called upon to lift up their heads, when such a 'redemption draweth nigh;' and well may that day be called 'the times of refreshment,' seeing the people of God are so often scorched with the fiery darts of Satan.

10. Then this petition shall wholly cease; then there will be no serpent to sting us; nor will the eye of justifying faith, to look upon the brazen serpent exalted, be necessary any more. The Lord will not only wipe away the tear of worldly grief, but also of godly sorrow, at that time. Then will the Church be without wrinkles, or any spot within her. In this respect it is the Church of God prayeth so earnestly for the Bridegroom's coming. For this it is they look for, and hasten in their prayers that day.

WATSON.

1649.

1. Heaven is the highest link of the saint's happiness. The lamp of glory will be ever burning, never wasting. As there is no intermission in the joys of heaven, so there shall be no expiration. When God has once planted His saints in paradise, He will never transplant them,—'they shall be for ever with the Lord.'

2. Prayer delights God's ear; it melts His heart; it opens His hand. Plead with Him earnestly, and either He will remove the affliction, or remove the impatience.

3. God being an infinite fulness, there is no fear of want for any of the heirs of heaven.

4. That grace is tried gold which can stand in the fiery trial and withstand fiery darts.

5. He that loseth his heart in the morning, in the world, will hardly find it again all the day after.

6. The Lord's Supper is the most spiritual ordinance ever instituted : here we have to do more immediately with Christ. In prayer we draw near through Christ : in this ordinance we become one with Him. In the Word preached we hear of Christ; in the Supper we feed on Him.

7. Though our sins go up to heaven as the smoke of a furnace, yet Christ's prayers go up as incense.

8. Men can never pray fervently that do not pray feelingly, like Samson, when he said, 'Shall I die for thirst?'

Daniel, in the den, prayed fervently and feelingly, and God did shut the lions' mouths, and did open the lions' den: 'The fervent prayer of a righteous man availeth much.'

9. Prayer is the wall and bulwarks of the land. God's vials of indignation are not poured out while the sluices of prayer are open.

10. When men cast off prayer, it is a sign they have cast off God; it is the brand of an apostate: 'thou restrainest prayer before God.'

11. Sin casts the soul overboard, and the loss of the soul is an unparalleled loss; it can never be made up again.

12. Mental prayer is not unheard—'Hannah spake in her heart.' When the heart is so full of grief that it can only groan in prayer, yet God writes that down: 'My groaning is not hid from Thee.'

13. God's ministers must have their hearts fired—not with passion, but with love; and as they are Christ's ambassadors, must come to sinners with an olive-branch of peace. The thunderbolt may crush, but the sun melts. It is better to love as a pastor than speak as an angel.

14. It is easy to turn white into scarlet, but not so easy to turn scarlet into white, yet God hath promised the repentant sinner to make the scarlet of a milk-like whiteness:—'Though your sins be as scarlet, they shall be white as snow.'

G U Y O N (M A D A M E).

BORN 1648—DIED 1717.

1. Banished from the presence of my Beloved, my Bridegroom, how could I be happy! I could not find access to Him, and I certainly could not find rest out of Him. I knew not what to do. I was like the dove out of the ark, which, finding no rest for the sole of its foot, was constrained to return again, but, finding the window shut, could only fly about without being able to enter.

2. I henceforth take Jesus Christ to be mine. I promise to receive Him as a husband to me. And I give myself to Him, unworthy though I am, to be His spouse. I ask of Him, in this marriage of spirit with spirit, that I may be of the same mind with Him,—meek, pure, nothing in myself, and united in God's will. And, pledged as I am to be His, I accept, as a part of my marriage portion, the temptations and sorrows, the crosses and the contempt, which fell to Him.

3. The misfortune is, that people wish to *direct God*, instead of resigning themselves to *be directed by Him*. They wish to take the lead, and to follow in a way of their own selection, instead of submissively and passively following where God sees fit to conduct them. And hence it is that many souls, who are called to the enjoyment *of God Himself*, and not merely to the *gifts of God*, spend all their lives in pursuing and in feeding on little consolations;

resting in them as in their place of delights, and making their spiritual life to consist in them.

4. Oh how excellent are the crosses of Providence! All other crosses are of no value.

5. I did not wish to speak of my troubles to others, or to make them known in any way. God had taught me to go to Him alone. There is nothing which makes nature die so deeply and so quickly as to find and to seek no earthly support, no earthly consolation.

7. I was then, indeed, only like a dead person raised up, who is in the beginning of his restoration, and raised up to a life of hope rather than of actual possession; but on this day I was restored, as it were, to perfect life, and set wholly at liberty. I was no longer depressed, no longer borne down under the burden of sorrow. I had thought God lost, and lost for ever; but I found Him again.

8. In Thee, O my God, I found it all, and more than all! The peace which I now possessed was all holy, heavenly, inexpressible. What I had possessed some years before, in the period of my spiritual enjoyment, was consolation, peace—the *gift* of God rather than the Giver; but now, I was brought into such harmony with the will of God, that I might now be said to possess not merely consolation, but the *God* of consolation; not merely peace, but *the God of peace*. This true peace of mind was worth all that I had undergone, although it was then only in its dawning.

9. My soul was not only brought into harmony with itself and with God, but with God's providences. In the

exercise of faith and love, I endured and performed whatever came in God's providence in submission, in thankfulness, and silence. I was now in God, and God in me; and where God is, there is as much simplicity as power.

10. Preach in a plain, simple manner; and, let me add, that the matter is still more important than the manner. Be careful *what* you preach, as well as *how* you preach. Preach nothing but the gospel—the *gospel of the kingdom of God.* And it is exceedingly desirable that you should preach it as a kingdom *near at hand;* as something not a great way off, but to be received and realised *now.* Aim at the heart.

FENELON.

BORN 1651—DIED 1715.

1. Such is God's greatness, that, in all His works, His own glory must be the sole end and intention.

2. God alone can work these miracles of grace. He interferes, as it were, between me and myself; He makes separation in my heart; He puts self at a distance; He wills that I should go forth from the limits of self, and give myself unto him without reserve, as to whom, from whom, and for whom I hold all that I am and have.

3. O God, men know Thee not. Thou art indeed the unknown God. Through Thee we live, and think, and delight ourselves in existence; yet we forget Him who giveth us all things richly to enjoy.

4. Light of the world! Sun of the soul! Brighter far than that which cheers the bodily sense; by Thee all things are seen, yet art Thou Thyself unseen!

5. The multitude of the wicked far exceeds the number of the righteous; even the good seem to be but half in earnest. Make haste to manifest Thyself; give glory to Thy name, and vindicate its majesty against those who blaspheme.

6. Vessel of clay! He who made thee has a right to destroy; but, far from seeking thy destruction, He labours to avert it. He menaces in mercy; and, if thou perishest, thou art self-destroyed.

7. God is not in haste to crush His enemies; He is long-suffering because He is everlasting; He is certain of His blow; He holds his arm long suspended, because His fatherly compassion is reluctant to smite, and because He knows how heavily His stroke falls.

8. O treacherous good! no longer will I call thee good, since thou dost but work our woe. And thou, which the world calls evil, and coward nature deems a weary load, the cross which God hath laid upon me, no evil shalt thou be to me!

9. Blessings for ever unto Thee, O my God, for that Thou hast made me a partaker of the cross of Christ, and a sharer in the sufferings of Him in whom Thou art well pleased!

10. How few there are who pray! For where are the men who desire the genuine good?

11. To be a Christian is to imitate Jesus Christ.

12. It needs not that God find aught in us, nor can He find aught in us, save that which He has given by His grace. Let us not, then, fear lest our sin and misery have placed us beyond the range of the divine mercy.

13. Give to truth, give to each individual truth, time to strike deep root in the heart.

14. Beware of exaggeration! Violent excitement exhausts the mind, and leaves it withered and sterile.

15. He loved us even to the death! May this love kindle ours; filling our souls with peace and joy; enabling us to resign grandeur, fame, and pleasure; to count as nothing all that time shall destroy; to will the will of God, and to watch in unwearied and blissful expectation for the coming of the Lord.

PICTET (A FRENCH DIVINE).

BORN 1655—DIED 1721.

1. Sure I am that the greatest number of sermons that are now made and printed, fail in point of simplicity. I bewail the misfortune of this age, which obliges preachers to lose so much time in polishing their discourses, because their hearers seek to be entertained with eloquence rather than to hear the word of God. It was not so in the beginning.

2. Ministers are bound to have no other aim than the glory of their Master; to preach, not themselves, but Jesus Christ; not to seek to shine by their eloquence, but to aim at bringing souls to the obedience of our Saviour.

3. The blood of Jesus Christ is ever living before God, and crying, Mercy, mercy, who is He that condemneth !

4. Union with Jesus Christ is the foundation of our hope.

5. The church, being the body of Him who is fairer than the children of men, how admirable must be its beauty !

6. We can do nothing without Christ, but He can do all things without us.

7. Christ is the Lord and Sovereign of the whole creation ; but He is especially the Saviour and Head of the Church.

8. We may say that the church contributes to the completion of Jesus Christ ; for, as the head, though the most eminent part of man, would be useless if separated from

the body, so we may say that Jesus Christ would not be a Head, if He had not a body to direct. He would not, indeed, be less happy in Himself, bur He would not be a head; and in this respect, He obtains His completeness by being united with the church, and gathering together all its members. Oh what an honour for the church, to be not merely the body of Christ, but in some measure to contribute to His completeness !

9. 'I will come on thee as a thief;' how terrible these words ! I who destroyed the first world with a deluge ; I who consumed Sodom with fire ; I who destroyed Jerusalem where My name was called ; I who removed My candlestick from the churches which the apostles founded! What shall we do, Lord, if Thou shouldst come on us and remove our light ? Let us prevent so terrible a calamity by a speedy return to Thee. For Thou wilt come in such an hour as we think not.

10. The body of the Saviour was formed out of the substance of the Virgin, lest any one should adopt the dream of the Valentinians, that His body was sent down from heaven.

11. All the sufferings of Christ were satisfactory (or propitiatory) ; not those only which He bore during the three hours' darkness, but those which He endured from the beginning of His life to His cross. For He could not suffer except as a surety ; for if we deny suretyship, Christ, being wholly innocent, could not have suffered.

12. Christ blesses us as did the priests of old (Rom. vi. 23) ; and His blessing is not bare words, like the blessing of a man ; but a real communication of spiritual gifts.

SUPERVILLE (A FRENCH DIVINE).

BORN 1657—DIED 1728.

1. What! do you preach the power of the gospel without feeling it yourself? Can you influence the hearts of others with the love of God, unless your own heart first burn within you? Do you urge others to be reconciled to God and be saved, and do you yourself neglect this great salvation.

2. O my soul! thou oughtest to make the cross of Jesus Christ thy highest knowledge, thy greatest glory, thy constant occupation.

3. He that would find God must seek Him in Christ Jesus.

4. You say, I have my faults, but at bottom I have a good heart. A good heart! Alas! it is this that deceives you, for it is the worst part of you.

5. The flesh, the old man, the old Adam, the law of sin which is in our members, all denote one and the same thing. This old man must be destroyed; this law in our members abolished; this flesh crucified; it must die without mercy.

6. Human virtues are like false coin, good in appearance, but indebted for its currency to the misery of mankind.

7. Ah! we were not able to stand when in innocence, how should we be capable of raising ourselves again, after we have been so sorely bruised by the fall.

8. Now Bethesda is everywhere, we may step down into the pool at any time, the waters are ever ready to perform the miracle, nor will the angel be wanting.

9. The politicians, the philosophers, the sages of the world, are but quacks. What have they done toward the cure of the human heart?

10. Man is not cured but by a miracle, by the working of the Spirit of God. We must have a heavenly physician, and this is Jesus Christ.

11. Under the law everything was shadow, under the gospel all is truth and reality. We have now the *true* Israel, the *true* deliverance, the *true* manna, the *true* tabernacle, the *true* Jerusalem, the *true* righteousness, the *true* atonement for sin, the *true* spiritual and reasonable service, the worship in spirit and in truth.

12. Blessed be God, we recover more by the second Adam than we lost by the first.

13. Here we have *Him*, who, by an adorable and incomprehensible mystery, hath united glory with worthlessness, the Godhead with the dust. Amazing union! which hath sanctified and ennobled our nature, without lessening the Godhead thus united with our flesh. Jesus has a manger for His cradle, partakes of our flesh and blood, is circumcised, cries as an infant, sucks His mother's breast. As man He suffers hunger and thirst, He watches, sleeps, and is weary; He weeps, He fears, He dies.

14. Christ did not take His human nature in heaven, nor did He prepare a heavenly substance in order to make a more than human appearance in the flesh; but choosing

to be our brother, He was made in all things like unto His brethren, sin only excepted.

15. Ah! my Saviour has undergone not bodily pains only; in His soul He was afflicted with sufferings inexpressible, not inflicted by the hands of men, but by God Himself. The floods of divine wrath overflowed Him. This caused His agony in the garden before the multitude laid hands on Him.

16. Divine justice is a fire which no victim except Jesus Christ could suffer, without being entirely consumed. God, the eternal Word made man, was able to bear our sins without being destroyed.

17. No, no! nothing less than an offering of infinite price can save me, and this I find in Jesus alone.

18. Constantly let us meditate on the worthiness of Him who died, and the unworthiness of those for whom He died.

HENRY (MATTHEW).

BORN 1662—DIED 1714.

1. Ignorant people have such a wonderful charity for all mankind, that they cannot bear to hear that any should go to hell; but whether you will hear, or whether you will forbear, I must tell you that there is a way which leads to hell, and great numbers of the children of men are walking in it. I dare not flatter you.

2. It is indeed a strait gate, but it is a gate, and it is open, not shut up and locked. We are not excluded, though admitted with difficulty; it is indeed a strait gate, but it leads to life, eternal life, and the life at the end will abundantly recompense the difficulty of the passage.

3. Is it so hard a thing to get to heaven? then up, and be doing, and strive to enter: we may sleep, and go to hell; but, if we would go to heaven, we must wake, and watch, and run.

4. Can we, with dry eyes and unrelenting hearts, behold so many immortal spirits, capable of endless bliss, ready to drop into endless misery? Have pity upon them; think of the happiness they lose, the ruin they fall into, and then, surely, you cannot but mourn over them.

5. Many sinners, but few saints; many weeds, but few flowers.

6. If you are not willing your ministers should ask you questions, come and ask them questions; desire to be

instructed. How gladly would I help the meanest in this congregation !

7. Remember, it is life, eternal life, we have in our eye; better be with a few in that land of the living, than with multitudes in the congregation of the dead.

8. Consideration is the first step towards conversion (Ezek. xviii. 28). The prodigal first came to himself, and then to his father (Luke xv. 17).

9. What ! would you have him to be like nobody ? The law of Christianity is a law of nonconformity to this world.

10. Pride keeps the Church's wounds open and bleeding.

11. When those that profess religion are griping and covetous, false and unjust, loose and intemperate, this gives occasion to those who seek occasion to speak against it. O Jesus, are these thy Christians !

12. God has His witnesses in the world, that bear their testimony against the wickedness of it; a remnant, that have not bowed to idols (Rom. xi. 4, 5); a virgin-company, that kept their purity when all the world wondered after the beast (Rev. xiii. 3).

13. The reason why sinners die, is not because there is no mercy for them in God, nor because Jesus Christ is either unable or unwilling to save them, but because they are not willing to come up to the terms on which the salvation is offered. He would, but they would not (Matt. xxiii. 37); He was willing to save them, but they were not willing to be saved by Him; this they may thank themselves for.

SHEPHERD (THOMAS).*

BORN 1665—DIED 1739.

1. They only do account it an easy thing to believe in Christ, who never were acquainted with themselves.

2. We have many hinderers in our way to heaven ; but few that care to go thither themselves, and fewer still that are helping others thither.

3. There is no great distance between an ungodly man's grave and his hell.

4. Great sinners, when brought home, are Christ's glory and triumph ; as the physician boasts of his mighty cures.

5. The joy that sinners have at their first conversion, is but an echo of the joy of Christ concerning them.

6. An even frame, not much lift up nor much cast down, I look upon as the best frame, most honourable to God, and most advantageous to the spiritual life.

7. Man is angry at the grace of God. His eye is evil, because God's eye is good.

8. Nothing in the world can hinder Christ's joy in the soul, or the soul's joy in Him.

9. Sweat came in with sin, and is a branch of the curse; therefore the Lord Christ thus sweats while He is answering for our sins, and removing the curse from us.

---

* Author of some old Hymns, under the name of 'Penitential Cries,' generally appended to Mason's Hymns.

10. Soul! because thou canst not weep for thy sins, Christ bleeds; because thy heart is hard, and thy eyes dry, and can send forth no tears, every pore of Christ's body does plenteously send forth tears of blood.

11. How dear are little children to God! He makes great account of them, and affords them a guard of angels (Matt. xviii. 10). They have their heavenly courtiers, angels of the highest order to attend them through the world.

12. Whilst thou art fooling away thy precious time among romances and play-books, the angels are searching into the knowledge of Christ; and their knowledge of Him feeds their admiring minds.

13. It is no virtue to be always doubting. The word bids us believe, but never bids us doubt.

14. True godly sorrow springs from faith. In order of nature, faith goes before repentance; but, in order of time, they both go together. True repentance springs from faith; from such faith as brings the wanderer back to his God. Faith inspires us with good thoughts of God, whereby we are persuaded that God is willing to entertain poor sinners, because He is gracious.

15. Angels shall sound the trumpet in the morning of the resurrection (Matt. xxiv. 31). They shall gather up the bodies of the saints. They will sort the dust of the godly from that of the ungodly, and cause every grain of dust to know its fellow. The same body that sinned with the soul, shall be damned with it; the same body that prayed and worshipped God with the soul, shall be glorified with it, on the joyous mountains of eternity.

HALYBURTON.

BORN 1674—DIED 1712.

1. Ye all have sinned! Oh, if ye knew what a world of evil is in that cursed thing, SIN! Sin is an ordinary word, a little word, and most men do apprehend that there is but little in it. But mistake it not; there is much in it; more than angels or men can ever discover.

2. In so far as we refuse compliance with the Gospel report, we are guilty of the death of Christ; for unbelief subscribes the Jews' charge against the Son of God, and asserts Him to be an impostor.

3. Every sin hath robbery in it. It is an endeavour to carry away some one or other of the crown jewels of heaven.

4. A Christian should be a man every way beyond others, and should have something peculiar in the whole of his conduct.

5. If your ears were not deafened by sin, you might hear the groans of the ground you tread upon, of the food you eat, of the raiment you put on.

6. It is only that strong and happy union between heaven and earth, God and man, in the person of Christ, that gives man any comfort, any strength or courage in his approaches to God.

7. Surely there is nothing evil if this be not so, to lose Christ, which is indeed to lose all that is good.

8. What ye want in yourselves, that ye have in Christ.

9. The approbation of God's way of saving sinners by Jesus Christ, to the praise of the glory of His grace, I take to be the true scriptural notion of justifying faith.

10. One view of forgiveness and pardoning mercy alienates the soul more from sin than twenty sights, nay, tastes, of hell.

11. The joy of the Lord is only to be retained when we walk tenderly and circumspectly; it is inconsistent, not only with the entertainment of any gross sin, but with a careless walk.

12. The night is far spent. 'Tis long since there was mention of His coming quickly. Darkness has continued long; and the growing of it, at this day, is not unlike the approach of the blackness of the midnight darkness, which, though terrible in itself, yet presages a speedy turn.

13. Live in the faith of the day breaking. Let this be your stay, your joy in this dark day, when the earth shakes and reels like a drunken man. All is cloudy and black; kingdoms tremble; crowns totter; and hearts are full of desponding fears. Fix this; dwell on it; the hope of it will be your comfort; cry for Christ, that He may turn, and be like a roe or a young hart upon the mountains of Bether. 'Even so, come, Lord Jesus.'

WATTS.

BORN 1674—DIED 1748.

1. Neither the acts of love, or zeal, or repentance, or fear, or worship, or any other acts of obedience, are appointed as the means of our justification, because these actions carry in them an appearance of our doing something for God, our answering the demands of some law; and this would make our justification by a law of works: but faith is that act of soul whereby we renounce our own works as the ground of our acceptance; acknowledging our own unworthiness, and giving the entire honour to Divine grace. We are saved by grace, that God may have the glory of all.

2. Christ has the keys of death; and the gates of eternal life are in His keeping.

3. The heart of a saint that comes near to God is pained at the memory of old sins; and together with a present sweetness of Divine love, there is a sort of anguish at the thoughts of past iniquities.

4. Mere sighs and groans are for persons at a distance; but when we get near to God, we speak to Him even in His ear; the heart is full and the tongue overflows.

5. I go to my best Friend, my Friend in heaven, when my friends here neglect me.

6. We eat, we drink, we sleep; that is the life of nature: we buy and sell, we labour and converse; that is the civil

life : we trifle, visit, tattle, flutter, and rove among a hundred impertinences, without any settled design what we live for; that is the idle life: and it is the kindest name I can bestow upon it. We learn our creed, we go to church, we say our prayers, we read chapters and sermons; these are the outward forms of our religious life. And is this all? Have we no daily secret exercises of the soul in retirement and converse with God? Have we nothing to do with God alone in a whole day together? Surely this can never be the life of a Christian?

7. Could sinners go on in sin if they thought the judgment day just opening upon them, and Jesus Christ at hand? Could we have such cold and lazy desires after a Saviour and his Salvation, if we thought our everlasting happiness or misery depended on the next day, the next hour, or the next moment? For we know not how soon the summons may come, and place us before His tribunal.

8. O happy state, O blessed mansions of the saints, when this body of sin shall be destroyed, and all the restless atoms that disquieted the flesh and provoked the spirit, shall be buried in the dust of death, and never rise again!

9. Then shall thy heart, O sinner, be ready to burst, not with penitence, but madness and overswelling sorrows; and yet it must not break nor dissolve, but will remain firm and hard for ever. This is, and must be, an eternal heartache, for there are no broken hearts in hell.

BOSTON.

BORN 1676—DIED 1732.

1. Faith is the hand that receives Christ and His righteousness as the all of salvation ; and repentance unto life consists in that godly sorrow for sin which flows from faith.

2. No sin of yours will ruin you, if you believe ; and nothing will save you, if you do not.

3. The outward means which the Lord usually makes use of to beget faith in one's heart is the word, the word of the gospel, preached, heard, or read. Rom. x. 17.

4. Melancholy is an enemy to gifts and grace, a great friend to unbelief, as I have often found in my experience.

5. I found it was no easy thing to part with sin ; and the impression on my spirit was that of my utter inability to put away sin. And I think I never had a more solid sense of the absolute need of Christ for sanctification.   I saw it was as easy for a rock to raise itself, as for me to raise my heart from sin to holiness.

6. I have sometimes wished for some drops of wrath to awaken me out of a secure frame ; but I found one drop, one arrow intolerable. Who knows the power of His wrath ? Tongue cannot express it. O precious Christ ! O precious blood ! Horror and despair had swallowed me up had it not been for that blood, the blood of God.

7. Come, sinner, enter into a marriage relation with Christ. Sin shall not stop the match if ye be willing.

He that could sanctify the virgin's substance, to make it a sinless piece of flesh, can easily sanctify you.

8. The body of Christ was not made of nothing, nor of anything but what belongs to Adam's family; that so He might be one of the family of Adam, a brother of those in whose name He was to act; and that so the same nature that sinned might suffer.

9. Beware of any standing controversy betwixt God and you; for if there be such, it will stare you in the face in a dying hour.

10. Doubts and fears are no friends to holiness of heart and life. It is little faith that breeds them in the hearts of the people of God; and little faith will always make little holiness.

11. The saints' dust is precious, locked up in the grave as in a cabinet till the Lord have further use for it. They are His precious fruit, that lie mellowing in the grave and ripening for a glorious resurrection.

12. The last ship for Immanuel's land is making ready to go. Therefore, now or never! The gospel is the Lord's farewell sermon to the world. The Lord has made a feast for the world these five thousand years, and the last dish is served up now. Oh receive it not in vain!

13. As the deluge caught the old world sleeping in deepest security, so at the second coming of Christ, the sinners of the last times will be drenched in slumbering stupidity.

14. Every pile of grass is a preacher of the loving-kindness of the Lord.

ERSKINE (EBENEZER).

BORN 1680—DIED 1754.

1. Love is the regnant attribute of the divine nature; 'God is love.' I do not find any other attribute so expressed in Scripture. We do not find it said, God is mercy, God is justice, God is holiness, God is power, or God is wisdom; no, the expression of this attribute has something peculiar in it : God is love.

2. It is a devilish humility that keeps you from believing; for the more unworthy you are of the grace or favour of God, the more fit you are for receiving the grace of God, at a throne of grace, by virtue of the covenant of grace.

3. The Son of God has been carrying on the war against the devil, wresting his captives out of his hand, and will never leave the field till He has driven Satan out of his kingdom ; and then we look for a new heaven and a new earth, wherein dwelleth righteousness.

4. The manna of heaven is rained down ; God's banqueting house is opened ; He is making to you a feast of fat things. Therefore, O starving sinner, come and take, and eat and drink abundantly ; for there is bread enough and to spare ; and, as every man and woman in the camp had a right to gather the manna, so has every soul a right to take Christ ; to eat His flesh and drink His blood.

5. Christ is the resurrection and life of a shattered creation ; if it were not kept by His power, it would sink to

nothing ; and, when He hath finished what He designed, He will take it and purge it from sin that had defiled it ; then He will erect a new heaven and a new earth, wherein dwelleth righteousness.

6. The marriage-house is ready; both the lower and the higher stories of it are ready; and that moment you believe, you enter into the rest of the blessed Bridegroom.

7. The best blood of the whole creation goes for the satisfaction of law and justice.

8. It was upon the credit of Christ's engagement to satisfy law and justice, that all the Old Testament saints were admitted into heaven.

9. Christ's first coming was to purchase a Bride for Himself by His obedience and death. His second coming will be to solemnize the marriage, and to fetch the Bride home to the royal palace, the house of many mansions that He is preparing for her reception.

10. This is the thing that begets faith, love, hope, and confidence—God's love in giving Christ. Have you seen God to be love ?

11. Faith is the beggar's hand, which comes, not to *give*, but to *get* Christ, and all with Him, for nothing.

12. If the promise does not belong to you, and to all to whom it is revealed, as a ground of faith, it is impossible to conceive how an unbeliever can make God a liar (1 John v. 10).

M'LAURIN.

BORN 1693—DIED 1754.

1. It is the glory of the world, that He who formed it dwelt on it; of the air, that He breathed in it; of the sun, that it shone on Him; of the ground, that it bare Him; of the sea, that He walked on it; of the elements, that they nourished Him; of the waters, that they refreshed Him; of us men, that He lived and died among us—yea, that He lived and died for us; that He assumed our flesh and blood, and carried it to the highest heavens, where it shines as the eternal ornament and wonder of the creation of God. It gives also a lustre to providence. It is the chief event that adorns the records of time, and enlivens the history of the universe. It is the glory of the various great lines of providence, that they point at this as their centre; that they prepared the way for its coming; that, after its coming, they are subservient to the ends of it, though in a way, indeed, to us at present mysterious and unsearchable.

2. It is one of the hardest tasks in the world to bring the heart to a sincere persuasion that sin is indeed as vile as God's word represents it; and that it deserves all that His law threatens against it.

3. A great many are not properly so sorry for their sins against God's law, as for the severity of God's law against their sins.

4. Though infinite goodness bestow undeserved favours, yet it is certain infinite justice will never inflict the least degrees of undeserved punishment.

5. If men could hate themselves as they do their neighbours, it would be a good help toward loving their neighbours as themselves.

6. Sin, in its very nature, is poison to the soul, tending to eternal death, separating it from God, who is its only life.

7. To judge truly of the matter, it is certain the liberty of man is not hindered by the grace of God, but enlarged and perfected by it.

8. A devout man, praying only for happiness, without praying for holiness, is a character yet unheard of.

9. Human corruption proves always too hard for human eloquence; it is ever found to have strong enough footing in the heart to stand it out against all the golden sayings of the tongue.

10. The meanest redeemed sinner can look upon himself as the child of God, a member of Christ, a temple of the Holy Ghost.

11. All men are convinced that they are sinners, but very few are convinced that they deserve to be miserable.

12. A principal hindrance to our embracing Christ's righteousness, is the want of a due sense of our own unrighteousness.

13. No man can pretend that the love of God tends to impair his health and waste his fortune, as the love of his lusts or his idols often does.

14. If mortifying our corruptions be uneasy, the satisfying them is impossible.

15. That which hinders the lovers of sin from acknowledging the glory of the cross is, that it shews so much of God's hatred of what they love.

16. The cross melts cold and frozen hearts; it breaks stony hearts; it pierces adamants; it penetrates through thick darkness. How justly is it called marvellous light! It gives eyes to the blind to look to itself; and not only to the blind, but to the dead. It is the light of life, a powerful light; its energy is beyond the force of thunder, yet it is more mild than the dew on the tender grass.

ADAMS (THOMAS).

BORN 1701—DIED 1784.

1. Oh when shall I feel the plague of sin, and long for a deliverance from it as I would from a sore disease of my body!

2. I seem to myself as a dark flint. By what kind of a stroke God will fetch light out of me I know not.

3. My sins brought Christ to me and me to Christ.

4. I see in other sinners what I am; in Jesus, what I should be.

5. I can say truly, I have great need of Christ; thank God, I can say boldly, I have a great Christ for my need.

6. I fly from myself to God; I appeal from myself to Christ.

7. My greatest obligation to God, next to the gift of Jesus Christ and His Spirit, is for commanding me to love Him with all my heart.

8. It is to be feared, that a secret wish to be saved, without holiness, is the great bar to our progress towards perfection.

9. If I grapple with sin in my own strength, the devil knows he may go to sleep.

10. Not to sin, may be a bitter cross; to sin, is hell.

11. Oh that sigh! Do happy people ever sigh? I find I want something which God will not suffer me to have;

and till we are of the same mind, life can be nothing at bottom but one perpetual sigh.

12. We can take reproof patiently from a book, but not from a tongue. The book hurts not our pride, the living reprover does; and we cannot bear to have our faults seen by others.

13. Christ says, 'Sit down in the lowest room'; but the lowest, according to St Paul, is so very low, that hardly a single man will sit down in it. Read Rev. iii. 17, 18, Gal. v. 19-21, Titus iii. 3.

14. Reading is, for the most part, only a more refined species of sensuality, and answers man's purposes of shuffling off his great work with God and himself, as well as a ball or a masquerade.

15. If we were but half Christians, the world would be at peace with us.

16. I know so much of Christ as not to be afraid to look my sins in the face.

17. Christ, by taking our sin on Himself, took it clean away from us; banished it out of the creation, and eternally annihilated it to every believer, who is as far from the charge of it before God, as if there never had been any such thing in the world. And if He did not do this for us, He did nothing. If we have one sin remaining that He did not expiate, we are still under a sentence of death.

18. I believe for the remission of sins; I believe for Christ's righteousness; I believe for power to love God and man; I believe for belief; and, God knows, I had rather be a believer than a king.

19. I go to Christ with faith for faith.

20. The Spirit, in the children of God, is like an organ: one man is one stop; another, another; the sound is different, the instrument the same, but music in all.

21. If we do not live down error, I am sure we shall never dispute it down.

22. The eager reading even of religious books may be dangerous, and a hindrance to those who are aiming at the true spirit of religion, if they have recourse to them instead of to God.

EDWARDS (JONATHAN).

BORN 1703—DIED 1758.

1. As it is the glory of the church of Christ that in all her members, however dispersed, she is thus *one;* one holy society, one city, one family, one body ; so it is very desirable that this union should be manifested and become visible.

2. The mighty struggles and conflicts of nations, those vast successive changes which are brought to pass in the kingdoms of the world, from one age to another, are, as it were, the travail-pangs of the creation, in order to bring forth this glorious event. And the Scriptures represent the last struggles and changes that shall immediately precede this event, as being the greatest of all.

3. This world is a dark place without Christ, and therefore is dark till He comes, and until His kingdom of glory is set up.

4. The Father had given Him the cup, and set it down before Him, with the command that He should drink it. This was the greatest act of obedience that Christ was to perform. He prays for strength and help that His poor, feeble human nature might be supported ; that He might not fail in this great trial ; that He might not sink, and be swallowed up, and His strength so overcome that He should not hold out and finish the appointed obedience.

5. Christ had an extraordinary sense of His dependence

on God, and His need of His help to enable Him to do God's will in this great trial. Though He was innocent, yet He needed help. He was dependent on God as man, and therefore we read that ' He trusted in God.'

6. The coming of Christ Jesus, I believe, made an exceedingly great addition to the happiness of the saints of the Old Testament who were in heaven ; and especially was the day of His ascension a joyful day among them.

7. It was necessary, not only that Christ should take upon Him a *created* nature, but *our* nature. He was formed in the womb of the Virgin, of the substance of her body, by the power of the Spirit.

8. Both Christ's satisfaction for sin, and His meriting happiness by His righteousness, were carried on through the whole time of His humiliation. Christ's satisfaction for sin was not by His last sufferings only, though it was principally by them ; but all His sufferings, and all His humiliation, from the first moment of His incarnation to His resurrection, were propitiatory or satisfactory.

9. The time of Christ's coming is spoken of as the morning, when Christ, who is the Sun, shall arise and appear ; and His happy kingdom, that He shall then set up, is represented as the day-time. But the time that goes before that is represented as night-time, or a time of darkness, and we that live in that time as being in a dark place. The word of prophecy is as a light shining in a dark place, or as the light of a bright star in this night, a light preceding the day of Christ's coming, like the morning star that is the forerunner of the day.

WESLEY (JOHN).

BORN 1703—DIED 1791.

1. What could strengthen our hands in all that is good, and deter us from all evil, like a strong conviction that the Judge standeth before the door, and that we shall shortly stand before Him?

2. The space from the creation of man upon the earth to the end of all things, is *the day of the sons of men;* the time that is now passing over us is *our day;* when this is ended, the *day of the Lord* will begin; but who can say how long it will continue? with the Lord one day is as a thousand years. From this expression some of the ancient fathers drew that inference, that what is called the day of judgment would be indeed a thousand years. And it seems they did not go beyond the truth; very probably they did not come up to it. For, if we consider the number of persons to be judged, and of actions to be inquired, it does not appear that a thousand years will suffice for the transactions of that day.

3. More especially will we speak, that by grace ye are saved through faith; because never was the maintaining this doctrine more seasonable than it is at this day. Nothing but this can effectually prevent the increase of the Romish delusion among us. It is endless to attack, one by one, all the errors of that church. But salvation by faith strikes at the root, and all fall at once where this is established.

It was this doctrine that first drove Popery out of these kingdoms, and it is this alone that can keep it out.

4. Thou ungodly one, thou vile, helpless, miserable sinner, I charge thee before God, the Judge of all, go straight to Him with all thy ungodliness. Go as altogether ungodly, guilty, lost, destroyed, deserving and dropping into hell; and thou shalt find favour in His sight, and know that He justifieth the ungodly. As such, thou shalt be brought unto the blood of sprinkling, as an undone, helpless, damned sinner.

5. Thus look unto Jesus. There is the Lamb of God who taketh away thy sins. Plead there no works, no righteousness of thine own; no humility, contrition, sincerity. In no wise. That were in very deed to deny the Lord that bought thee. No; plead thou singly the blood of the covenant, the ransom paid for thy proud, stubborn, sinful soul.

6. Who are they that are justified? The ungodly,—the ungodly of every kind and degree, and none but the ungodly. It is only sinners that have any occasion for pardon; it is sin alone which admits of being forgiven. Forgiveness has an immediate reference to sin, and to nothing else. It is our *unrighteousness* to which the pardoning Lord is merciful; it is our *iniquity* that He remembers no more.

7. If God doth not justify the ungodly, and him that worketh not, then Christ hath died in vain; then, notwithstanding His death, can no flesh living be justified.

8. There is scarce a greater help to holiness than a continual tranquillity of spirit, the evenness of a mind stayed upon God, a calm repose in the blood of Jesus. All fear freezes and benumbs the soul.

HERVEY.

BORN 1713—DIED 1758.

1. We are, I grant it, justified by works. But whose; The works of Christ, not our own.

2. The salvation of sinners does not interfere with the justice of the supreme Legislator. On the contrary, it becomes a faithful and just procedure of the Most High, to justify him that believeth on Jesus.

3. The righteousness by which we are justified is both legal and evangelical: legal in respect to Christ, who was made under the law that He might obey all its commands; evangelical in respect to us, who work not ourselves, but believe in the great Fulfiller of all righteousness. We are justified by works, if we look to our Surety; we are justified without works, if we look to ourselves.

4. The ground of our comfort, the cause of our justification, is, not the grace of faith, but the righteousness which is of God by faith; not the act of believing, but that grand and glorious object of a sinner's belief, the Lord our Righteousness. Faith recommends to God, and justifies the soul, not for itself or its own worth, but on account of what it presents and what it pleads.

5. We ourselves are often the dreamers, when we imagine others to be fast asleep.

6. The beginning of our cure is to be sensible of our disorder.

7. Few applied to the blessed Jesus, in the days of His flesh, but the sons and daughters of affliction. The levee of that Prince of Peace was crowded by the lame, the blind, the diseased.

8. True faith in Christ and His righteousness arises from the ruins of self-sufficiency and the death of personal excellency.

9. We never maintain that any sacrifice whatever, not even the propitiation of Christ's death, was intended to *make God merciful;* only to make way for His eternal purposes of mercy, without any prejudice either to the demands of His law or the rights of His justice.

10. If you doubt whether Christ sustained the wrath of God, let us follow Him to the garden of Gethsemane. He had no remorse to alarm His spotless conscience, yet fearfulness and trembling came upon Him. What cause can be assigned for this amazing anguish? None but the wrath of His Almighty Father, who was now become an inexorable Judge, treating Him no longer as the Son of His love, but as the Surety for numberless millions of guilty creatures.

11. It was Immanuel, the incarnate God, who purchased the Church with His own blood. The divine nature of our Saviour communicated its ennobling influences to every tear He shed, to every sigh He heaved, and every pang He felt.

12. We can perform no good work till we are interested in Christ and accepted of God.

13. Be always cheerful as well as serious, that you may win men to Christ.

ROMAINE.

BORN 1714—DIED 1795.

1. Do you desire from your heart that Christ should soon come, in all His glory, to judgment? Are you preparing and looking out for it as an event that may not be far off? If you are, then you are safe.

2. Does not the present state of the world, as to religion, greatly resemble our Lord's description of the men on whom that day shall come unawares, as a thief in the night?

3. The cause of every possible complaint is in you, whether you feel it or not. You have an abyss of corruption; so have I; and perhaps felt it deeper than you have or will feel it. But I have a teacher who makes this whole body of sin profitable, and to the increase of my faith, and to the magnifying the grace of my Almighty Saviour. My daily lesson is to carry my burden to Him, and He carries both me and it; and, while we thus go on lovingly together, He often lets me look into the hell within; but He keeps my conscience sprinkled with His atoning blood; and even I do feel its sovereign virtue to cleanse me from all my sins, if they were ten million times more and greater than they are. Thus believing, yet groaning under my dreadful load, I hear the Father's testimony, and I honour it, ' *Thy sins and iniquities will I remember no more.*'

4. In books I converse with men, in the Bible I converse with God.

5. John xvi. 14, 15, is a very favourite text of mine. If you look to the Greek, you will consider the word translated *show* a gross mistake. It belongs to the ear, and not to the eye; not to seeing, but to speaking,—to the word, which, preached clearly, begets faith; and, which believed, nourishes faith. I would render the word, He shall clearly declare or preach, and so manifest the things of Christ, that they shall become the object of faith, and hope, and love.

6. Peace being broken between God and man, the breach was made up by our great Peacemaker. The Gospel is the open proclamation of it, inviting sinners to be reconciled, and to enjoy the benefits of a free trade between heaven and earth.

7. When I feel guilt, I quiet my conscience with the sprinkling of the blood of Jesus. When the miseries of sin are present, the love of God in Christ turns them into blessings.

8. In my walk, in my warfare, in my duties, in my friendships, in everything, I live by the faith of the Son of God; whereby a man may be as certain that he is alive in Christ as that he is alive to this world.

9. You are looking, not at the object of faith—at Jesus —but at your faith. You would draw your comfort, not from Him, but from your faith; and because your faith is not quite perfect, you are as much discouraged as if Jesus was not a quite perfect Saviour. How sadly does the sly spirit of bondage deceive you? For what is your act of believing? Is it to save you? Are you to be saved *for* believing?

WHITEFIELD.

BORN 1714—DIED 1770.

1. Oh, Prayer, prayer! It brings and keeps God and man together. It raises up man to God, and brings down God to man.

2. It is remarked of Old Testament saints, that they rose early in the morning; and particularly of our Lord, that He rose a great while before day to pray. The morning befriends devotion; and if people cannot use so much self-denial as to rise early to pray, I know not how they will be able to die at a stake for Jesus Christ.

3. Good works have their proper place. They justify our *faith*, though not our *persons;* they follow it, and evidence our justification in the sight of men.

4. Do not say I preach despair. I despair of no one, when I consider God had mercy on such a wretch as I, who was running in a full career to hell.

5. Give the world the lie. Press forward. Do not stop, do not linger in your journey; but strive for the mark set before you.

6. If any here do expect fine preaching from me to-day, they will go away disappointed. I came not here to shoot over people's heads, but, if the Lord be pleased to bless me, to reach their hearts.

7. Why should I lean upon a broken reed, when I can

have the Rock of Ages to stand upon, that shall never be moved?

8. O grey-headed sinners! I could weep over you. Your grey hairs, which ought to be your crown, are now your shame.

9. Come, little children, come to Christ. Come while you are young. Do not stay for other people. If your fathers and mothers will not come to Christ, come you without them.

10. What if thou hadst committed the sins of a thousand? What if thou hadst committed the sins of a million worlds? Christ's righteousness will cover, Christ's blood will cleanse thee from the guilt of all.

11. It is very remarkable that the Old Testament ends with the word *curse;* but the New with a precious blessing, even the grace of our Lord Jesus Christ.

12. God is not only a help, but a *present* help; the gates of the New Jerusalem stand open night and day.

13. Did you ever hear any of the devil's children compose an ode, that the devil is 'our refuge,' that the god of this world is a present help in time of trouble? Did you ever hear any say that the forty-sixth Psalm was founded on a lie?

14. What will you do when the elements shall melt with fervent heat? when this earth, with all its fine furniture, shall be burnt up: when the angel shall cry that time shall be no more?

15. There is no river to make glad the inhabitants of hell, no streams to cool them in the scorching fire.

16. Fly, sinner, fly! God help thee to fly! Hark, hear

the word of the Lord! See the world consumed, the Avenger at thy heels! Before to-morrow you may be damned for ever!

17. We do not live up to our dignity, till every day we are waiting for the coming of our Lord from heaven.

18. I did not speak that word strong enough, which says, ' He that believeth not shall be damned.' It is said of one of the primitive preachers, that he used so to speak that word ' damned,' that it struck all his hearers. We are afraid of speaking that word for fear of offending such and such, who yet despise the servant for not being so honest as his Master.

BERRIDGE (JOHN).

BORN 1716—DIED 1793.

1. None can redeem a world but the Maker of it.

2. I marvel much that any who allow the imputation of Christ's *death*, should object to the imputation of His *life*.

3. Working for life is the law of Moses; believing for life is the law of Jesus.

4. None can come to Jesus except the Father draws them. Yet sinners do not perish because they *cannot* come, but because they *will not* come.

5. Truly, my friend, your cross is just the same with my own. I am not able to walk a step without a crutch. The wood of it comes from Calvary. My crutch is Christ; and a blessed crutch He is. Oh let me lean my whole weight on Thee whilst I am walking through the wilderness.

6. No prophet used 'verily, verily,' before Christ, nor any apostle after Christ; it seems an expression peculiarly belonging to Him who is truth itself, and therefore only fit for Him to use.

7. If we desire to be holy, we must seek to be happy in the Saviour's love.

8. Holiness, as well as pardon, is to be had from the blood of the cross.

9. All fancied sanctification, which does not arise

wholly from the blood of the cross, is nothing better than Pharisaism.

10. What utter destruction the Lord's own servants would make in His vineyard, if the Lord Himself did not hold the vines in His right hand !

11. A furnace seems a hot atmosphere to breathe in, and a deadly path to walk in ; but it is really a place of liberty.

12. Everlasting thanks for a Surety, whose blood is of infinite value, and who can save to the uttermost.

13. The Lord help us to gird up our loins and trim our lamps. The Lord make us watchful and prayerful, looking and longing for the coming of the Bridegroom.

14. A Christian never falls asleep in the fire or in the water, but grows drowsy in the sunshine.

15. How easily we can mistake frothy mirth for gospel joy ; yet how wide is the difference ! Joy in the Lord, as it is the most delightful, so it is the most serious thing in the world, filling the soul with holy shame and blushing, drawing tears of sweetest love. Laughter is not found in heaven. All are too happy there to laugh.

16. Much reading and thinking may make a popular minister ; but much secret prayer must make a powerful preacher.

17. Much secret prayer will solemnize your heart, and make your visits savoury as well as your sermons. The old Puritans visited their flocks by house-row. The visits were short ; they talked a little for God, and then concluded with prayer to God. An excellent rule, which prevented tittle-tattle, and made visits profitable.

18. All decays begin in the closet ; no heart thrives without much secret converse with God ; and nothing will make amends for the want of it. I can read God's Word, or hear a sermon at times, and feel no life ; but I never rise from secret prayer without some quickening.

19. Never am I well but when at home with Jesus.

20. O heart, heart ! what art thou ? A mass of fooleries and absurdities ; the vainest, foolishest, craftiest, wickedest thing in nature. Yet the Lord Jesus asks me for this heart; wooes me for it, died to win it ! O wonderful love ! adorable condescension !

21. I want His fountain every day, His intercession every moment; and would not give a groat for the broadest fig leaves, or the brightest human rags to cover me. A robe I must have, of one whole piece, broad as the law, spotless as the light, and richer than an angel ever wore, the robe of Jesus.

PIKE (SAMUEL).

BORN 1717—DIED 1773.

1. The perfect work of Christ is presented, in the gospel, to be directly believed on, as the only, the sure, the immediate ground of a sinner's peace and hope before God. And if this testimony, believed on in the conscience, will not convey peace, I know not what will or can.

2. Christ Himself is the *object* of faith ; the truth, or gospel of Christ, is the *matter* of faith; the divine evidence of the truth is the *ground* of faith ; the declaration and hearing the truth is the *medium* of faith ; and the Spirit of truth the *author* of faith.

3. If a person strives to perform any duties, or aims to exert any acts, in order to obtain peace with God, he contradicts the truth of the gospel ; yea, the very turn of his thought and the desire of his mind are contrary to the perfect freedom of grace in Christ, which the gospel was written to testify.

4. When a person receives the divine truth, his thoughts are not at all occupied about the nature of faith, or about the workings of his own mind, any more than we are engaged in examining into the nature of light and vision at the time that we are gazing with pleasure at any object. But what he is thinking about is the nature, evidence,

---

* Author of the well known Work, 'Brief Thoughts on the Gospel.'

suitableness, and importance of what is testified in the
divine word concerning Jesus Christ, as a free and complete Saviour for sinners.

5. If a person's attention, for the ease of his mind and
conscience, is drawn to the experiences of his own heart,
instead of the free grace revealed in the gospel, then,
though he accounts himself to believe in Christ, yet he
has only something like the truth imprinted on his imagination in a delusive way ; and, as his soul is not drawn to
it and by it, it has not really taken possession of his heart
and conscience.

6. All those exercises, and prayers, and efforts are
wrong, which suppose that some act must be exerted in
order to gain an interest in Christ ; that the knowledge of
our peculiar interest is the proper relief of the guilty conscience ; that the truth of the gospel believed is not
sufficient to comfort the soul; that the Holy Spirit conveys
the assurance of special interest into the mind without
scriptural evidence, whispering something more to the
soul than what is contained in the divine word.

7. The self-deceiver has no notion that God freely
justifies the ungodly. He thinks that God first implants
a principle of holiness in the heart, draws forth grace
into exercise, and then the person is justified in consequence of such an exercise, and has peace of conscience
from the good quality of his own actings. Under the
power of these sentiments, he avoids a direct trust in the
divine mercy revealed, having no idea of any such freeness of grace as shall give hope and peace, merely from
what the gospel testifies concerning the free and complete

redemption in Jesus Christ. As these actings of mind do not flow from the belief, but from the disbelief of the truth, the hope of the soul terminates upon a wrong object. For his chief comfort hinges on the idea he has got of the nature of his own acts and experiences; so that, in reality, the mind does not recur to a free Christ for relief, but to the marks and signs of interest ; the soul does not lean on the Rock of Ages, but upon the supposed validity of its evidences ; does not take shelter in Christ, but in its own frames and feelings ; the soul being encouraged or discouraged, distressed or comforted, just as it thinks it has or has not exerted the act of faith aright. Thus the whole matter turns, not upon the question whether the gospel be true, but whether the inward feelings and experiences are right.

BRAINERD (DAVID).

BORN 1718—DIED 1747.

1. I felt insatiable longings after God this day. I wondered how poor souls live that have no God. The world, with all its enjoyments, quite vanished. I longed exceedingly to be dissolved, and to be with Christ. Oh my weary soul longs to arrive at my Father's house!

2. Oh how divinely sweet it is to come into the secret of His presence, and abide in His pavilion!

3. None knows but those who feel it, what the soul endures when shut out from the sensible presence of God. It is more bitter than death?

4. I exhorted the people to love one another, and not to set up their own frames as a standard to try all their brethren by.

5. Filling up our time *with* and *for* God is the way to rise up and lie down in peace.

6. Oh how dark it looked to think of being unholy for ever! This I could not endure.

7. There are many with whom I can talk *about* religion; but, alas! I find few with whom I can talk *religion itself*.

8. I longed to spend the little inch of time I have in the world more for God. My soul, my very soul, longed for the ingathering of the poor heathen. I was tenderly affected toward all the world, longing that every sinner

might be saved, and could not have entertained any bitterness towards the worst enemy living.

9. My soul was drawn out for the interest of Zion, and comforted with the lively hope of the appearing of the kingdom of the great Redeemer. These were sweet moments! I felt almost loath to go to bed, and grieved that sleep was necessary.

10. If I cannot behold the excellencies of God as to cause me to rejoice in Him for what He is *in Himself*, I have no solid foundation for joy. To rejoice only because I apprehend I have an interest in Christ, and shall be finally saved, is a poor, mean business indeed.

11. My soul centred in God as my only portion; and I felt that I should be for ever unhappy if He did not reign.

12. I viewed the infinite excellency of God till my soul even broke with longings that He should be glorified. I thought of dignity in heaven; but instantly the thought returned, 'I do not go to heaven to get honour, but to give all possible glory and praise.' Oh how I longed that God should be glorified on earth also! Oh I was made for eternity, if God might be glorified!

13. I was born on a Sabbath-day; I was new-born on a Sabbath-day; and I hope I shall die on a Sabbath-day. I long for the time. Oh why is His chariot so long in coming!

14. Oh that His kingdom might come; that all might love and glorify Him for what He is in Himself, and that the blessed Redeemer might see of the travail of His soul, and be satisfied! Oh come, Lord Jesus, come quickly. Amen!

BROWN (JOHN, OF HADDINGTON).

BORN 1722—DIED 1787.

1. Notwithstanding my eager hunting after all the lawful learning which is known among the sons of men, God hath made me generally preach as if I had never read another book but the Bible.

2. Often we read history as atheists or deists, rather than as Christians. To read of events, without observing God in them, is to read as atheists; to read, and not observe how all events conduce to carry on the work of redemption, is to read as deists.

3. The doctrine of grace reigning through righteousness is good to live with, and good to die with.

4. I have lived sixty years very comfortably in this world; yet I would gladly turn my back on all to be with Christ.

5. Many a comely person I have seen; but none so comely as Christ. Many a kind friend I have had; but none like Christ, in loving-kindness and in tender mercies.

6. Reading tires me, walking tires me, riding tires me; but, were I once with Jesus above, fellowship with Him will never tire.

7. I have served several masters, but none so kind as Christ. I have dealt with many honest men, but no creditor like Christ.

8. Nothing is more common, easy, or agreeable to

corrupt nature, than to preach a multitude of the precious truths of God in a broken and disjointed manner, without ever preaching the Gospel of Christ.

9. The least neglect to hold forth Christ as God's free gift and our all, in any privilege or duty ; or the least recommendation of sincerity, repentance, &c., as the ground of our warrant to receive Jesus Christ, or as the condition of our title to salvation, tends to pervert the Gospel.

10. The Gospel preacher, when offering relief to sinners, ought to represent the persons for whom Christ offered Himself, as a propitiation, under the character of *men, many, unjust, ungodly, without strength, enemies to God, sinners, condemned in law, lost,* &c. He is to invite men to Christ, not as *elect,* or as *sensible* sinners duly convinced, or good-hearted ; but as *men, sons of Adam, simple, foolish, scorners, stout-hearted, far from righteousness, wicked, disobedient, gainsaying, heavy laden with guilt and trouble,* thirsting for happiness in anything, however vain and vile, self-conceited, weariers of God by their iniquities, who have spoken and done evil things as they could ; nay, as many as they find out of hell.

11. No mark of grace ought to be given but such as can be traced up to a believing of the record which God hath given of His Son.

12. What hard, knotty timber must we be, that the Lord hath to hack us so much, in order to render us plain and smooth !

13. Can virgin-love be better placed than on a Divine Husband ? Can early years be better spent than in fellowship with Him ?

NEWTON (JOHN).

BORN 1725—DIED 1807.

1. What some call providential openings, are often powerful temptations. The heart, in wandering, cries, 'Here is a way opened before me!' but, perhaps, not to be trodden, but rejected.

2. A Christian should never plead spirituality for being a sloven; if he be but a shoe-cleaner, he should be the best in the parish.

3. Many have puzzled themselves about the origin of evil: I observe that there is evil, and that there is a way to escape it; and with this I begin and end.

4. Christ has taken our nature into heaven, to represent us; and has left us on earth, with His nature, to represent Him.

5. The religion of a sinner stands on two pillars,—namely, what Christ did for us in His flesh, and what He performs in us by His Spirit. Most errors arise from an attempt to separate these two.

6. A Christian in the world is like a man transacting his affairs in the rain. He will not suddenly leave his client because it rains; but the moment the business is done he is gone: as it is said in the Acts—'Being let go, they went to their own company.'

7. When a Christian goes into the world because he sees it his call, yet, while he feels it also his cross, it will not hurt him.

8. If an angel were sent to find the most perfect man, he would probably not find him composing a body of divinity, but lying a cripple in a poorhouse.

9. Man is not taught anything to good purpose till God becomes his teacher: and then the glare of the world is put out, and the value of the soul rises in full view.

10. God deals with us as we do with children: He first speaks; then gives a gentle stroke; at last, a blow.

11. We must go to the foot of the cross to understand what the Scripture declares of God's holiness, justice, and truth, and the wonderful method by which they are brought to harmonise with the designs of His mercy and grace in the salvation of sinners.

12. Worldly men are alway true to their principles; and if we were as true to ours, the visits between the two parties would be short and seldom.

13. Much depends on the way we come into trouble. Paul and Jonah were both in a storm, but in very different circumstances.

14. A dutiful child is ever looking forward to the holidays, when he shall return to his father; but he does not think of running from school before.

15. If two angels came down from heaven to execute a divine command, and one was appointed to conduct an empire, and the other to sweep a street in it, they would feel no inclination to exchange employments.

16. I am satisfied that the almighty power which sustains the stars in their orbits is equally necessary to carry me with safety, honour, and comfort through the smoothest day of my life.

HORNE (BISHOP).

BORN 1730—DIED 1792.

1. The power of Christ will be manifested in all, by the destruction either of sin or the sinner. The hearts which now yield to the impressions of His Spirit are broken only in order to be formed anew, and to become vessels of honour fitted for the Master's use. Those which continue stubborn must be dashed in pieces by the stroke of eternal vengeance.

2. Christ beseeches kings, no less than their subjects, to be reconciled to Him, and by Him to the Father, since a day is at hand when mighty men shall have no distinction but that of being mightily tormented.

3. Let faith teach thee how to sleep and how to die ; while it assures thee that as sleep is a short death, so death is only a longer sleep ; and that the same God watches over thee in thy bed and in thy grave.

4. Thou, O Christ, art everlasting truth ; all is vanity and falsehood, transient and fallacious, but the love of Thee.

5. The all-righteous Saviour Himself wept over sinners ; sinners read the story, and yet return again to their sins !

6. The Spirit and the bride say, Come ! Arise, O Lord Jesus, from Thy throne of glory, and come quickly ; let not the man of sin prevail against Thy church, but let the long depending cause between her and her adversaries be judged and finally determined in Thy sight.

7. Vain were the idols of the ancient world, Baal and Jupiter; as vain are those of modern times, Pleasure, Honour, and Profit.

8. Thus will the Lord, our Saviour, provide for us on earth and conduct us to heaven ; where we shall dwell to 'length of days,' even the days of eternity, 'one fold under one Shepherd ;' a fold into which no enemy enters, and from which no friend departs.

9. Earth is the land of the dying : we must extend our prospect into heaven, which is 'the land of the living.'

10. The hope of the church was always in Messiah. Of old she prayed for the mercy of His first advent ; now she expecteth His second.

11. The coming of Christ is twofold : first, He came to sanctify the creature, and He will come again to glorify it. If creation be represented as rejoicing at the accomplishment of the former, how much greater will the joy be at the approach of the latter. And not only they, but ourselves also, who have the first-fruits of the Spirit, groan within ourselves, waiting for the redemption of the body, when, at the renovation of all things, man, new-made, shall return to the days of his youth, to begin an immortal spring, and be for ever young.

HILL (SIR RICHARD).

BORN 1732—DIED 1808.

1. How long might one live with some persons, who are looked upon as very good Christians, and not know whether they had any souls or not!

2. If you will be the world's favourite, you must be neither too like God nor too like the devil.

3. The most dangerous infidels are not the most open infidels.   There is a set of men who persuade themselves that they believe Christianity, whilst in truth they are reasoning Christianity quite out of doors.

4. When a poor unawakened soul, who has long lingered under some bodily disease, dies, it is often said, 'It is happy for such a one that he is released.'   A dreadful release!—from earth to hell!

5. Scarcely two persons run the same road to destruction; but there is but one way to happiness.   'I am the Way,' saith Christ.

6. There are some ministers who, if they have given their hearers a sip of pure gospel wine, and brought their souls into a glowing ardour, immediately throw a gallon of cold water upon them, whereby all the flame is quenched; or, to vary the metaphor, since the Scripture makes use of both (Isa. lv. 1), if they have given them a taste of gospel milk, they cannot be satisfied till they have curdled it with a pailful of legal vinegar.   Such ministers may mean well,

but it will not do : the heart gets hard, guilt cankers the
conscience, and the obedience which is produced (if there
be any at all), is at best slavish—never filial. They would
guard against Antinomianism, whilst in truth they produce
it, by drawing the flaming sword of the law, and thereby
'guarding' the poor guilty sinner's free approach to Christ,
'the Tree of Life,' from whom alone fruit unto holiness is
to be found.

7. Watchfulness will not avail without prayer, nor
prayer without watchfulness.   'Watch and pray,' saith our
Lord.

8. Either take Christ or Moses for your husband, for
you cannot have both.   If you are married to Christ, you
are divorced from the law (that is, as a covenant by which
you are to be saved, but not as a rule of life); but if you
are wedded to Moses, you have no part in Christ; and you
will find Moses to be as bloody an husband as Zipporah
did of old.

HORSLEY.

BORN 1733—DIED 1806.

1. Every sentence of the Bible is from God, and every man is interested in the meaning of it.

2. The apostles were, by infinite degrees, the best-informed of all philosophers; and the prophets of the primitive church were the soundest of all divines.

3. It is a gross mistake to consider the Sabbath as a mere festival of the Jewish Church, deriving its whole sanctity from the Levitical law. The abrogation of that law no more releases the worshippers of God from the observation of the Sabbath, than it cancels the injunctions of filial piety, or the prohibitions of theft and murder. The Christian stands obliged to the observance of a Sabbath. By keeping a Sabbath, we acknowledge a God and declare we are not atheists; by keeping one day in seven, we protest against idolatry, and acknowledge *that* God who made the heavens and earth; and by keeping our Sabbath on the first day of the week, we protest against Judaism, and acknowledge *that* God who, having made the world, sent His only begotten Son to redeem mankind. The observation of the Sabbath is a public weekly assertion of the two first articles in our creed—the belief in God the Father Almighty, the Maker of heaven and earth; and in Jesus Christ, His only Son, our Lord.

4. He who forgave the sinner that perfumed His feet;

He who called Saul the persecutor to be an Apostle of the faith ; He who from the cross bore the companion of His last agonies to Paradise ;—HE hath said, 'Him that cometh to Me, I will in no wise cast out.'

5. What, then, shall be the joy of those to whom the King shall say, 'I was an hungered, and ye gave Me meat ?' &c. O rich requital of an easy service ! Love the duty ; heaven the reward ! Who will not strive to be foremost to minister to the necessities of the saints ; secure of being doubly repaid ;—*here*, in the delight of doing good ; *hereafter*, in a share of this glorious benediction !

6. Every man may be allowed to say that he will not believe without sufficient evidence ; but none can, without great presumption, pretend to stipulate for any particular kind of proof, and refuse to attend to any other.

7. Christ's body was plainly the mortal body of a man. It suffered from hunger, from fatigue, and violence, and needed the refection of food, of rest, and sleep.

8. After His resurrection, He had no longer any local residence on earth. He was become the inhabitant of another region, from which He came occasionally to converse with His disciples ; His visible ascension, being not the necessary means of His removal, but a token to His disciples that this was His last visit ; an evidence to them that the heavens had now received Him, and that He was to be seen no more on earth till the restitution of all things.

9. The sudden and universal notoriety that there will be of our Saviour's last glorious advent, is signified by the image of the lightning, which, in the same instant, flashes upon the eyes of spectators in remote and opposite stations.

BOOTH.

BORN 1734—DIED 1806.

1. Preaching the Gospel is proclaiming glad tidings of salvation for the guilty.

2. It is hence apparent, that God, in the bestowment of blessings on the children of men, is not influenced by the purity of their hearts, the piety of their lives, or the worthiness of their characters; but by a regard to His own eternal perfection; to the supreme excellence of His own revealed name; and to the everlasting honour of His own immense goodness.

3. If the testimony of God to an apostate, guilty, and wretched world, concerning His incarnate Son, and relative to the riches of His own grace, be not a sufficient warrant for the most ungodly person upon earth to believe in Jesus, it is not easy to conceive of any Divine declarations which could have been made, that would have authorised any of those whom the Scriptures call *sinners*, or the guilty in a *perishing condition*, to believe in Christ.

4. To consider any man as born of God, but not as a child of God; as a child of God, but not as believing in Jesus Christ; as believing in Jesus Christ, but not as justified; or as justified, but not as an heir of immortal felicity; is, either to the last degree absurd, or manifestly contrary to the apostolic doctrine.

5. 'Repent ye, and believe the Gospel.' This may be

the meaning of the exhortation:—Repent; relinquish all your wrong notions, relating to the way and the manner of finding acceptance with the Deity. 'Believe the Gospel;' which opens a most unexpected avenue for the communication of this blessing; which brings you glad tidings of a salvation, fully procured by the incarnate God, and freely offered to the unworthy sinner.

6. Is the heavy-laden sinner invited to Christ? it is, not as qualified by being burdened, but as guilty and perishing, that he must apply to the Saviour; taking all his encouragement so to do, from the testimony of God concerning Jesus.

7. Does any one ask, What is my warrant for believing in Jesus Christ? The answer is, not anything done by you, not anything wrought in you; but the word of grace, or the testimony of God concerning Jesus.

8. Faith in the blood of Jesus, and that peace which is connected with it, far from stupefying the believer's conscience, render it more sensible to that which is evil, more awake to the secret operations of innate corruption, and more jealous of his own heart.

9. You make no profession. The reason is, I presume, you have nothing, of experimental Christianity, to profess. No faith, for instance, in the blood of Jesus; no 'repentance from dead works;' no love to God; no subjection of conscience to the authority of Christ; and, therefore, unregenerate, dead in sin, and under the curse of a broken law. You make no profession. But does that supersede the dominion of God over you, or the authority of His precepts, and leave you to live as you please?

MILNER (JOSEPH).

BORN 1744—DIED 1797.

1. The church has arms which the men of the world understand not.

2. The little success at Athens evinces that a spirit of literary trifling in religion, where all is theory and the conscience unconcerned, hardens the heart effectually.

3. Omnipotent energy alone can produce or preserve true holiness.

4. To believe, to suffer, to love, not to write, was the primitive taste.

5. The first Christians, with the purest charity to the *persons* of heretics, gave their *errors* no quarter.

6. It should ever be remembered that Christian light stands single and unmixed, and will not bear to be kneaded into the same mass with other systems, religious or philosophical.

7. The primitive Christians knew the doctrine of the election of grace, but not the self-determining power of the human will.

8. Beware of philosophy, is a precept which as much calls for our attention now as ever.

9. The notions of proud philosophers vary in different ages; but they seldom fail in some form or other to withstand the religion of Jesus.

10. A Trinitarian speculatist may be as worldly-minded

as any other ; his *doctrine*, however, contains that which alone can make a man fix his affections on things above.

11. Persecution frequently does in this life, in part, what the last day will do completely, separate wheat from tares.

12. An artificial and polished arrangement of sentences is lost upon a vulgar audience ; and those who affect it are, it is to be feared, little moved themselves with the importance of divine things, and are far more solicitous for their own character as speakers than for the spiritual profit of their hearers.

13. What a number of elaborate sermons have been preached to no purpose ! Even the truth that is in them is rendered, in a great measure, useless, by the wisdom of words with which it is clothed ; while plain, colloquial addresses to the populace, by men fearing God, and speaking of divine things in fervour and charity, has been attended with the demonstration of the Spirit ; and souls have been rescued from sin and Satan.

CECIL (RICHARD).

BORN 1748—DIED 1810.

1. The blessed man is he who is under education in God's school, where he endures chastisement, and by chastisement is instructed.

2. A stubborn and rebellious mind in a Christian must be kept low by dark and trying dispensations.

3. We cannot build too confidently on the merits of Christ as our only hope ; nor can we think too much of the mind that was in Christ as our great example.

4. If you have set out in the ways of God, do not stumble at present difficulties. Go forward. Look not behind.

5. The history of all the great characters of the Bible is summed up in this one sentence :—They acquainted themselves with God, and acquiesced in His will in all things.

6. The most likely method we can take to hasten the removal of what we love, is, to value it too much ; to think on it with endless anxiety ; to live on its favour with solicitude. It shall soon either become a thorn in our side, or be taken away.

7. A Christian will find his parenthesis for prayer, even through his busiest hours.

8. God is omniscient as well as omnipotent : and omniscience may see reason to withhold what omnipotence could bestow.

9. A Christian has advanced but a little way in religion

when he has overcome the love of the world; for he has still more powerful and importunate enemies: self—evil tempers—pride—undue affections—a stubborn will. It is by the subduing of these adversaries that we must chiefly judge of our growth in grace.

10. What we call 'taking steps in life' are most serious occurrences; especially if there be in the motive any mixture of ambition. *'Wherefore gaddest thou about to change thy way?'*

11. Remember always to mix good sense with good things, or they will become disgusting.

12. It is always a sign of poverty of mind when men are ever aiming to appear great; for they who are really great never seem to know it.

13. How many people go out of their sphere under good pretences!

14. Whatever, below God, is the object of our love, will, at some time or other, be the matter of our sorrow.

15. A Christian must stand in a posture to receive every message which God shall send. He must be so prepared as to be like one who is called to set off on a sudden journey, and has nothing to do but to set out at a moment's notice; or like a merchant who has goods to send abroad, and has them all packed up and in readiness for the first sail.

JONES (THOMAS S., D.D., EDINBURGH).

BORN 1754—DIED 1837.

1. In matters of religion, all the doctrines which men are required to believe, and all the duties which they are commanded to perform, are contained in the Bible; and if anything is taught or enjoined which is not found in, or fairly deducible from, the doctrines and precepts of the sacred volume, it is an imposition, and ought to be rejected.

2. Faith cannot be separated from holiness, nor holiness from faith; and, should the separation be attempted, neither holiness nor faith can be attained.

3. The law of God is a charter of rights. With the preservation of that charter, everything dear to God and valuable to man is eternally connected. To permit the law to bend to the criminal here, would be attended with consequences of injustice, fatal beyond all calculation.

4. Genuine repentance flows from the cross of Christ.

5. The cross of Christ, mildly, regularly, and constantly, influences the understanding by the conviction of its truth. It engages the heart by the immensity of the divine goodness and grace; it directs and enforces the conduct of all who feel its influence, by the persuasion of duty, propriety, and interest.

6. Study the doctrine of the cross: believe it, and it will take off your chains; it will open the prison-house of Satan.

7. The sufferings of Christ exhibited, in a new and more amiable light, the divine character,—threw a lustre around the works of providence and grace before unknown, and kindled new and transcendent glories both in earth and heaven.

8. It must be the highest degree of presumption in mortals to attempt to limit either the power of the grace of God or the virtue of the death of Christ.

9. A religion without feeling must be a religion without faith, without hope, without peace, without comfort, without piety, without devotion, without morals, without love to God or love to mankind.

10. Despised and scorned as the repentance of a sinner is, by the proud and hardened infidel, that event is, in the estimation of glorified spirits, an object of great magnitude and importance. It is a new creation, from which are reflected new illustrations of the wisdom, power, mercy, grace, and goodness of God. It is a resurrection of the dead in sin to an endless life of holiness and glory.

11. Trial is intended to discover what is in man; to shew his strength or his weakness, his virtue or his vice, his religion or his irreligion.

LOVE (DR).

BORN 1757—DIED 1825.

1. True love to Christ, though it begins in, and is excited by, a sight of His suitableness to us (Heb. vi. 18), yet does not terminate here; but is led up thereby to rest ultimately in Him for what He is in Himself.

2. The fourth petition of the Lord's Prayer sounds like the language of pilgrims and strangers seeking their sustenance in this foreign land from day to day.

3. God loves not only a hearty and generous giver (2 Cor. ix. 7), but a hearty and generous receiver; that is, one who accounts the God he pleads with to be such a giver. The glory of His perfections is much more acknowledged by such a person than by others.

4. The great sight at the last day will be *God looking out of the eyes of flesh.*

5. 'So then it is not of him that willeth, nor of him that runneth, but of God that sheweth mercy' (Rom. ix. 16). It is as if the apostle had said, 'When you see a man willing and running, reflect that this willing and running do not come from the man himself, as the author of these, but from God who sheweth mercy to him.'

6. The divine dominion is founded on God's matchless excellences.

7. What if heaven and hell be set in the centre of the universe as the Shechinah of the divine glory, to be beheld

by innumerable worlds of upright intelligence, who have never been put into a state of probation, that they may thereby be instructed in the perfections of the divine nature.

8. Every man has something that he rests on for obtaining justification and happiness. Faith is his putting Christ instead of *that;* his so coming to Christ, and to rest upon Him, as to abandon *it*.

9. Faith has *confidence* in its nature, otherwise we could not have ' access with confidence by the faith of Christ.'

10. Stillness of spirit is like the canvas for the Holy Spirit to draw His various graces upon.

11. Observe how frequently the work of sanctification is ascribed to God under the title ' The God of peace.'

12. We ought to beware of speaking against loving Christ for His benefits; for the glory of God is eminently displayed in those benefits; and it is in these that He Himself is manifested to us. Observe with what complacency the apostle speaks of ' the unsearchable riches of Christ' (Eph. iii. 8); and how he gives thanks on behalf of the Colossians for 'the hope which is laid up' for them in heaven (Col. i. 3, 5). Observe, too, the language of the prodigal : ' How many hired servants of my father's have bread enough and to spare, and I perish with hunger' (Luke xv. 17). And see the Lord's own invitations : Isa. lv. 1-3 ; John v. 40, &c. Christ Himself may really be loved for His divine excellences which appear in His gracious actings towards us.

STEWART (DR ALEXANDER).

BORN 1764—DIED 1821.

1. Faith is credit given to a declaration or assertion, on the authority of the person who makes it, whether that assertion be directly expressed or only implied. When our Lord said to the nobleman of Capernaum, ' Thy son liveth; the man *believed the word* that Jesus had spoken, and went his way,' confident that he would find his son alive and well. When Jesus said to the blind man, ' Go, wash in the pool of Siloam,' the man *believed the assurance implied* in our Lord's injunction, that he would by this means receive his sight ; 'therefore he went his way, and washed, and came again seeing.'

2. If the thing declared and proposed to our faith be a matter of no importance, and fitted to excite no interest, the belief of it will produce no sensible effect, and will admit of no direct evidence. An observer cannot discover whether the thing reported meets with credit or not. But if the matter asserted appear to be of importance, it will, *when believed*, excite emotion, and perhaps prompt to action. If *not believed*, whatever be its importance, it will produce neither action nor emotion. The unequivocal expression of the emotions, accompanying the belief of an interesting declaration, or the action prompted by such belief, is the outward *evidence* of faith.

3. Faith in Christ, in respect of its reality and efficacy,

may be called *living* faith ; whereas its counterfeit, which can have no efficacy, is properly called *dead* faith. This dead, or unproductive faith, is not a different *kind* of faith from the true ; it is, strictly speaking, not faith at all, even as a counterfeit piece of money is not money, or as a dead man is no man.

4. To 'live by faith,' or 'walk by faith,' is to have the life regulated by a habitual prevailing regard to those doctrines and invisible realities which are revealed to us in Scripture. A person may be said to live a life of faith, when the influence of spiritual, invisible objects prevails in regulating his judgment, his affections, and his conduct.

5. There cannot be a more direct proof of the inveterate blindness and hardness of the human heart than this,— that we do not believe many things which God declares, even when we are convinced that it is He that speaks. Yet, that this is the fact, we are assured by Him who knows what is in man, and who cannot lie. One cannot conceive more audacious impiety than thus to discredit the God of truth, and, in effect, to 'make Him,'—*i.e.*, to treat Him as if He were,—'a liar.'

6. Though there is much guilt and depravity in unbelief, it does not follow that there is any merit in faith. A man cannot claim reward for simply believing that to be true which he knows God has affirmed. So that, when our justification is made to depend on our believing the truth, nothing can more expressly preclude every plea of merit on our part. 'It is of faith, that it might be by grace.'

HALL (ROBERT).

BORN 1764—DIED 1831.

1. I hope I am not censorious; but I am persuaded that much of the *liberality* so much talked of, is rather a fashionable cant, than any genuine candour of heart.

2. Lax notions of the person of Christ, a forgetfulness of His mediation, place the mind in a deistical state, and prepare it for the most licentious opinions.

3. O my friend, what an infinity of time I have lost; and how ardently do I long to do something, which shall convince the world I have not lived in vain!

4. I am afraid a vicious taste is gaining ground, both among preachers and hearers; all glare and paint, little to the understanding, and nothing to the heart.

5. I have serious apprehensions, that the *ostentatious* spirit, which is fast pervading all denominations of Christians in the present times, will draw down the frown of the Great Head of the Church, whose distinguishing characteristic was humility. He did not strive, nor cry, nor cause His voice to be heard in the street.

6. To pray *immediately* to Christ, to cast ourselves upon His power and grace, appears to me the best antidote to despondency. I have no doubt we are much wanting to ourselves, in not having more direct dealings with the Saviour, or not addressing Him in the same spirit in which He was applied to for the relief of bodily disease.

7. A Christian should look upon himself as something sacred and devoted. For that which involves but an ordinary degree of criminality in others, in him partakes of the nature of sacrilege; what is a breach of trust in others, is, in him, the profanation of a temple.

8. The wheels of nature are not made to roll backward; everything presses on towards eternity; from the birth of time an impetuous current has set in, which bears all the sons of men to that interminable ocean. Meanwhile, heaven is attracting to itself whatever is congenial to its nature, is enriching itself with the spoils of earth, and collecting within its capacious bosom whatever is pure, permanent, and Divine, leaving nothing for the last fire to consume, but the objects and the slaves of concupiscence; while everything which grace has prepared and beautified, shall be gathered and selected from the world, to adorn that eternal city which hath no need of the sun, neither of the moon, to shine in it.

9. Prayer touches the only spring that can insure success. By speaking, we move man; but by prayer, we move God.

10. He who has given His spirit, will never suffer His work to be stopped by the want of the riches of the earth; He will sooner turn the very stones of the street into the precious metals, than suffer the means to be wanted of carrying on this work.

11. Never did the mighty God more fully display the greatness of His power, than when He shewed Himself mighty to save to the uttermost.

12. You have taken hold of nothing, you have grasped only shadows, if you have not taken hold of Christ, your Life.

HALDANE (ROBERT).

BORN 1764—DIED 1842.

1. All religions but that of the Bible, share the glory of recovering men to happiness between God and the sinner. All false views of the gospel do the same thing. The Bible alone makes the salvation of guilty men terminate in the glory of God as its chief end. Can there be a more convincing evidence that the Bible is from God?

2. The expression 'dead to sin' (Rom. vi. 2) has no reference whatever to the *character* of believers, but exclusively to their *state* before God, as the ground on which their sanctification is secured.

3. The believer is one with Christ as truly as he was one with Adam; he dies with Christ as truly as he died with Adam. Christ's righteousness is his as truly as Adam's sin was his.

4. Jesus Christ suffered the penalty of sin, and ceased to bear it. Till His death He had sin upon Him; and, therefore, though it was not committed by Him, yet it was His own, inasmuch as He took it on Him. When He died on account of sin He died to it, as He was now for ever justified from it. He was not justified from it till His death, but from that moment He was dead to it. When He shall appear the second time, it shall be without sin.

5. Unless we keep in mind that we are dead to sin and alive unto God, we cannot serve Him as we ought.

6. The freedom from the moral law which the believer enjoys, is a freedom from an obligation to fulfil it in his own person for his justification. But this is quite consistent with the eternal obligation of the moral law as a rule of life to the Christian.

7. It is not the first end of law to curse men, but only what it demands since the entrance of sin. Such is the right of the law.

8. Christ was made under the law; but it was a *broken* law; and consequently He was made under its curse.

9. A good conscience is a conscience discharged from sin by the blood of Christ.

10. How can there be love without a sense of reconciliation with God; and how can the fruits of joy and peace be brought forth till the conscience is discharged from guilt?

11. Doubts of a personal interest in Christ are evidences either of little faith or of no faith.

12. The creation, which, on account of the sin of man, has been subjected to vanity, shall be rescued from the present degraded condition under which it groans; and, according to the hope held out to it, is longing to participate with the sons of God in that freedom from vanity into which it shall at length be introduced, partaking with them in their future and glorious deliverance from all evil.

13. The heavens and the earth will pass through the fire, but only that they may be purified, and come forth anew, more excellent than before.

FOSTER.

BORN 1770—DIED 1843.

1. Sometimes prayer is delayed from the sense of recent guilt. No wonder there should be an indisposition then. But will time wear the guilt away? And what will be the best security against renewed sin? Do not defer praying till more guilt come between. Do not, lest death come between!

2. How marvellous and how lamentable that the soul *can* consent to stay in the dust, when invited above the stars!

3. God is transcendently worthy of all love and devotion, the infinite perfection of all excellences united.

4. Does this dead stillness of conscience appear an awful situation? Why? Because we foresee that it will awake; and with an intensity of life and power proportioned to this long sleep, as if it had been growing gigantic during its slumber! It will rise up with all that superiority of vigour with which the body will rise at the resurrection. It will awake! Probably in the last hours of life; but if not then, it will nevertheless awake at the last day!

5. Let us seek that our consciences may ever be in the divine keeping rather than our own.

6. Life is expenditure. We have it but as continually losing it; we have no use of it but as continually wasting it.

7. That fire (of the great day) will leave no more controversies to be decided between God and false divinities. It will be a funeral flame, as to the dominion of the power of evil in this world; but, like Elijah's fire, it will not be lighted till all is ready for the sacrifice.

8. This *pertinacious* going forth of the soul to God, as granting pardon and justification through Jesus Christ—this is the essential thing.

9. Do justice to the divine mercy, by believing its thousandfold declarations and promises.

10. An interval of more than forty years makes all the difference between the morning of life and its evening. What a solemn and mighty difference it is, that whereas we then beheld life before us, we now behold death.

11. We must think daily of holding ourselves in readiness for setting off on the last great journey.

COLERIDGE.

BORN 1772—DIED 1834.

1. Tertullian had good reason for his assertion that the simplest Christian, if indeed a Christian, knows more than the most accomplished irreligious philosopher.

2. I am not ashamed to confess that I dislike the frequent use of the word *virtue*, instead of *righteousness*, in the pulpit; and that in prayer or preaching before a Christian community it sounds too much like Pagan philosophy.

3. Truths, of all others the most awful and interesting, are too often considered as *so true* that they lose all the power of truth, and lie bed-ridden in the dormitory of the soul, side by side with the most despised and exploded errors.

4. The doctrine of election is in itself a necessary inference from an undeniable fact ; necessary, at least, for all who hold that the best of men are what they are through the grace of God.

5. From what you know of yourself, of your own heart and strength, dare you trust to it.

6. Christianity is not a theory or a speculation, but a life ; not a philosophy of life, but a life and a living process.

7. The gospel is not a system of theology, nor a syntagma of theoretical propositions. It is a history, a series of facts and events related and announced. These do indeed involve, or rather I should say, they at the same

time *are* most important doctrinal truths, but still they are *facts* and declaration of *facts*.

8. A Christian cannot speak or think as if his redemption by the blood, and his justification by the righteousness of Christ alone, were future or contingent events, but must both say and think, I *have been* redeemed, I *am* justified.

9. Here is a sacrifice, a sin-offering, and a High Priest who is indeed a Mediator; who, not in type or shadow, but in very truth, and in His own right, stands in the place of man to God, and of God to man; and who receives as a Judge what He offered as an Advocate.

10. The agent and personal cause of the redemption of mankind is the co-eternal Word and only-begotten Son of the living God, incarnate, tempted, agonizing, crucified, submitting to death, resurgent, communicant of His Spirit, ascendant, and obtaining for His church the descent and communion of the Holy Spirit the Comforter.

11. I believe Moses, I believe Paul; but I believe in Christ.

12. Sin is the disease. What is the remedy? Charity? Pshaw!—Charity is the health, the state to be obtained by the use of the remedy, not the sovereign balm itself. Faith of grace, faith in the God-manhood, the cross, the mediation, the perfected righteousness of Jesus, to the utter rejection and objunction of all righteousness of our own,—faith alone is the restorative. The Romish scheme is preposterous; it puts the rill before the spring. Faith is the source, charity, that is, the whole Christian life, is the stream from it.

HOWELS.

BORN 1778—DIED 1832.

1. Man is not only bad, but bad enough to rival even the devil in wickedness.

2. All the malice of men and devils cannot make him miserable whom Christ makes happy.

3. Christ is life ; others only live.

4. God has His universities in this lower world. Here He educates His family. Here they graduate. The Son of God Himself studied here below ; and here He was qualified to assume the reins of universal government.

5. Some have taken more pains to win hell than it has cost martyrs to win a crown of glory in heaven.

6. The wicked have two hells ; one in time, and the other in eternity.

7. When God means to make a creature happy, He makes Him obedient.

8. As a nation, what have we done? We have cherished in our bosoms the serpent Popery ; and it is at the present moment endeavouring to sting us to death.

9. Happy is the man who is drawn by prosperity to God.

10. If you would trace your inability to its source, you must trace it to an indisposition strengthened by ten thousand acts of sin.

11. I am disposed to think I shall be more grateful to

God in heaven for the bitterest than for the sweetest dispensations here on earth.

12. It is the invitation of Christ which gives you a right to approach Him.

13. Do not trifle with sin.

14. Triumph over your feelings—by faith !

15. Do not be content with swimming on the surface of divine truth ; make it your element ; *dive* into it.

16. He who is weary of God will soon make a hell for himself, even in this world.

17. Unworthy as you are, no one is worthy of your heart but God.   Give it to Him wholly and unreservedly.

18. If you seek Christ, carry nothing with you.   All you need in life, in death, and for eternity, is to be found in Him.

19. Do you only pray for yourself ?   You have never yet prayed aright.

SCHIMMELPENNINCK.

BORN 1778—DIED 1856.

1. There are two sorts of prayer: one, grounded on the word and promises of God, asking for particular things; the other, a groaning which cannot be uttered—a sense of the superincumbent weight of death and bondage upon creation, when the Spirit helps our infirmities—a cry of misery like that of the Israelites in Egypt. Our Lord knew both sorts. He prayed for specific objects; He groaned in spirit at the grave of Lazarus.

2. We too much regard God as one to go to when it pleases us, instead of as one whose active energy and love are ever operating upon us.

3. Heaven begins when faith in Christ drops the seed of eternal life into the soul; increases when the soul quits the body; is perfected when, at the Lord's coming, it is united to a glorified body.

4. The atonement is received by faith; righteousness by union with Christ. Reconciliation or peace is through the Son; the perception of sin through the Spirit. The Spirit never gives peace but as He reveals the Son.

5. There is a great resemblance between the Epistle to the Ephesians and that to the Colossians; yet is there this difference :—the Apostle in the Ephesians speaks of the Church as the fulness of Christ, and in the Colossians speaks of Christ as the fulness of the Church.

6. The abiding conviction that we are the Lord's, produces that holiness, love, spirituality, and nearness to
God, which is the Christian's privilege. The joy of
knowing you are the Lord's, stimulates and strengthens.
Seek, then, in your own experience, to make your calling
and election sure. The assurance of faith is the well
from which sanctification flows.

7. The Lord is always a sanctuary or hiding-place to
His children ; in every place, in every company, they may
hide in the secret of His presence from the strife of
tongues about them. Better never enter into society, even
into that of Christians, than go without taking our hiding-
place with us.

8. The lowest possible view that a Christian can take,
is seeking to be saved. We should wish to be with Jesus,
to be in His love, to glorify Him, to witness for Him.

9. Though Christ was a Son, yet learned He obedience
by the things which He suffered. In any instance that
we give up our own will without sacrificing conscience, we
are gainers. If but my dog exercise my patience, and
make me yield my will to his, he is a blessing to me.

10. Look to the blood of Jesus for pardoning grace ; to
the high priesthood of Jesus for sustaining grace ; to the
glory of Jesus for animating and strengthening grace.
Christ imparts His fulness not at once, but in detail. He
imparts life at once in a sense of pardon, but builds up
into His likeness by bringing home the details of His life
and character.

11. Hagar enters the wilderness with a bottle of water,
given by Abraham. A mere bottle of water, though filled

from the source and given by a believer, is no provision for the wilderness. We must have the well itself, and this was near Hagar all the time; but it was only when God opened her eyes that she saw it. She never knew her need of the well till the bottle was expended. Nor do we see the necessity of the living water till the tanks of our own righteousness, or of notions learnt from others, are found to fail.

12. True faith is the grave of anxiety, as of unbelief.

13. It is of much more consequence to our peace to love others, than to know that they love us.

CHALMERS (DR).

BORN 1780—DIED 1847.

1. It is quite competent to believe, even in the duller and darker frames of the mind; for belief does not look inwardly upon the frames, but stays itself by looking outwardly upon the word.

2. There is a great running after ministers in our day, and this argues a desire of something or other;—but, desire of what? Is it to be regaled by the eloquence of the preacher? Is it because you are lured by the report of his high and far-sounding popularity? Is it because you want a feast for your imagination or your intellect, or any of your sensibilities? That is not a desirousness which will help you forward, but rather prove an impediment in the way of your salvation.

3. A believing view of eternity would absorb all our griefs and all our provocations.

4. The righteousness of Christ imputed to those who believe, is a phrase so familiar that it loses its impression. But hearken diligently to this joyful intimation, and your soul shall live: Your sin put to Christ's account, and His righteousness put to your account, totally alter your relation with God.

5. My God, spiritualise my affection! Give me to know what it is to have the intense and passionate love of Christ.

6. I long for mutual and confiding intercourse. May He no longer be lightly esteemed by me, but as altogether lovely! I desire to feast with Him, and Him with me. I would sit down with great delight under the canopy of His Mediatorship, rejoicing in the abundance of peace and love.

7. God is both the Rock of salvation, and the Monarch of heaven and earth.

8. We are called upon to be joyful, because God cometh in judgment. It will be a day of terror to the wicked, but of triumph and establishment to the righteous, when the new heavens and new earth shall emerge from the wrecks of an older economy. On that day may we be counted worthy to stand before the Son of man!

9. Let us wait in faith for the coming of the Son of God. Let us, in the faith of the Gospel, both rejoice and work righteousness.

10. I would learn of Thy holy oracles. I would take the sayings of the Bible simply and purely as they are, and exercise myself on the trueness of these sayings.

11. Let me believe in the midst of heaviness. Let me believe in the dark.

12. We do not steady a ship by fixing the anchor on aught that is within the vessel. The anchorage must be without. And so of the soul, when resting, not on what it sees in itself, but on what it sees in the character of God, the certainty of His truth, the impossibility of His falsehood.

13. Yet come the enlargement when it will, it must come, after all, through the channel of a simple credence given to the sayings of God, accounted as true and faithful sayings.

NETTLETON.

BORN 1783—DIED 1844.

1. Zeal without prudence will defeat its own end. Zeal, untempered with love and compassion for souls, will soon degenerate into harshness and cruelty of manner and expression, which will have no other effect on an audience than scolding, or even profane swearing.

2. The uplifted arm of vengeance is yet stayed. The collected wrath yet waits a moment. A voice from the mercy-seat, a warning voice, is heard. The Saviour calls. Haste then, O sinner, haste to Christ, the only refuge from the storm. Then, safe from the fear of evil, at a distance you shall only hear the thunders roll; while pardon, and peace, and eternal life are yours.

3. You may destroy the sinner's earthly plans, break up all his interest in the concerns of time, fill his mind with all the solemn realities of death, judgment, and eternity, bring him under the most powerful convictions of sin, and the selfish principle may be more active than ever, in building up a righteousness, or in quarrelling with God about the terms of salvation.

4. It is sometimes taken for granted that, if the sinner had clear views of the character of God, he would love Him. But facts prove the contrary. Sinners in the last stages of conviction, who have lost all interest in the concerns of time,—sinners, too, on a dying bed, who care nothing for the world, feel more opposition than ever.

5. Sinners, must I leave you where I found you, unreconciled to God? Your business is not with a fellow-mortal. I have done; and the whole remains to be settled between God and your own souls. However hard you may think this message, it is not mine. God beseeches, God commands your compliance now. And will you raise your feeble arm to oppose? God is on the throne; and have you an arm like God? However opposed you may be, yet God is on the throne, and what can you do?

6. And now all things are ready; and God is inviting and beseeching you to accept his message. What is the reply of your heart? Do you not like the terms of this treaty? You are required only to be reconciled to God. What can be more reasonable than this? Is it hard that you should be required to love God, to feel sorrow for sin, to confess and forsake it? Is this hard, or is sin so lovely and desirable that it appears hard and unreasonable that you should be required to hate it with all your heart?

7. Is sin so noble a thing in itself, and so desirable in its consequences, that you cannot part with it? that you will lay down your life, your eternal life, for its sake? Your *love* of sin is all the excuse you have, or can have. Or, will you plead your *inability?* What! *cannot* be reconciled to God! *cannot* feel sorrow for sin! *cannot* cease to rebel against the King of heaven! What an acknowledgment is this! Out of thine own mouth wilt thou be condemned. If, indeed, you are so opposed to God that you *cannot* feel sorrow for sin, this is the very reason why you ought to be condemned. The harder it is for you to repent and love God, the more wicked you are.

PAYSON.

BORN 1783—DIED 1827.

1. Look back to the time when you imagined your-selves to be convinced of sin, and say whether you were then convinced, or whether you have at any time since been convinced, of the exceeding sinfulness of *unbelief*, If not, there is great reason to fear that you are deceived, that you have mistaken the form for the power of godliness.

2. If there is one fact, or doctrine, or promise in the Bible, which has produced no practical effect upon your temper or conduct, be assured that you do not truly believe it.

3. The Bible tells us that an enemy came and sowed tares. Now, if any man chooses to go further than this, and inquire where the enemy got the tares, he is welcome to do so ; but I choose to leave it where the Bible leaves it. I do not wish to be wise above what is written.

4. If with a careful and enlightened eye we trace the path of a numerous church, we shall find it strewed with the fallen, the fainting, the slumbering, and the dead, who set out in their own strength, and have been stopped, ensnared, and overthrown by various obstacles and enemies.

5. The symptoms of spiritual decline are like those which attend the decay of bodily health. It generally commences with loss of appetite, and a disrelish for

spiritual food, prayer, reading the Scriptures, and devotional books. Whenever you perceive these symptoms, be alarmed, for your spiritual health is in danger; apply immediately to the Great Physician for a cure.

6. Unless we strenuously aim at universal holiness, we can have no satisfactory evidence that we are the servants of Christ. A servant of Christ is one who obeys Christ as his master, and makes Christ's revealed word the rule of his conduct. No man then can have any evidence that he is a servant of Christ any further than he obeys the will of Christ. And no man can have any evidence that he obeys the will of Christ in one particular, unless he sincerely and strenuously aims to obey it in every particular—for the will of Christ is one.

7. God commands *all* men to repent. Christians have enough to repent of daily; and if they are not in a penitent frame, they justify impenitent sinners.

8. Let your Great Physician heal you in his own way. Only follow His directions, and take the medicine which He prescribes, and then quietly leave the result with Him.

9. To a person who had been frustrated in a benevolent design : ' I congratulate you, and anticipate your eventual success. I do not recollect ever to have succeeded in anything of importance, in which I did not meet with some rebuff, at the commencement.'

10. Anticipated sorrows are harder to bear than real ones, because Christ does not support us under them. In every slough we may see the footsteps of Christ's flock who have gone before us.

BROWN (DR JOHN).

BORN 1785—DIED 1858.

1. By far the greater part of mankind are 'without hope.' A large proportion of them have no *faith*, and where there is no faith, there *can be* no *hope;* and there are not a few who, though they have a species of faith (of which they would very willingly get quit if they knew but how), have yet no hope. They know that, whatever they may have to *fear* from death, and judgment, and eternity, they have nothing to *hope* from them, and therefore they do not believe and hope; but, like the demons under whose influence they act, 'they believe and tremble.'

2. Habitual unholiness is a stronger proof that a man's hopes, whatever they be, do not rest on the faith of the truth, than anything wearing the form of evidence, which can be brought forward on the other side.

3. It is dreadful to think what multitudes, under the influence of these delusive hopes, contrive not only to live, but even to die, without much disquietude in reference to the interests of their eternity; continue till the last, 'saying, Peace, peace, to themselves, while there is no peace'; 'go down to the grave with a lie in their right hand'; ascertain the reality and extent of their mistake when it is too late to rectify it, and first 'read their sentence at the flames of hell!' Alas! could the secrets of eternity be made audible to the ears of flesh, how often, in the hour of death, would

be heard, in quick and awful succession, from the darkness in which the parted spirit has evanished, the shriek of surprise, the groan of despair !

4. The ground of the sinner's hope is in God alone. That ground is sometimes represented to be the sovereign, self-moved benignity of God; at other times the obedience to death of His incarnate only-begotten Son; and, at other times, the untrammelled revelation of mercy in 'the word of the truth of the gospel.'

5. The ground of the sinner's hope never varies   It is 'the same yesterday, to-day, and for ever.' The ground of the hopes of the accomplished saint, who, by the word, and providence, and Spirit of God, has been made meet for that inheritance on which he is just about to enter, is precisely the same as when a hopelessly lost sinner, driven from all the false confidences in which he had been accustomed to seek and find shelter, 'he fled for refuge to lay hold on the hope set before him in the gospel,' and found it.   Our first hope is our last hope : 'the beginning of our confidence' is the end of our confidence.

6. Believing the gospel and absolute despair of salvation are plainly incompatible states of mind.   A man may believe what men falsely call the gospel, and what he mistakenly thinks the gospel, and yet remain a stranger to the hope of eternal life.   A man may think that he *believes* what is really the gospel, while he only *speculates* about it, and remain a stranger to the hope of eternal life.   But the *real* gospel cannot be *really* believed without, in the degree in which it is believed, producing hope.

EVANS (REV. J. H.).

BORN 1785—DIED 1849.

1. Guilt upon the conscience always leads away from God.

2. The shining of God's face upon His child is a substitute for every loss.

3. Be great students of the cross of Christ; it is the great means of resisting Satan.

4. You will find Him an unfading flower in a fading world.

5. There is no rest but in Jesus.

6. The dimmest eye that ever looked at the brazen serpent has eternal life.

7. Faith is not sense, nor sight, nor reason; but a taking God at His word.

8. What strengthens faith? Secret prayer; close dealings with conscience over the blood of atonement.

9. That is the most absolute faith which trusts God in the dark.

10. Our aim is not to preach nicely arranged essays; we have to do with man's conscience, with heaven and hell, with God and salvation.

11. How is faith strengthened? By being much exercised with the *object* of faith.

12. The only plank between the believer and destruction is the blood of the Incarnate God.

13. A sense of God's love in the soul will make a man of a tender conscience.

14. Our gospel is a free-grace gospel; it is to him that 'worketh not, but believeth.'

15. The great secret of all happiness is knowing the way to the cross.

16. It is a great thing to live upon the blood; but I want *one* thing more; I want to live upon Him who shed it.

17. A whole-hearted sinner will never know anything of a full Christ.

18. Nothing darkens the soul like indulged sin.

19. The life of a natural man is one departure from God. He is not only not quite right; he is *altogether wrong.* Every step he takes is a step of departure farther from God.

20. There is not one sin we ever commit but has its effects upon our souls in after years.

21. It requires a whole Trinity to keep a saint of God.

22. A citizen of the New Jerusalem travelling home-wards, is our true standing and our real position; everything below that is below ourselves and our high calling.

23. It is the man of prayer that receives large communications from God.

24. Put all you have beside your dying bed; put all upon your coffin, and then weigh it.

25. My brother, do you and I know, to a certainty, that the Son of God shall not come this day? Do we know, to a certainty, that we shall not this day hear the trump of the archangel? Why was it said, eighteen hundred years ago, 'The coming of the Lord draweth nigh'? That men might watch for it; looking for the coming of the day of God.

JAMES (JOHN ANGELL).

BORN 1785—DIED 1859.

1. It is *by* faith, not *for* faith, that we are justified. Nothing can be a greater corruption of the truth than to represent *believing* as accepted instead of righteousness, or to be the righteousness that saves the sinner.

2. We have a modern *subjectivity* rising up, which aims to substitute an intuitional consciousness for simple faith, and to give us an inward light for the objective glory of the Sun of righteousness.

3. What are all thy sorrows, thy cares, and thy losses, viewed in the light of this happy condition? Tell me of thy poverty and many privations, I will reply, 'Yes; but then think of thy justification!' Tell me of thy disappointed hopes and blasted schemes; 'Yes, but thy justification!' Tell me of thy change of circumstances, and the painful contrast of the present with the past; 'Yes, but thy justification!' Tell me of thy friends departed, and thy now desolate condition; 'Yes, but thy justification!' Thus, to every tale of want or woe, when that tale comes from the lips of a believer in Christ, I will bring up that one sweet, soothing melody for the troubled spirit,—justification by faith.

4. Faith is a mightier conqueror of the world than even death. We shall do more to gain the victory by looking up into heaven than by looking down into the grave.

5. If *profiting* (not pleasing) is the end of *preaching*, how much of failure is perpetually going on !

6. Better, far better, not to speak at all, but go home in silence, than to enter upon all kinds of general conversation as soon as the service is over.

7. We do not think enough of Christ's second coming. What would be said of the wife who, when her husband was away in another country, could be happy without him, and be contented to think rarely of him. On the contrary, the loving wife longs for her husband's return. Oh, when will he come back ! is her frequent exclamation. Wife of the Lamb, church of the Saviour, where is thy waiting, hoping, longing for the second coming of thy Lord ? Is this *thy* blessed hope, as it was that of the primitive church. O Christian, are these not wanting here ? Every morsel of that bread thou eatest at the sacramental table, every drop of wine thou drinkest, is the voice of Christ saying to *thee*, I will come again, and receive you to myself ; and should draw forth thy longing desires, Come, Lord Jesus ; even so, come quickly.

8. The night is long, and dark, and stormy, but the morning must come ; and oh what a sunrise will it be !

9. Christian, why weepest thou ? Look up ! heaven is smiling above you ! Look on ! heaven is opening before you ! Let your tears, if they must fall, be as the drops of rain which fall in the sunshine, and reflect the colours of the rainbow. The last tear of earth will soon be wiped away, amid the first smile of heaven ; and that smile will be eternal.

10. If the man that trembles at death be a coward, he that trifles with it is a fool.

11. How little the writers of the New Testament say about death, compared with what they do about the heavenly glory ! It would seem as if they scarcely saw it, and as if it were lost amidst the blaze of the celestial splendour, and appeared only like a dark spot floating on the disc of the heavenly luminary !

12. It is a fearful thing to come to a deathbed with a religion so feeble as to leave the poor soul in dreadful doubt as to its state.

BICKERSTETH (EDWARD).

BORN 1786—DIED 1850.

1. The natural tendency of our hearts is ever to confound the Church and the world, and to make the lines between the two indistinct. One great purpose of the Scripture, that we may be guarded against so fatal a mistake, is to make the distinction manifest.

2. But oh how ungrateful have we been! Covetous and earthly-minded, selfish and worldly, proud, ambitious, full of vainglory, delighting in war and victory, and glorying over others; our iniquities in our own land, and in every land where we have gone, have been continually testifying against us, and filling up a fearful measure of guilt. England ought to be deeply humbled before God, instead of being lifted up with pride. Yet God has spared us, and preserved His church in the midst of us; and for its sake, and His great name's sake, He has delivered us from our foes even when we justly merited His wrath, and has blessed us that we may be a blessing. How often have our monarchs, our statesmen and our heroes, our Parliament and our whole country, been unfaithful to God! and how often has He revived us, by giving us faithful witnesses of His word to withstand error, and boldly testify His truth!

3. The church is in its preparation only for its future glory. The temple is only building, the lively stones are

only gathering, polishing, and finishing for their respective places. As soon as an individual Christian is mature, he is removed; the harvests of each season, as soon as they are ripe, are gathered in, and a fresh growth succeeds. We see, therefore, but indistinctly and partially the fulness of God's wisdom and love in all that He is doing. What will be the coming maturity? If the present truth be so precious, what will be the fulness of truth and glory in the day of Christ, when all the saints are gathered together in the glorified bodies of the resurrection, in the presence of Christ, when we shall see Him as He is, and know as we are known? Oh happy day, the Lord hasten it, and bring us each one to partake of it!

4. Glorious was the scene when Enoch was translated; or when Elijah's chariot of fire and horses of fire appeared in the whirlwind, and took him to his glory; yet more glorious was the scene, when, surrounded by His disciples, the risen Saviour slowly and majestically ascended. How unspeakably glorious, then, will be that full result of His resurrection and ascension, when, crowding from every country, in glorious resurrection-bodies shining as the sun, at one and the same moment, the myriads and myriads of His saints, of every age, are all gathered into his presence, where is fulness of joy, and are ever with the Lord!

5. O glorious state! unspeakably desirable! No sin, no curse, no death, no sorrow, no pain, no temptation; God Himself with us for ever, and our God: all holiness, all blessing, all life, all joy, all bliss, all victory and triumph for evermore! What a scene of glory must this be! Come, Lord Jesus, quickly come!

WOLFE (REV. C.).

BORN 1791—DIED 1823.

1. The gospel is a word in season to him that is weary; it speaks, therefore, to him that is weary; to him that is seeking rest and finding none; and to him it brings relief, refreshment, and repose.

2. The gospel finds you a bruised reed; it props and supports you. It finds you weeping; and it wipes away all tears from your eyes. It finds you fearful, cheerless, disquieted; and it gives you courage, hope, and tranquillity. There is a wilderness before it, and the garden of Eden behind. Before it is lamentation, and mourning, and woe; behind it come thanksgiving and the voice of melody.

3. How should even the innocent pleasures of life sink in your estimation, when you think of those pleasures that are at the right hand of God!

4. Where will you find a man that has not some thorn in his side?

5. To whom do our thoughts belong? On what objects do they delight to repose; and how many of them would you wish to conceal from the pure and everlasting gaze of your Creator?

6. Choose which master you will serve, mammon or God? Choose which wages you will receive, death or immortality? Think before you decide, which master loves you most, which would sacrifice most for you?

7. Times and seasons may change ; the everlasting gospel is still the same.

8. The burden of the man of the world is gathering as he proceeds ; that of the Christian is becoming lighter and more easy.

9. We are here in a state of education for heaven ; it should be nothing less than the business of an education.

10. The wicked thinks there is a chance that God may not be in earnest, and upon that chance he plunges in, body and soul.

11. How has God's mercy been shewn ? By visiting the sentence on sin to the uttermost. He did not fling us His mercy indolently from His throne ; but He executed sentence to the uttermost upon His only-begotten Son. His mercy does not consist in extinguishing His justice, but in executing it upon the head of the Son in whom He was well-pleased. Awful mercy ! Terrible forgiveness ! Mercy that we must not dare to trifle with !

12. Christ is " God manifest." He is the *Word*, God *heard;* the *light*, God *seen;* the *life*, God *felt*.

IRVING (EDWARD).

BORN 1792—DIED 1834.

1. I cannot help observing what an entireness this (Rev. xxii.) bespeaketh in the very words of Scripture, and how it confirmeth the doctrine of verbal inspiration.

2. This is my view of the Apocalypse. It was intended to be at once the chart, and the pole-star, and the light of the Christian church, over the stormy waves of time, until the Great Pilot who walketh upon the waters and stilleth the waves should again give Himself to the sinking ship, and make her His abode, His ark, His glory, for ever and ever.

3. God's glory is the one great object of a creature's being.

4. All that can be *felt* of God is in the Holy Ghost ; all that can be *known* of God is in the Son ; and all that *is* of God is in the Father.

5. The Faithful Witness is He who in the age to come shall cast the liar out of the earth, and the great lie out of creation.

6. Death is the seal of the fallen creature.

7. Christ is known to be very God, not because the names of very God are taken and applied to Him, but, which is far stronger, that the names applied to Him are the names taken and given to God.

8. This symbol of stars (Rev. i. 20) doth signify that

all true light is dispensed to the world by Christ's ministers, until the Sun of righteousness arise and eclipse them all with the glory of His light.

9. Christ wants love, and nothing less than love can please Him. He is troubled with the falling away of our love, and He laments over it. Man all over, even in His glory, He mourns over a brother's weaned affections, and He condescends to remonstrate with him on the subject. How beautiful, how sublime, is such condescension in God's Anointed One, who ever hath and holdeth the love of God, and of all elect angels, and of all glorified saints, thus to make His moan over His turtle-dove upon the earth ! My soul, be lifted up with admiration ; and learn thus lowly to entreat the love of the lowliest !

10. As it is Christ's personal office to inform and instruct His ministers, or to speak unto the angels of the churches, so it is the Spirit's personal office to speak unto the churches.

11. The Holy Spirit bindeth the churches : spirits of darkness bind the world.

12. The Holy Ghost cometh not with some indescribable influence to work some formless effect; but he doth come unto us for that same end for which he came unto the Virgin, in order to beget sons of God !

13. The world is drenched in guilt. The red waters of its guilt flow up unto the very lip, and in a few, few instants, shall overwhelm its life. In blood, in a deluge of blood, its height of hope shall be drowned, its star of hope quenched. The day is far spent. The night is at hand !

14. True humility doth not speak much of itself; but sitteth still, and listeneth and learneth.

15. You might as well think to change times and laws, and to reverse the stable ordinances of God, as think in your own strength to withstand Satan's assaults, or redeem your souls from his dominion; because it is the dominion of sin, whose strength is the law, whose constancy is the unchangeable God, who hath said, The soul that sinneth, it shall die. Can you say unto disease, Depart? Can you say to pain, Gnaw my vitals no more; or to sorrow, Poison my peace no longer, and no longer consume my verdure? Can you say to the clay-cold lips, Breathe upon me once more; or to the death-bound tongue, Speak to me again, that my soul may be comforted, and my hopes revived? Can you say to the grave, Give me back my dead, thou devouring grave; or to corruption, Feed not on my darling? Canst thou, O man, abrogate or reverse any one of these bitter stings which trouble thy soul's good condition from the cradle to the grave?

NEVINS.

BORN 1797—DIED 1835.

1. I feel that I must not only pray more, but *differently;* and that my praying more will not answer any good purpose, unless I also pray differently. I find that *quality* is to be considered in praying, as well as *quantity;* and, indeed, the former more than the latter.

2. It displeases God that we should be always dwelling on our wants, as if He had never supplied one of them. How do we know that God is not waiting for us to praise Him for a benefit He has already conferred, before He will confer on us that other which we may be now so earnestly desiring of Him?

3. Say you, ' I cannot trust myself'? But can you not trust Christ? If there is danger that you will prove faithless, yet, is there any danger that He will? It is because you are not to be trusted that you should trust Him, who is able to keep that which is committed to Him. If you trust Him for strength, you are as sure of being supplied, as of being pardoned, if you trust Him for that.

4. Yes, when saints become anxious, it is not long ere sinners become anxious. The inquiry of the three thousand on the day of Pentecost, ' Men and brethren, what shall we do?' was preceded by the inquiry of the one hundred and twenty who ' all continued with one accord in prayer and supplication.' Generally, I suppose, that is the *order.* First, saints inquire, and *then* sinners. And whenever in

any congregation, religion does not flourish, one principal reason of it is, that the saints are not inquiring.

5. Some sinners repent with an *unbroken* heart. They are *sorry*, and yet go on as did Pilate and Herod.

6. A sinner must *come to himself*, as did the prodigal, before ever he will come to Christ.

7. When a Christian backslides, it is as if the prodigal son had reacted his folly, and left his father's house a second time.

8. Some sinners lay down their burden elsewhere than at the feet of Jesus.

9. Human friends can weep with us when we weep; but Jesus is a friend, who, when He has wept with us, can wipe away all our tears.

10. Procrastination has been called a thief—the thief of time. I wish it were no worse than a thief. It is a murderer; and that which it kills is not time merely, but the immortal soul.

11. The obstacle in the way of the sinner's conversion possesses all the *force and invincibleness* of an *inability*, with all the *freeness and criminality* of an indisposition.

12. How many indulge a hope which they dare not examine!

13. If the mere delay of hope—hope deferred—makes the heart sick, what will the death of hope—its final and total disappointment—despair—do to it

14. Genuine benevolence is not stationary, but *peripatetic*. It *goeth* about doing good.

15. It is easier to do a great deal of mischief than to accomplish a little good.

VINET.

BORN 1797—DIED 1852.

1. Stripped of the great fact of expiation, and all that cluster of ideas connected with it, what, I ask, is Christianity?

2. The sensibility which frequently overflows in tears, often leaves in the heart a large place for selfishness.

3. It is absolutely impossible that a *true* religion should not present a great number of mysteries. It teaches more truths than all others; but each of these truths has a relation to the infinite, and, by consequence, borders on a mystery.

4. Mysteries multiply with discoveries. With each new day there is associated a new night. We purchase increase of knowledge with an increase of ignorance.

5. The things of the heart are not truly comprehended but by the heart.

6. Great souls pass through the world without being understood.

7. Christianity has not left to infidelity the satisfaction of being the first to tax it with folly. It has hastened to bring this accusation against itself. It has professed the bold design of saving men by a folly (1 Cor. i. 23).

8. Christianity is something more than an assemblage of dogmas; it is the principle of a new life.

9. Christianity has given to truth a dignity independent of time and numbers. It has required that truth should be believed and respected for itself.

10. Men believe so much in man, so much in numbers, so much in antiquity, and so little in truth! Christianity was designed to produce a race of men who should believe in truth, not in numbers, nor in years, nor in force; men, consequently, who should be ready to pass for fools.

11. Oh, then, let us daily ask God to form around us an immense void, in which we shall see nothing but Him,— a profound silence, in which we shall hear nothing but Him!

12. It is not known how difficult it is to believe in the midst of a crowd that does not believe.

13. Faith, which is the *vision* of the *invisible* and the *absent* brought *nigh*, is the energy of the soul and the energy of life. It is the point of departure for all action; since to act is to quit the firm position of the present, and stretch the hand into the future.

14. The greater part of men live by faith in powerful men. A small number of individuals lead the whole human race.

15. The cross, the triumph of grace, is the triumph of law.

16. We believe in the wreck of humanity (the fall); we believe that its unfortunate ship has perished; the remains of that great catastrophe float upon the waves.

17. The King of heaven can sign nothing but an

honourable peace. When He pardons, it cannot be at the expense either of His justice or His holiness. The honour of His government has suffered no stain.

18. Sages of the earth, Christ is the key of your problems, the completion of that philosophy which you resume without ceasing, but never finish ; troubled spirits, He is your peace ; lovers of wealth, He is your true treasure ; men, He is the word which solves the enigma of life, and conquers the power of death. He alone re-binds us to the author of our being, and to universal order.

HEWITSON.

BORN 1812—DIED 1850.

1. It is as sinful to doubt God's willingness to save me as to doubt His existence.

2. No amusement is innocent which takes away the soul from Jesus.

3. Our faith overcomes by identifying us with the Son of God.

4. No small part of meekness lies in waiting on the Spirit for strength to perform all our works unto the Lord.

5. May we, like Rahab, hang out the scarlet thread in the sight of the Lord, and, like her, be delivered from the overflowing scourge when it passes through.

6. How little I am like Jesus, who, when He walked on earth, was "in heaven;" who, as has been beautifully said, always repelled sin, but touched it at every point.

7. The warfare is hot; we need God's armour always, and *all* God's armour.

8. If we would let God's thoughts, as they are revealed in the word, come in and fill the chamber of our minds, how different our views and feelings would be regarding both God and ourselves; both His thoughts toward us, and our standing in His sight? What an ado unbelief sometimes stirs up within us, as if all were over! Were God's thoughts then to be let in, it would be like Jesus coming into the midst of the mourners, and saying,

Why make ye this ado, and weep? The damsel is not dead, but sleepeth. As the minstrels and other mourners are put out of the house by Jesus, so must *our thoughts* be put out of our hearts by God's thoughts. Then, all being still, the sweet voice of the Redeemer will be heard, Maid, arise!

9. The cross now, the crown to-morrow; now the bed of languishing, to-morrow the throne of Jesus.

10. I find that to say, *Come quickly*, is the result only of close walking with God.

11. Nothing but the blessed hope of Christ's glorious appearing, and of our being partakers of the glory when He appears, can draw us away from and lift us upward from among the temptations, and cares, and enjoyments of the present scene.

12. Rend, ye heavens, and give us back our Lord! Open, and let us in to our incorruptible inheritance.

13. These two facts, Christ dead, and Christ living, give us peace of conscience and participation in the life of God. Christ dead, is our all for pardon and peace; Christ living, is our all for life and holiness.

14. Yet a little while, and He will place the crown on your now oftentimes aching brow.

15. The morning is drawing on apace; the streaks of day-dawn are beginning to appear in the east.

16. Faith sees already the dawning light, the first streaks of day, on the tops of the eastern hills. Faith, not fancy, sees the Lord just on the point of leaving the right hand of the Father; and she raises her unheeded voice amid the sleeping, dreaming virgins, "Behold, He cometh with clouds!"

M'CHEYNE.

BORN 1813—DIED 1843.

1. It is all the gift of the sun, that the grass is of that refreshing green, and all the rivers are lines of waving blue. It is all the gift of the sun, that the flowers are tinged with their thousand glories; that the petal of the rose has its delicate blush, and the lily, that neither toils nor spins, has a brightness greater than Solomon's. Now, this is the way you may be justified. You are dark and vile in yourselves, but Christ's glory shall be seen in you.

2. Amazing love, that calls you to a feast (Prov. ix. 1-6), and not to hell!

3. When you lift up your eyes in hell, or when Jesus comes, you will cry, 'Lord, Lord;' but all diligence will then be too late. When the boat has left the shore, it is vain for you to run.

4. The way of salvation, by Jehovah our Righteousness, was sweet to Paul. His soul rested here with great delight. He came thus to God in secret, thus in public, thus in dying.

5. For every sin of yours, here is a stripe in Jesus. For the sins of infancy, here are the sufferings of His infancy; for the sins of youth, here are the sufferings of His youth; for the sins of manhood, here are the sufferings of His manhood.

6. His obedience is divine obedience. For your unholy life, here is His divinely holy life to cover you. Here are

His holy thoughts to cover your unholy thoughts; here His holy words to cover your unholy words; here are His holy actions to cover your unholy actions. There is something infinitely vast and glorious in the righteousness of God.

7. If Christ was sufficient for one sinner, then He must be sufficient for all. The great difficulty with God was, not how to admit *many* sinners into His favour, but how to admit *one* sinner. If that difficulty has been got over, then the whole has been got over.

8. I know that, if any of you have tasted the sweetness of Christ, you would be content to abide in Him for an eternity.

9. God's anger is like a river dammed up. It is getting higher and higher, fuller and deeper, every day.

10. Little children, if you would take Jesus for a Saviour, then you might carry all your griefs to Him; for Jesus knows what it is to be a little child.

11. God has an infinite sense of justice. His eyes behold the things that are equal. Now, when He sees the blood of His Son sprinkled on any soul, He sees that justice has had its full satisfaction in that soul; that that man's sins have been more fully punished than if he had borne them himself eternally.

12. If the word concerning Christ does not break your heart, it will make it as the nether millstone.

13. You will be incomplete Christians, if you do not look for the coming again of the Lord Jesus.

14. Soon we shall see Him as He is; then our trials shall be done. We shall reign with Him, and be entirely like Him. The angels will know us, by our very faces, to be brothers and sisters of Jesus.

POWERSCOURT (LADY).

DIED 1836.

1. It needs a great stretch of faith sometimes, when the enemy comes in like a flood, to believe that God is as much at peace with me, through Christ, as with those already above; that Abraham now in glory is not safer than I.

2. What simplicity there seemed to be in Christ's words after His resurrection! He seemed to enjoy the travail of His soul when distributing His peace.

3. It is worth being afflicted to become intimately acquainted with, and to learn to make use of, the chief among ten thousand, the altogether lovely.

4. The poor world may have a reprieve *here* from suffering, but the child of God may not, would not, if he might. Happy confidence; He will not keep back one needful stroke! Is it not strange that the moment He is acting most the part of a parent, is just the moment we are most apt to forget we are His children?

5. He is never more wounded in the house of His friends, than when they *murmur.* Nothing seems so to overcome His forbearance with the Israelites.

6. Let us come in the simplicity of sickness, in the helplessness of want; to trust is to be healed, to touch the hem of His garment is to be whole; but let us *keep touching* Him, for virtue is ever coming from Him.

7. Let us get well acquainted with our Physician ; let us take lodgings in His neighbourhood ; let us see Him every day.

8. We are not to *flee* from Satan, but to *resist*, that he may flee from us.

9. We have a right to wear a sweeter smile than even angels wear.

10. I am quite weary of this heart,—Satan's workshop, —always going on, hammer, hammer, hammer, stealing every grace given, to manufacture into some adornment for the ideal self.

11. It is underground work here ; our roots taking a firmer grasp of the Rock of Ages, in order to our springing up and flourishing in the courts of our God.

12. I believe the Lord explains the meaning of words by His providences.

13. He has shewn His love in trusting His cause to us, and lent us as volumes of His library for the perusal of the world.

14. Perilous times ! when Christians have time to play with idols ; have time to feast the world ; to nestle themselves as the world ; to go rounds of formality ; have time to pick faults in their neighbours, their brethren ; have time to amuse themselves with religious dissipation !

15. Angels know the bliss of power, *we* the happiness of weakness.

16. Blessed be God, His blood can cleanse us not only from all the evil that we see, but what *He* sees. Many chambers within are unopened yet to us. We see but through the crevice ; yet His blood gets entrance and drowns all.

17. Alas, what idolatry, what mockery, what mummery around me! May He quickly come and set all things in order, for this confusion is the earnest of hell!

18. From Scripture it seems to me that a minister's chief business commences instead of finishes when a soul is brought to life.

19. Having to reign with Christ we must come into the same school to learn to govern.

20. Our risen hands must not touch anything below accursed in Satan.

21. We are afraid of being *desperate Christians!* Oh, let us be desperate. The church needs extremity; a great *tug* out of the world.

22. Our kingdom is not from hence. We should be looking at earth as from heaven, instead of looking at heaven from earth, as though present things were already past, and future things already present.

23. What a thunderclap of hallelujah when all the prayers of all saints for our poor world, long, long laid up, shall all be answered in one event!

APPENDICES

BIOGRAPHICAL INFORMATION
(Added to this 1994 reprint)

ABBOT, GEORGE (1562-1633)   Page 125
Archbishop of Canterbury (1611) and leader in the reign of James I, Abbot lost favour on the accession of Charles I on account of his commitment to the Protestant and Calvinistic constitution of the Church of England.

ADAMS, THOMAS (1701-1784)   Page 266
Rector of the country parish of Wintringham, 1724-84, Adams would have been unknown to posterity had it not been for his evangelical conversion during his ministry and his consequent book, *Private Thoughts on Religion*.

A KEMPIS, THOMAS (1379-1471)   Page 53
Medieval Dutch mystic whose classic *On the Following* (or *Imitation) of Christ* (probably written 1415-1424), despite defective theology, has gone through over 6,000 editions because of the value of its main theme.

ATHANASIUS (*c.* 296-373)   Page 16
Bishop of Alexandria, Egypt, devoted his life, and suffered five exiles, for the resolute defence of the truth of Christ as God incarnate. His testimony and powerful writings against the Arians had a decisive influence.

AUGUSTINE OF HIPPO (354-430)　　　Page 32

The greatest theologian between Paul and Luther, Augustine was converted in 386 and became bishop of Hippo (N. Africa) in 396. His enormous influence upon subsequent church history came through his extensive writings. He showed that grace and faith, not free-will and works, lie at the heart of true Christianity although he inconsistently retained the Roman Catholic view of the church. See B. B. Warfield, *Studies in Tertullian and Augustine,* 1930.

BACON, FRANCIS (1561-1626)　　　Page 123

Rose to fame as a lawyer and parliamentarian in the reign of Elizabeth I and achieved higher honours under James I. Despite brilliant abilities, his public career was a failure and it was only in scientific and literary work that he became great.

BALE, JOHN (1495-1563)　　　Page 74

English Reformer and Bishop of Ossory (Ireland) in the reign of Edward VI. His *Select Works* were published by the Parker Society, 1849.

BASIL THE GREAT (*c.* 329-379)　　　Page 25

A leading anti-Arian theologian and bishop of Caesarea (370). In his greatest work, *De Spiritu Sancto,* he opposed low views of the Holy Spirit.

BATES, WILLIAM (1625-1699)　　　Page 208

Influential Puritan leader and preacher in London, known for his moderate principles and emphasis upon practical piety. Ejected from St Dunstan's in the West in 1662, he later ministered at Hackney.

BAXTER, RICHARD (1615-1691)★[1]   Page 194

Minister at Kidderminster, Worcestershire (1641-1660), Baxter sprang to fame with his *Saints' Everlasting Rest,* 1650. A popular Puritan preacher, he was silenced in 1662 and thereafter, living in or about London, he devoted his time to writing. Most of his best material appears in his *Practical Works* (4 vols., Soli Deo Gloria, 1991).

BERNARD OF CLAIRVAUX (*c.* 1091-1153)   Page 42

French monastic figure and church-leader in the early medieval tradition. His spiritual writings remain as one of the few lights in an otherwise dark century.

BERRIDGE, JOHN (1716-1793)   Page 280

The bachelor and partly-eccentric Vicar of Everton, Bedfordshire (1755-93), who became a bold, uncompromising evangelist after fruitless years when he had preached 'salvation partly by faith and partly by works'. His epitaph, composed by himself, describes him as 'An Itinerant Servant Of Jesus Christ, Who Loved His Master And His Work, And After Running On His Errands Many Years, Was Called Up To Wait On Him Above'.

BEVERIDGE, WILLIAM (1638-1707)   Page 232

Anglican theologian who, in a period of growing apostasy, maintained a clear evangelical witness which was perpetuated in his writings. He was Bishop of Asaph from 1704.

---

[1] ★Names thus marked are authors whose books (or books on whom) have been or are currently being published by the Trust. See pp. 382-384.

BICKERSTETH, EDWARD (1786-1850)   Page 336
Anglican preacher, author and hymn-writer who, almost
from his ordination in 1815, threw his energies into the
support of many evangelical and Protestant agencies,
especially the Church Missionary Society. Many of his
sixteen books enjoyed wide popularity.

BINNING, HUGH (1627-1653)   Page 206
Professor at Glasgow University at the age of 18, he was
ordained at 22 and died at 25. Few Scots Christians have
exercised such an influence in such a brief life. Though of
'prodigious learning' Binning lived according to his dying
words, 'One line of the Bible is worth more than all human learning' (See his *Works,* reprinted by Soli Deo Gloria).

BOOTH, ABRAHAM (1734-1806)   Page 298
Baptist pastor of the Prescott St. Church, London, from
1768 to his death, Booth by example and by his writings
demonstrated that Calvinistic orthodoxy could be com-
bined with evangelistic zeal.

BOSTON, THOMAS (1676-1732)★   Page 259
Scots evangelical pastor in the remote parish of Ettrick
(from 1707) whose name became familiar throughout
Scotland for his writings, especially *Human Nature in its
Fourfold State.* His autobiography (Banner of Truth reprint,
1988) is a classic.

BRADFORD, JOHN (*c.* 1510-1555)★   Page 90
Called to the ministry of the Word early in the reign of
Edward VI, Bradford soon became one of the King's six
itinerant chaplains. His preaching was especially used in

Lancashire and Manchester (his birthplace). Imprisoned for his fearless Protestantism under Mary Tudor, he was burned to death on July 1, 1555 when he 'endured the flame as a fresh gale of wind in a hot summer's day'. The two volumes of his *Works* (Banner of Truth reprint, 1979) are among the most valuable and popular of all the writings of the English Reformers.

BRAINERD, DAVID (1718-1747)★ Page 286
Missionary to the North American Indians who died at the age of twenty-nine in the home of Jonathan Edwards at Northampton. Edwards' *Life of Brainerd* became one of the most influential of all missionary biographies.

BROOKS, THOMAS (1608-1680)★ Page 199
Puritan pastor in London, ejected in 1662. 'Of all the Puritans he is the most readable if we except John Bunyan' (C. H. Spurgeon).

BROWN, JOHN (1785-1858)★ Page 329
United Presbyterian minister, famous for his work in Rose Street and Broughton Place congregations in Edinburgh (1822-58). His expository preaching (of which nine works on the New Testament were published) constituted, in the words of William Cunningham, 'a marked era in the history of scriptural interpretation in this country'. His dying words affirmed that he was 'wonderfully well'.

BROWN, JOHN (of Haddington) (1722-1787)★ Page 288
Grandfather of the above and a leader in the Secession Church. The British Museum contains twenty-six editions of his *Self-Interpreting Bible*.

BROWNE, SIR THOMAS (1605-1682)   Page 175
After graduating at Oxford (M.A., 1629) Brown studied
medicine on the Continent and then, from 1637, lived
quietly at Norwich where he was knighted by Charles II
in 1671. His *Religio Medici* was said to be his greatest work.
A number of his Tracts appeared after his death.

BUCHOLTZER, ABRAHAM (1529-1584)   Page 103
A Lutheran theologian who pastored several German
churches.

BULLINGER, JOHANN HEINRICH (1504-1575)   Page 84
Swiss Reformer and successor to Zwingli in Zurich.
Through his writings and contacts with English exiles he
exercised considerable influence upon the English Reformation. Four volumes of his *Decades* were published by
the Parker Society, 1849-52.

BUNYAN, JOHN (1628-1688)★   Page 212
Baptist pastor at Bedford where he suffered twelve years
imprisonment for nonconformity. His *Pilgrim's Progress*
(1678) is said to be translated into more languages than any
book except the Bible, but Bunyan's other writings are
also of great value.

BURGESS, ANTHONY (d. 1664)   Page 237
Member of the Westminster Assembly and minister of
Sutton Coldfield, Warwickshire, from 1635 to the Great
Ejection of 1662. Author of Puritan volumes of outstand-
ing worth (and strangely overlooked by nineteenth century
publishers) dealing with Justification, Original Sin,
Assurance and the Law of God.

CALAMY, EDMUND (1600-1666)   Page 157
Westminster divine and, as minister of St Mary
Aldermanbury (1639-62), one of the most prominent of
the London Puritans. Declined a bishopric and suffered
under Charles II.

CALVIN, JOHN (1509-1564)★   Page 88
The last of the Continental leaders of the Reformation
who, though spending almost his entire ministry at
Geneva, was 'the one international reformer'. He com-
bines profundity with simplicity, and doctrinal grasp with
close attention to careful exegesis. Few other theologians
of the past continue to have such a wide readership at the
present time.

CARYL, JOSEPH (1602-1673)   Page 171
Prominent Westminster divine and Puritan pastor who is
best remembered today for his 500 sermons on Job, delivered over twenty-four years, although their publication has
never been repeated since 1676.

CECIL, RICHARD (1748-1810)★   Page 302
Prominent Anglican evangelical leader who ministered in
London from 1780 to his death and was a founding member of the Eclectic Society (an evangelical fraternal) which
met fortnightly in his vestry.

CHALMERS, THOMAS (1780-1847)   Page 323
'The chief Scottish man of his time' (Thomas Carlyle),
who as a preacher and teacher of students exercised
enormous influence. First moderator of the Free Church
of Scotland on the Disruption of 1843. His works run to
twenty-four volumes.

CHARNOCK, STEPHEN (1628-1680)*   Page 214
One of many to be converted while at Emmanuel
College, Cambridge, he later served in London, Oxford
and Ireland. Silenced in 1660 he was joint pastor with
Thomas Watson from 1675. His lecture-sermons on *The
Existence and Attributes of God,* published posthumously,
'are one of the noblest productions of the Puritan epoch'
(J. I. Packer).

CHAUCER, GEOFFREY (*c.* 1340-1400)   Page 50
Foremost English poet of the Middle Ages who gave much
of his life to the service of the King but did his finest
literary work amid the troubles of later life when he had
fallen from favour. His (unfinished) *Canterbury Tales*
portrays the life of his times.

CHEMNITZ, MARTIN (1522-1586)   Page 101
The most eminent Lutheran theologian of the second half
of the 16th century. Librarian at Konigsberg; lecturer at
Wittenberg; then preacher at Brunswick (from 1554),
where he died.

CHRYSOSTOM, JOHN (*c.* 347-407)   Page 30
Bishop of Constantinople and greatest preacher of the Greek
church, his work was characterised by love for Scripture,
missionary zeal and fearless reformation of morals. On
account of the latter he was twice exiled by the Empress
Eudoxia, whose son brought his body back to Constantinople for re-burial thirty-one years after his death.

CLEMENT OF ALEXANDRIA (*c.* 155-*c.* 220)   Page 8
Christian philosopher who taught at Alexandria. While a

Christian apologist, and an opponent of Gnosticism, Clement's understanding of Scripture was affected by Platonic and Stoic ideas.

CLEMENT OF ROME (*fl. c.* 90-100)   Page 1
A leading member and presbyter in the church at Rome towards the end of the first century. Numerous writings have been attributed to him but the only genuine one is an Epistle to the Corinthians.

COLERIDGE, SAMUEL TAYLOR (1772-1834) Page 316
Poet, critic and philosopher who, with William Wordsworth, inaugurated a literary revival at the beginning of the 19th century. Speculative and original rather than controlled by Scripture, Coleridge is Christian only in the broadest sense of the word.

COOPER, THOMAS (1517-1594)   Page 94
Vice-Chancellor of Oxford before becoming Bishop of Lincoln (1570) and Bishop of Winchester. 'Much noted for his learning and sanctity of life', his work against the Roman Catholic mass was reprinted by the Parker Society.

CRADOCK, WALTER (*c.* 1610-1659)   Page 166
Foremost Welsh preacher and evangelist of the mid-17th century. 'The enemies of religion throughout North Wales for a hundred and fifty years afterwards were accustomed to call all serious people, *Cradockians*' (T. Rees, 1883).

CRANMER, THOMAS (1489-1556)   Page 71
Archbishop of Canterbury, and cautious architect of the reformation in the Church of England, he was finally

martyred for his evangelical witness to the truth of Scripture.

CRISP, TOBIAS (1600-1643)   Page 161

Rector of Brinkworth, Wiltshire (1627-41), whose vigorously-worded sermons, published posthumously, occasioned repeated controversies on Antinomianism. Crisp over-reacted to the legalistic strain of his early ministry and at times jeopardised orthodoxy by loose and unguarded statements on the freeness of divine grace.

CYPRIAN (*c.* 200-258)   Page 13

Latin church father who, though converted from paganism little more than a dozen years before his martyrdom, exercised wide influence as Bishop of Carthage and, more permanently, through his prolific writings.

DAVENANT, JOHN (1576-1641)   Page 137

Lady Margaret Professor of Divinity at Cambridge and Bishop of Salisbury from 1621 to his death. His *Exposition of Colossians* has been his most enduring work.

DE VALENTIA, JACOBI (1468-1491)   Page 63

Nothing is known about this fifteenth-century figure.

DENT, ARTHUR (?-1607)   Page 108

Rector of South Shoebury, Essex from 1580 to his death. One of the early Puritans and persecuted for nonconformity, he was author of the widely read, *The Plain Man's Path-way to Heaven* (1601). With his last breath he repeated the text, 'I have seen an end of all perfection, but thy law is exceeding broad'.

DICKSON, DAVID (1583-1663)★   Page 142
Scottish church leader. 'Few that lived in his day were more honoured to be instruments of conversion than he' (Wodrow). After 23 years' ministry at Irvine, Ayrshire, he served, successively, as professor of divinity in Glasgow and Edinburgh.

EDWARDS, JONATHAN (1703-1758)★   Page 289
Preacher, theologian and apologist for the Great Awakening, whose ministry at Northampton, Massachusetts, was followed by labours among the Indians. Edwards remains the most useful and widely read of all the authors of colonial America.

EPHRAEM THE SYRIAN (*c.* 306-379)   Page 21
A leading scholar of the Syriac-speaking church, he wrote several commentaries on Scripture. He was a popular preacher, hymn-writer and poet, nicknamed 'the lyre of the Holy Spirit'.

ERASMUS, DESIDERIUS (1467-1536)   Page 61
Scholar and humanist who pioneered a return to the plain sense of Scripture and by his publication of the Greek New Testament (1516) was a leading instrument of the Reformation. But he wanted reform without disunity or, in Luther's phrase, he wished to walk on eggs without breaking them. He had neither the resolution nor the doctrinal grasp to be a reformer himself.

ERSKINE, EBENEZER (1680-1754)   Page 261
Scots evangelical pastor who, deposed from the Church of Scotland ministry for opposing patronage, became the

founder of the Secession Church. His sermons were once among the most popular titles in Scottish literature.

EVANS, JOHN (1680-1730)   Page 331
Successor to Dr Daniel Williams, he became an eloquent and popular preacher in Westminster. Doddridge's *Rise and Progress* is said to be influenced by a work by Evans.

FENELON, FRANÇOIS de SALIGNAC
de la MOTHE (1651-1715)   Page 244
French Roman Catholic Archbishop of Cambrai who was on the side of orthodoxy in the Jansenist controversy. His defence of Madame Guyon illustrated his sympathies; his preaching against worldly glory offended the King; but his submission to the Papacy in controversy was indicative of a major failure in his thinking.

FISHER, EDWARD (*c.* 1601-1655)   Page 180
A member of the Guild of Barber-Surgeons and of a Presbyterian church in London whose book *The Marrow of Modern Divinity* (London, 1645) was largely compiled from Reformed and Puritan authors. Its republication in Scotland in 1718 was the occasion of a controversy which quickened the life of Scottish pulpits.

FLAVEL, JOHN (1627-1691)*   Page 210
Puritan preacher who spent almost his entire ministry (from 1650) in Devon. His writings, certainly among the most valuable left by the Puritans, show why his work was so greatly blessed. Archibald Alexander, first Professor of Theology at Princeton Theological Seminary, was converted through reading Flavel.

FLEMING, ROBERT (1630-1694)   Page 216
Trained at St Andrews under Samuel Rutherford, Fleming
was serving his first pastoral charge at Cambuslang when
the persecuting reign of Charles II began. Silenced, and
for a time imprisoned, he went into exile in Holland
in the late 1670s and became minister of the Scots congregation at Rotterdam. His best-known publication was
the *Fulfilling of the Scriptures*.

FOSTER, JOHN (1770-1843)   Page 314
English nonconformist minister who was more effective
with his pen than in the pulpit. His *Essays* and *Reviews*
were widely read by his contemporaries.

FOXE, JOHN (1516-1587)   Page 92
Converted in the latter years of the reign of Henry VIII,
in exile under Mary Tudor, Foxe was a friend of many
of the reformers and the great work of his life became
his record of ancient and contemporary Christian history
published in his *Book of Martyrs* (1563, enlarged 1570)
—a work chained to the reading desk in every parish
church by order of Queen Elizabeth.

FRASER OF BREA, JAMES (1639-1699)   Page 235
A Covenanting divine who suffered imprisonment and exile
for his faith. He wrote a treatise on justifying faith which
went through many editions.

FULGENTIUS (468-533)   Page 34
Bishop of Ruspe in North Africa. Strongly Augustinian in
theology, he wrote and preached against the errors of Arius
and Pelagius.

GOODWIN, THOMAS (1600-1680)★   Page 155
One of the eminent Puritan divines and leader of the
Dissenting Brethren, whose views he represented at the
Westminster Assembly. His books have often been reprinted.

GRAY, ANDREW (1633-1656)   Page 222
The ministry of this Scottish divine lasted only three years,
but made a deep impression. His printed sermons proved
popular long after his death.

GREGORY OF NAZIANZUS (330-389)   Page 23
Gregory was known as 'the Theologian' for his sturdy
defence of the orthodox Trinitarian faith against the Arians
and others. His oratory and eloquence made him a compelling preacher.

GREGORY THE GREAT (540-604)   Page 37
A formidable pope, he ranks as one of the four original
'Doctors of the Church'. His *Dialogues* simplified the
doctrines in Augustine's *City of God* and proved very
influential.

GUALTER, RODOLPHUS (1519-1586)   Page 99
Swiss Reformer and son-in-law of Zwingli. He succeeded
Bullinger as pastor at Zurich. His commentaries were highly
esteemed.

GUYON, JEANNE MARIE BOUVIER
de la MOTHE (1648-1717)   Page 241
A French Quietist and devotional writer who was prone
to the errors of mysticism. Her works include 'A little bird
I am', a beautiful poem written in prison.

HALDANE, ROBERT (1764-1842)★ Page 312
A Scottish evangelist, writer and philanthropist. His teaching on the Epistle to the Romans occasioned revival in Europe and his commentary on that epistle is his abiding memorial.

HALE, SIR MATTHEW (1600-1676) Page 159
Lord Chief Justice of England (1671-1676). He was a member of the Westminster Assembly and a friend of Richard Baxter.

HALL, JOSEPH (1574-1656) Page 134
He represented James I at the Synod of Dort and later became Bishop of Norwich. His devotional works are his best.

HALL, ROBERT (1764-1831) Page 310
An English Baptist minister whose fame rests largely on his pulpit oratory.

HALYBURTON, THOMAS (1674-1712) Page 255
A champion of Reformed truth and regarded as one of Scotland's greatest theologians. His *Memoirs* have often been reprinted.

HAMILTON, PATRICK (1503-1528) Page 82
Zealous for the biblical truth that Luther had rediscovered, Hamilton became the proto-martyr of the Scottish Reformation. He was burnt in St Andrews for his testimony to Christ.

HENRY, MATTHEW (1662-1714) Page 251
Presbyterian minister and famous biblical exegete. His

Exposition of the Old and New Testaments is a devotional classic.

HERBERT, GEORGE (1593-1633)	Page 153
Early Anglo-Catholic priest and poet. 'The King of Love my Shepherd is' is one of his abidingly popular hymns.

HERVEY, JAMES (1714-1758)	Page 273
A devotional writer of gentle spirit. His *Theron and Aspasio* proved significant. William Romaine preached his funeral sermon.

HEWITSON, W. H. (1812-1850)	Page 348
A minister of profound thought, fervour and piety, well captured in *Select Letters and Remains* (1853, ed. John Baillie).

HILDEBERT (1056-1133)	Page 39
Hildebert is famous chiefly for his literary works in excellent Latin. A powerful preacher, he became Archbishop of Tours.

HILL, SIR RICHARD (1732-1808)	Page 294
An M.P. and a controversialist, he championed the Calvinistic Methodist cause. Rowland Hill, the preacher, was his brother.

HOOKER, RICHARD (c.1554-1600)	Page 113
'The judicious Hooker' was an accomplished apologist for the Church of England against the Puritans. His *Laws of Ecclesiastical Polity* is his magnum opus.

HORNE, GEORGE (1730-1792)	Page 292
Bishop of Norwich. Though a High Churchman, he had

sympathies with John Wesley and his Methodists in their zeal.

HORSLEY, SAMUEL (1733-1806)   Page 296
Held different Anglican bishoprics. A High Churchman who strongly defended orthodox views of the Trinity and of Christ's deity.

HOWE, JOHN (1630-1705)   Page 219
English nonconformist minister who strove in vain to promote unity among Presbyterians and Independents.

HOWELLS, WILLIAM (1778-1832)   Page 318
A Church of England preacher whose evangelical sermons gave him a wide popularity.

HUME, ALEXANDER (1560-1609)   Page 120
A Scottish clergyman with Puritan convictions who was also a poet and hymnwriter.

HUS, JOHN (1373-1415)   Page 56
Czech reformer, preacher and theologian. Hus insisted on the Bible's unique authority and Christ's Lordship over the Church. He suffered at the stake for his faith.

IGNATIUS (*c.* 40-107)   Page 3
Bishop of Antioch and called 'the Godbearer'. He wrote seven famous letters to churches attacking heresy. He 'attained to God' by execution in Rome.

IRENAEUS (*c.* 130-*c.* 200)   Page 5
Bishop of Lyons. As a boy, Irenaeus heard Polycarp preach.

His claim to fame rests on his *Against Heresies.*

IRVING, EDWARD (1792-1834)★   Page 340
Eloquent Scottish minister at one time assistant to Dr
Thomas Chalmers. Having adopted 'charismatic' views
and error on Christ's person, he was excommun-
icated and became a deacon in the Catholic Apostolic
Church.

JAMES, JOHN ANGELL (1785-1859)★   Page 333
Independent minister of Carr's Lane Chapel, Birmingham.
His best-known book is *The Anxious Enquirer.*

JANEWAY, JAMES (1636-1674)   Page 227
Ejected by the Act of Uniformity of 1662, he became a
very popular preacher in Rotherhithe, London.

JEROME (*c.* 345-*c.* 419)   Page 27
Attracted by the ascetic monastic life, Jerome became a
biblical scholar of linguistic brilliance. His greatest triumph
was his Latin *Vulgate.*

JONES, THOMAS (1754-1837)   Page 304
For nearly forty years the minister of Lady Glenorchy's
chapel, Edinburgh. Thomas Chalmers wrote of Jones's 'habitual excellence in the pulpit'. His collected *Sermons* (1816)
indicate something of his vivid, powerful preaching.

KNOX, JOHN (*c.* 1514-1572)★   Page 86
A Christian leader of strong conviction and enormous
courage, Knox proved to be the principal theologian and
architect of the Reformed Kirk of Scotland.

LATIMER, HUGH (1485-1555)   Page 66
Bishop of Worcester. He won fame as a vigorous preacher
who sealed his testimony at the stake in Oxford in 1555.

LEIGH, EDWARD (1602-1671)   Page 173
A member of the Westminster Assembly and an M.P. for
eight years. His writings are mainly compilations.

LEIGHTON, ROBERT (1611-1684)   Page 188
Archbishop of Glasgow. He is best remembered for his
notable commentary on First Peter.

LINDSAY, DAVID (*c.* 1570-1627)   Page 132
Presbyterian divine who ministered in Scotland and wrote
several books.

LOCKYER, NICHOLAS (1611-1685)   Page 183
A fervent Puritan divine who frequently preached to the
House of Commons and became a chaplain of Cromwell.
Ejected in 1662, he went to Rotterdam.

LOVE, JOHN (1757-1825)   Page 306
Presbyterian divine who helped to found the London
Missionary Society in 1795. Nearly all his publications were
posthumous.

LUTHER, MARTIN (1483-1546)   Page 68
The great German reformer who rediscovered the New
Testament gospel and broke the power of the Roman
Church. He translated the Bible into German.

MACARIUS THE EGYPTIAN (301-391)   Page 18
Called 'the Elder' or 'the Great', Macarius was extremely

ascetic and lived for sixty years with a colony of monks in the Egyptian desert.

M'LAURIN, JOHN (1693-1754)   Page 263
Profound and eloquent Presbyterian theologian and evangelical leader. He was very active in social work, including financial help to the impoverished Jonathan Edwards.

M'CHEYNE, ROBERT MURRAY
(1813-1843)★   Page 350
'The saintly M'Cheyne' devoted all the energies of his short life to preaching Christ. Andrew Bonar's *Life and Remains of Robert Murray M'Cheyne* is a classic.

MARSHALL, WALTER (1628-1680)   Page 229
Presbyterian divine ejected in 1662. His chief work, *The Gospel Mystery of Sanctification*, proved immensely popular.

MEDE, JOSEPH (1586-1638)   Page 144
Great English biblical scholar of encyclopaedic knowledge. His expository fame rests on his *Clavis Apocalyptica,* a premillennial study which had profound influence.

MELANCHTHON, PHILIP (1497-1560)   Page 77
German Reformer and Lutheran humanist. He systematised Luther's teachings and was mainly responsible for the Augsburg Confession.

MESTREZAT, JEAN (1592-1657)   Page 150
A learned theologian and excellent preacher, he was one of the pillars of the French Reformed Church. He preached a famous series of sermons on Hebrews.

MILNER, JOSEPH (1744-1797)   Page 300
An ardent evangelical clergyman, he became a popular
preacher. His best known work is his *History of the Church
of Christ*.

MILTON, JOHN (1608-1674)   Page 177
Famous English poet and controversialist. In his *Paradise
Lost,* the finest flower of humanism in English literature,
he sought to 'justify the ways of God to man'.

NETTLETON, ASAHEL (1783-1844)★   Page 325
A New England evangelist of note with a single-minded
zeal for souls. Hundreds were converted under his ministry. He opposed the doctrine of conversion taught by
Charles Finney and the New Haven theology, in part
because it would be 'calamitous to revivals'.

NEVINS, WILLIAM (1797-1835)   Page 343
Educated at Yale and Princeton Theological Seminary,
Nevins served the First Presbyterian Church, Baltimore
from 1820 to his death at the age of 37. His *Select Remains*
(New York, 1836) show his character and work to have
been similar to that of R. M. M'Cheyne.

NEWTON, JOHN (1725-1807)★   Page 290
A converted slave-trader who became an Anglican clergy-
man. Newton wrote such popular hymns as 'Amazing
Grace' and 'How sweet the name of Jesus sounds'.

OWEN, JOHN (1616-1683)★   Page 196
Widely regarded as the greatest English theologian of all
time. He became Vice-Chancellor of Oxford University

and was a member of the Savoy Conference (1658). Owen wrote voluminously and much of his work is still in print.

PALEARIO, AONIO (1500-1570)   Page 79
One of the most prominent humanists of his age. He was declared a heretic for his writings and burnt at Rome.

PASCAL, BLAISE (1623-1662)   Page 204
Eminent mathematician, thinker and theologian. His *Thoughts* is an apologetic classic. He emphasised God's grace alone as the basis of salvation.

PAYSON, EDWARD (1783-1827)   Page 327
Congregational minister in Portland, Maine. Of deep spirituality, his printed sermons made him one of the best-known of last-century American preachers.

PEARSON, JOHN (1613-1686)   Page 186
Bishop of Chester. An erudite and profound divine, author of *Expositions of the Creed,* he championed episcopacy at the Savoy Conference.

PERKINS, WILLIAM (1558-1602)   Page 117
Noted English Puritan preacher and pastor at Cambridge. He was one of the founders of the tradition of English practical divinity.

PETRARCH, FRANCESCO (1304-1374)   Page 46
Early Italian poet and scholar, and 'the Father of Humanism'. He tried to reconcile piety with the love of the world.

PICTET, BENEDICT (1655-1724) Page 246
Swiss theologian who wrote valuable controversial, doctrinal and devotional works.

PIKE, SAMUEL (1717-1773) Page 283
An Independent minister. One of the Tuesday lecturers at Pinner's Hall who later embraced Sandemanian views.

POWERSCOURT, LADY (d. 1836) Page 352
Pious, Dublin-based aristocrat known principally for the collection of her *Letters and Papers* which was published two years after her death.

QUARLES, FRANCIS (1592-1644) Page 147
English religious poet. He is best remembered for his *Divine Emblems* (1635), derived in part from Jesuit sources.

QUESNEL, PASQUIER (1634-1719) Page 225
French Jansenist theologian whose views were condemned by Pope Clement XI. His works emphasised the value of close study of the Bible in increasing true devotion.

RALEIGH, SIR WALTER (1552-1618) Page 110
Famous English soldier, courtier, explorer and man of letters. He was beheaded on a charge of conspiracy.

ROLLOCK, ROBERT (1555-1599) Page 115
First Principal of Edinburgh University. A powerful and learned preacher, the author of many books.

ROMAINE, WILLIAM (1714-1795) Page 275
A warm evangelical Calvinist and friend of Whitefield.

Romaine was a compelling preacher who attracted large crowds. He is best known for his *The Life, Walk and Triumph of Faith*.

RUTHERFORD, SAMUEL (1600-1661)★   Page 164
Pre-eminent in Scotland as a theologian and pastor. Most of his famous *Letters*, devotional classics, were written from prison.

SANDYS, EDWIN (1516?-1588)   Page 96
A fervent and learned Archbishop of York who opposed Romanism. He helped to translate the Bishops' Bible.

SAVONAROLA, HIERONYMUS (1452-1498)   Page 58
Italian preacher and reformer. Excommunicated for denouncing papal corruptions, he was hanged as a 'schismatic and heretic'.

SCHIMMELPENNINCK, MARY ANNE
(1778-1856)   Page 320
An author greatly influenced by Pascal. She abandoned Quakerism for Moravianism.

SHEPHERD, THOMAS (1665-1739)   Page 253
Shepherd abandoned the Church of England for an Independent pastorate. His publications were chiefly sermons but included some hymns still in common use.

SIBBES, RICHARD (1577-1635)★   Page 140
'The heavenly Dr Sibbes' succeeded Thomas Goodwin as curate of Holy Trinity, Cambridge. This Puritan divine's many works have often been reprinted. It was said

that 'Heaven was in him before he was in heaven'.

STEWART, ALEXANDER (1764-1821)   Page 308
Scots minister in the Highland parish of Moulin
(1786-1805), where he became a living Christian through
a visit of Charles Simeon in 1796 and saw a revival in 1800.
From the parish of Dingwall (1805-1819) he retired to
Edinburgh. The parents of Alexander Duff, missionary to
India, were among those influenced by his ministry at
Moulin.

SUPERVILLE, DANIEL (1657-1728)   Page 248
A Protestant theologian who ministered very acceptably
in Rotterdam.

SUTTON, CHRISTOPHER (1565-1629)   Page 128
A Canon of Westminster, then of Lincoln. His devotional
books, written with much fervour, enjoyed great popularity.

TAULER, JOHANNES (*c.* 1300-1361)   Page 44
A German Dominican mystic who preached homely,
practical sermons with popular appeal. He was highly
esteemed by Luther.

TAYLOR, JEREMY (1613-1667)   Page 191
Anglican bishop and writer, called 'the Spenser of prose'
(Coleridge). He is now best remembered for his *Holy
Living* (1650) and *Holy Dying* (1651).

TERTULLIAN (*c.* 160-*c.* 220)   Page 11
Brilliant theologian of the patristic period who elucidated

Trinitarian and Christological doctrines. He became a Montanist.

TRAPP, JOHN (1601-1669)   Page 169
'Oh, rare John Trapp!' (Spurgeon). He wrote a commentary on the Bible marked by scholarship, industry and humour. He was also one of the prime preachers of his time.

TRELCATIUS OF LEYDEN (1542-1602)   Page 105
Wrote *A Brief Institution of the Common Places of Sacred Divinity* which includes a rejoinder to Cardinal Bellarmine.

VINET, ALEXANDRE RUDOLPHE (1797-1847)   Page 345
Swiss theologian who was Professor of Theology at Lausanne. He stressed personal experience, a good conscience and moral conduct.

WATSON, THOMAS (d. 1686)*   Page 239
A man of considerable learning, he achieved fame and popularity as vicar of St Stephen's, Walbrook. He wrote prolifically in a lucid, homely and graphic style. His best known work is his *Body of Practical Divinity.*

WATTS, ISAAC (1674-1748)   Page 257
Evangelical leader in the difficult period between the Puritans and the Evangelical Revival. He is best remembered for popular hymns such as 'When I survey the wondrous cross'.

WESLEY, JOHN (1703-1791)   Page 271
Founder of Arminian Methodism. A man of great courage

and organising ability, he evangelised very widely in the open air. His *Journals* is a classic.

WHITEFIELD, GEORGE (1714-1770)★ Page 277
Unrivalled preacher of great eloquence and passion, Whitefield was indefatigable in preaching in the United Kingdom and America.

WILCOX, THOMAS (1622-1687) Page 201
Little is known about this seventeenth-century divine despite being the author of the popular tract *A Choice Drop of Honey from the Rock Christ*.

WOLFE, CHARLES (1791-1823) Page 338
Irish poet and curate. He is remembered almost solely for his famous lines on the burial of Sir John Moore.

WYCLIFFE, JOHN (*c.* 1329-1384) Page 48
'The Morning Star of the Reformation'. A brilliant scholar, he castigated clerical immorality and Roman abuses, holding the Bible to be the only guide for faith and practice.

AUTHORS REPRINTED

The following authors in the present volume
have been republished by the Banner of Truth Trust
and most remain currently in print

BAXTER, RICHARD
  The Reformed Pastor.
BOSTON, THOMAS
  Memoirs of Thomas Boston;
  Human Nature in its Fourfold State.
BRADFORD, JOHN
  The Writings of John Bradford.
BRAINERD, DAVID
  See *The Diary of David Brainerd* in *The Works of Jonathan*
  Edwards, Vol. 2.
BROOKS, THOMAS
  The Works of Thomas Brooks;
  Heaven On Earth; Precious Remedies.
BROWN, JOHN of Edinburgh
  Discourses and Sayings of Our Lord.
  Commentaries on: *Hebrews; 1 Peter; 2 Peter, Chapter 1.*
BROWN, JOHN of Haddington
  See *John Brown of Haddington*, by Robert Mackenzie.
BUNYAN, JOHN
  The Works of John Bunyan.
CALVIN, JOHN
  Sermons on Deuteronomy; Sermons on 2 Samuel; Sermons
  on Job; Sermons on Ephesians; Sermons on Timothy & Titus.
  Commentaries on: *Genesis; Jeremiah & Lamentations;*
  Daniel; Hosea; Joel, Amos & Obadiah; Jonah, Micah &
  Nahum; Habakkuk, Zephaniah & Haggai; Zechariah &
  Malachi.

NETTLETON, ASAHEL

See *The Life and Labours of Asahel Nettleton,* by B. Tyler
& A. Bonar.

NEWTON, JOHN

The Works of John Newton;

The Letters of John Newton.

See *The Thought of the Evangelical Leaders: Notes on the
Eclectic Society (John Newton and Anglican Evangelicals),*
edited by J. H. Pratt.

OWEN, JOHN

The Complete Works of John Owen;

The Epistle to the Hebrews;

The Death of Death in the Death of Christ.

Also: *Communion With God; Apostasy From the Gospel;
The Glory of Christ*—modernised and abridged by Dr.
R. J. K. Law.

RUTHERFORD, SAMUEL

Letters of Samuel Rutherford.

See *Samuel Rutherford and His Friends* and *Grace in
Winter,* both by Faith Cook.

SIBBES, RICHARD

The Works of Richard Sibbes.

WATSON, THOMAS

*All Things for Good; The Doctrine of Repentance; A Body of
Divinity; The Ten Commandments; The Lord's Prayer; The
Beatitudes; The Godly Man's Picture: Drawn with a
Scripture Pencil.*

WHITEFIELD, GEORGE

George Whitefield's Journals;

George Whitefield's Letters 1734-1742;

Select Sermons of George Whitefield.

See *The Life of George Whitefield,* by Arnold Dallimore.